writing with mentors

ALLISON MARCHETTI • REBEKAH O'DELL

writing with mentors

HOW TO REACH EVERY
WRITER IN THE ROOM
USING CURRENT, ENGAGING
MENTOR TEXTS

FOREWORD BY **PENNY KITTLE**

HEINEMANN • Portsmouth, NH

Heinemann
361 Hanover Street
Portsmouth, NH 03801–3912
www.heinemann.com

Offices and agents throughout the world

The authors and publisher wish to thank those who have generously given permission to reprint borrowed material:

Figures 2.3, 3.5, and 3.6: "Pharrell Williams: Just Exhilaratingly Happy" by Ken Tucker. Posted March 6, 2014, via www.npr.org. Review and excerpts thereof reprinted with permission from WHYY, Inc.

Library of Congress Cataloging-in-Publication Data
Marchetti, Allison.
   Writing with mentors : how to reach every writer in the room using current, engaging mentor texts / Allison Marchetti and Rebekah O'Dell.
        pages   cm
   Includes bibliographical references and index.
   ISBN 978-0-325-07450-4
   1. English language—Composition and exercises—Study and teaching (Secondary)
2. Mentoring in education. 3. Mentoring of authors. I. O'Dell, Rebekah. II. Title.

   LB1631.M38548 2015
   428.0071'2—dc23   2015012918

Editor: Katie Wood Ray
Production: Hilary Goff
Cover and interior designs: Suzanne Heiser
Author photo: Allison Fiebert, Capture Photography
Typesetter: Kim Arney
Manufacturing: Steve Bernier

Printed in the United States of America on acid-free paper
19 18 17 16 15   VP   1 2 3 4 5

Dedication

For Joe. You're every word, you're every line.
For Peter, whose story has just begun.
—AHM

For Taylor, whose teaching legacy can be found
on every page of this book.
For Evan, my glue.
—RO

Contents

Foreword

I remember my first year of teaching in flashes of panic and despair, joy and exhilaration, young faces and sand blowing across the playground. Year one was a rollercoaster of screaming third graders and me barely holding on to the last car as we whipped around turns and accelerated into dips. All year I felt one grip away from being flung into the heat of a California desert afternoon.

I arrived with a flimsy understanding of everything, and that vulnerability wasn't hard to spot: I was friendless, adrift, and unsure. I soon mastered recess, dismissal, and lunch count, even tears (theirs) during math and tears (mine) while reading aloud *Where the Red Fern Grows*. But there was so much to learn about teaching and so little time to sit beside colleagues and labor over an idea, a unit, or a child's learning problem. No matter how hungry I was to learn, I didn't know who or what to study.

I mostly remember feeling alone.

I taught in four states before I worked in a school district that helped me think through my teaching with colleagues. So many teachers still learn to find mentors in books or we starve. Luckily, in my second year, a colleague handed me books by Donald Graves and Lucy Calkins. I mentored myself to their passion and purpose: watchful and filled with questions. With their wisdom I was able to isolate and try to understand recurring errors in my teaching of writing. I developed strategies. I got better.

Great teachers have an unstoppable drive to figure things out. We imagine that our classrooms might be places where, as Rebekah and Allison say, "the craft of writing is truly studied, not assigned, and we study it together," but we need mentors to show us how. You have two here in your hands. You'll see how they entice students to practice the moves of writers and when (and how) to be deliberate in teaching; you will see vibrant writing workshops in heterogeneous courses and in IB. You will understand how to immerse students in the trial and error that characterizes all learning. You will find ways to improve collaborative work and watch students sharing thinking, mentoring each other.

In *Writing with Mentors* you will see the landscape of workshop teaching through one focus: mentor texts. The book is packed with QR codes which link to texts you can use in your classroom tomorrow (like a diverse list of critical reviews, which will lift analysis to an authentic, lively place), and the authors offer smart advice for organizing these texts online for easy student access. With so many texts already gathered, it is as if Allison and Rebekah have done all the shopping for you—bringing you weeks of meals planned and all of the ingredients you need—but they will also cook beside you as you sift and toss and dance in your kitchen. The authors show you how to use mentor texts to inspire, to focus writers on structure, and to amplify the power of sentence structure and word choice. Most of all, they show you the handover that occurs when a teacher positions herself as one of many teachers in any classroom: the texts you study and the other writers in the room.

Allison and Rebekah demonstrate the limitless possibilities of daily practice in finding words to shape ideas. The student samples that will thrill you here are the product of an immersion in excellent models and the time to practice freely in notebooks. It is the regular-ness of this time that leads young writers to experiment and play, finding better words than the day before and taking on the nuances of voice from writers they admire. The authors even include a list of common questions writers have in conferences and how we might respond, always pointing students to mentor texts. This is an exciting book packed with vision. I read it in small chunks with my notebook beside me.

In my classroom I have a framed poster advertisement from 1998 for Don Graves' book *How to Catch a Shark: and Other Stories of Teaching and Learning*. Don is 19-years-old and shirtless in the photograph, gleefully clutching one fin of the shark he and his friend have just hauled in. I smile every time my eyes land on that photo; I see the sunset from his deck and hear his laughter. Don gave me the courage to write. So many teachers are afraid to put their voices out into the world. We know why. Criticism has fins that puncture enthusiasm. Rebekah O'Dell and Allison Marchetti show such courage here: not only to write for you, but the courage to trust their students to make almost all the decisions about their work—at all stages.

When we lost Don Graves in 2010 it silenced a voice that had led hundreds of thousands of teachers for a generation. Tom Newkirk, in a breakfast at NCTE in 2013, called for voices to carry his wisdom forward. Allison and Rebekah were there that morning and became determined to write this book that you now hold in your hands. They quote Graves who believed we must help students "figure out how to solve writing problems . . ." as these two have figured out how to solve teaching problems. I love their expansive thinking of ways to work like writers, now and long past high school.

I am certain Don would have celebrated these wise, kind, and fearless advocates for young writers. This book vibrates with joy and possibility. Lucky you to have it in your hands.

—Penny Kittle
North Conway, NH

Acknowledgments

Writing a book is the most wonderful and most terrifying thing we have ever done. Without a doubt, this book would not be held in our hearts or printed in your hands without the support, influence, and insight we have received from so many people. Our debt of gratitude is large. This acknowledgment represents only tiny pieces of what we feel.

Thank you . . .

To our students, past and present, for all you have taught us. We come to school excited to teach because of your energy, your creativity, your courage, your spirit—both as people and as writers.

To our teachers who inspired us to become teachers and taught us how to do it right. To Maggie Huminski, Jeannette Faber, Barry Gibrall, Mattie Flowers, Mary Bevilaqua, Sara Kajder, and Margo Figgins. Your influence on our lives can be seen in our classrooms every day.

To our school home, Trinity Episcopal School. In particular, thank you to Dr. Tom Aycock, Rob Short, and Sarah McDermott who hired both of us when you had an opening for only one. We are eternally grateful for that decision. Thank you for your willingness to let us play and experiment in our classrooms. Thank you for the daily (and sometimes minute-by-minute) encouragement and support you have offered us through this process—high-fives and emails and text message pep talks.

To our colleagues and friends at Trinity—especially Betsy, Maria, Christina, Chris M., Chris W., and Francis—for cheering us on and making us laugh.

To our many teacher-writer mentors who have taught us how to teach and whose books are worn with admiration and use. This book was written on the shoulders of your work. Thank you for what you have done for us, for our students, and for the profession. We want to be all of you when we grow up: Troy Hicks, Penny Kittle, Chris Lehman, Kate Roberts, Nancie Atwell, Kelly Gallagher, Jeff Anderson.

To everyone at Heinemann. You have made our dreams come true. A special thank-you to Tom Newkirk who got the dream rolling. Thank you for your call to action. Ever since the morning of the Donald Graves breakfast, we felt a responsibility to your calling. We still do.

To Katie Wood Ray, *our* mentor in every way. We will never, ever forget the first time your name popped up in our inbox. We called each other and screamed. First, we thank you for your own work. Without your books, we might never have discovered the power of mentor texts. Your research, your writing—all of it makes our work possible, both in our classrooms and in this book. Second, we thank you as our tireless, inspiring editor. Thank you for shepherding this project from an email to a book in the course of one year. Thank you for your wisdom and expertise as a writer and teacher of writing—you have taught us how to write all over again. Thank you for your close reading of many drafts, for your wisdom, for being our greatest cheerleader. Thank you for your generosity in sharing all that you have with us. We are constantly amazed by you and are so very grateful.

To our parents, who have always fiercely protected and promoted our dreams.

To our families who have sacrificed so much so that we can run after our dream of being writers. In particular, thank you to our husbands, who have kept daily life running—meals cooked, houses cleaned, children fed—so that we could write, who have lost their wives to their laptops for many, many months, who have both forced us to take breaks and insisted we get back to work, and who have steadily encouraged us every step of the way.

Introduction

HOW THIS BOOK CAME TO BE

Something shifted in us the morning of the Donald Graves breakfast at NCTE13.

Awed, sitting in the same room as all of our teaching idols and mentors, we listened as Tom Newkirk passed the torch to the next generation of innovative writing teachers:

"We're getting older," he joked. "We need *you* to continue the work."

We came to the breakfast that morning as inspired teachers largely tethered to our local context. We left as inspired educators who felt a responsibility to share well beyond our school and our city. For us, it was a catalyzing moment. We had always *wanted* to be in the conversation, but it wasn't until Tom Newkirk said that he *needed* us to be in the conversation, to continue the good work of Graves, Atwell, and Kittle, that we jumped.

That night, sprawled across our hotel beds as we worked on our presentation for the next day, our whole outlook changed. Tomorrow's presentation wasn't just a presentation—it was a contribution to something larger, something that might have a life past our 8:30 AM presentation slot. Looking back, before that night, the presentation we had made was for us—in the way a writer might write for herself. We were trying to understand something about ourselves as teachers, something about our students. But the breakfast changed everything. Suddenly we were thinking bigger, thinking with a sense of, "How could we contribute to this larger conversation?" Take-out cartons in hand, we excitedly made revisions to our presentation, edging toward this newfound sense of possibility.

A few days later, after we returned home from Boston, our blog, *Moving Writers*, was born, and it—and the incredible reader support we have found there—gave us the confidence and inspiration to write this book.

What You Will Find in This Book

This book was written to help you understand the potential that writing with mentors has for your students.

We've organized it into nine chapters that mimic the scaffolded instruction we use to support writers in our own classrooms, beginning with the teacher. As you look at the contents, you'll see that Chapter 1 offers a new way of thinking about mentor texts and the central role they can play in writing instruction. In Chapter 2, we explore what it means to be a teacher who puts her full faith in professional writers and leverages this faith as far as it can go in the classroom. We take you to our most trusted sources for finding mentor texts—sources that never tire and never feel old, sources we promise will excite both you and your students. Finally, we share our criteria for selecting the best mentor texts these sources have to offer.

In Chapter 3, we move into the classroom, offering a practical explanation of how a teacher might move from this trust in professional writers and discovery of rich texts to planning for instruction. In Chapters 4 through 8, we walk you through our work with students and mentors from the first day of school to the last—from the early stages of inspiration to the final moments of publication. We share lessons that demonstrate the enormous potential of mentors at every stage of the writing process.

Finally, we close with a chapter that explains why we teach with mentors at all, because it's the influence of writers that will endure long after our students have left our classrooms. With the help of mentors, we cultivate independence in our writers and help them build lasting writing lives.

You'll notice that chapters are punctuated with brief invitations (A Way In) to engage in the work your students will be doing or to think about your classroom and how the approach we're describing might work for you and your students. For these invitations, we suggest you reserve some space in your writer's notebook or find a small, separate notebook for the jotting and thinking you'll do over the course of this book.

Other chapters will engage you in some observational work: You'll listen as we "teach aloud," offering a window into our thinking as we search for, curate, and plan with mentor texts or talk to students about how to seek help and inspiration from the work of professional writers. And then you'll listen some more to the voices that really matter: the students'. You'll watch some of our students collect thinking, plan, play, draft, start over, write some more—with mentors at their side every step of the way. These students represent a wide variety of ability levels, from the most emerging writers to students who have always wanted to grow up to become writers, but they all have one thing in common: The quality of their writing has been markedly improved by the influence of mentor texts.

Although we've written this book with upper middle to high school–aged students in mind, the mentor text approach to writing instruction is relevant to a wide range of writers at all grade levels. In fact, mentor text instruction has traditionally occurred in the primary grades, well-documented in books like Katie Wood Ray's *Study Driven*, Ralph Fletcher's *What a Writer Needs*, and Ruth Culham's *The Writing Thief*. And while the texts we refer to are geared toward a more mature audience, the philosophy and organizational tools, as well as the ways of talking to students about mentors, are timeless and ageless. We have always taught by the mantra "Good teaching is good teaching," and we use elementary school materials all the time and adapt them for high school.

Our hope in this book is to show you a way mentors can help you teach anything you need or *want* to teach in writing. A way that will stimulate both you and your students. A way that is grounded in the work of real writers and the real reading you do every day. A way that naturally differentiates instruction for your students while preserving your time and energy. A way that is sustainable and fresh and will serve your students well long after they leave your classroom.

CHAPTER ONE

A Classroom Where Mentors Matter

T he room is filled with the quiet buzz that always accompanies writing as students dig in to their study of critical reviews. Reed skims several restaurant reviews by Pete Wells, restaurant critic for the New York Times, pausing to jot down notes in the margins. Studying the reviews gives him a feel for what kind of information he might need in his own review—service notes, food descriptions, and so on. Nearby, Ari prepares for drafting. She studies John Green's review of Eleanor & Park, searching for a possible structure for her own work. Further along in the process, Cole checks his commas against The A.V. Club's Ryan Smith's punctuation in a game review of Titanfall. A few students gather around a laptop with Pete Wells' review of M. Wells Steakhouse. They are studying how Wells uses hyperlinks to extend his writing and further connect with his audience. Others listen to Ken Tucker's Fresh Air podcast of his review of Pharrell Williams' album G I R L as they ready their own podcasts for publication. Their ears perk up as the words and rhythms of Tucker's writing soak in.

Meanwhile, I move around the room, clipboard in hand, stopping to confer with different students. I pause at Niki's desk. "How's it going?" I ask. She explains she wants to show how It's Kind of a Funny Story is different from the other novels she's read about high school drama, but she can't find the words. I read her beginning and scan my mental filing cabinet for a mentor text that might help her move forward. "This is a great start," I say, pointing to her opening paragraph.

"You might take a look at John Green's review of Eleanor & Park. *He shows how Rowell's book stands apart and is different in a sea of young adult love stories. He does this same thing in his review of* The Hunger Games *and* The Dead and the Gone." *I wait until she locates the reviews at nytimes.com and promise to return later to see how her piece is coming along.*

A small group of writers calls from the opposite side of the room. "I don't know what else to put in," I hear one of them say. The students working on movie reviews tell me their writing feels incomplete, that their pieces are missing something, but they don't know what. I suggest they take a break from their own writing and return to A. O. Scott's review of The Fault in Our Stars. *When they find it, they decide to walk through the review again, paragraph by paragraph, and jot down the kinds of details Scott includes in his review. Nearby, Jake works with Joshua Alston's review of a* Modern Family *episode to learn how to express disappointment in a product while maintaining a professional tone. "I thought it would be more useful since the other reviews were mostly positive and praised the products," he tells me.*

Before I know it, the bells rings. Papers flutter. Binders snap shut. "Good work today, writers!" I shout above the clamor. In seconds, the classroom is empty. I conferred with five writers—not nearly as many as I would have liked. But I feel confident the others were in good hands. As another group of students files in, I pause for just a moment, grateful for the mentors in the room— Green, Wells, Smith, Tucker, Scott, Alston—and the teaching they made possible.

—Allison

From Reed's review of a local restaurant

[The] inside is different than any other restaurant, in the sense that it is cluttered and dirty. The lock to the bathroom door is broken, and there are words and pictures scribbled all over the walls. Waiters are screaming, dropping things, pushing customers out of their way, and it sometimes takes over an hour to get a table. Despite these unwelcoming aspects of the restaurant, it serves and is known for some of the best Italian food in the state.

Consider the scene above. Students are spread out around the room; some are working individually while others are working in small groups. There are brainstormers and drafters and publishers and readers and thinkers and rethinkers and tinkerers—everyone moving, everyone caught in his or her own flow, everyone writing, and everyone *engaged with mentor texts*. It might seem chaotic. It might seem impossible. But it's not. This is what mentor texts can make possible in your classroom, and this book is about the instructional approach we use to carry out this teaching in our classrooms.

We aren't the first teachers to use mentor texts in our writing instruction. It's a practice we learned from our own teaching mentors—Nancie Atwell, Penny Kittle, Kelly Gallagher, Ralph Fletcher, Katie

Wood Ray, and Jeff Anderson to name just a few. These teachers first showed us the enormous potential of teaching writing by showing students "what's possible from the best writers" (Kittle 2008, 39).

Mentor texts are model pieces of writing—or excerpts of writing—by established authors that can inspire students and teach them how to write, and they have become the single most important element of our writing instruction. We used mentor texts sparingly in the beginning—mainly to introduce students to a new genre of writing or to illustrate a specific skill—but our dalliance with these texts and the authors behind them quickly turned into a full-on love affair when we realized all that they enable.

Mentor texts enable student writers to become connected to the dynamic world of professional writers. Mentor texts enable independence as, over time, students are able to find and use the inspiration and craft elements found in the sentences and pages of their favorite writers. Mentor texts enable complete creativity and individuality to emerge in student writing and in writing instruction. Mentor texts enable a teacher, whose planning time and knowledge of every potential genre of writing is limited, to reach every writer in the room, on any given day, whatever the writers' needs. Mentor texts enable all of us—teachers and students alike—to do far more than we could ever do on our own.

From Niki's book review of *It's Kind of a Funny Story*

Many teen books of this day and age deal with romance as a main focal point in their stories. Some seem to be rather quickly formed and slightly unbelievable for the depth of love the characters have for each other. But *It's Kind of a Funny Story* [by Ned Vizzini] centers around self-discovery and the road to happiness, which is a refreshing read in comparison. Craig's hesitant relationship with Noelle is slow and steady, neither of them quite mentally ready for a real romance, which is a rational decision to make. It's not a book about sad teens finding love to make themselves happy again. It's more a book about a sad teen finding happiness within himself on his own terms, and if there's a slight romance along the way, then that's nice. Coincidentally, Vizzini writes with personal experience, which makes the book feel even more genuine. In fact, the whole basis of the book centers around his experience in a psychiatric hospital when he was younger.

Creating Conditions for Writers and Mentors

In the opening vignette, students are in so many different places at once—both physically scattered about the room and in different phases of the writing process. While mentor texts are at the heart of it all, this picture might seem overwhelming. Even though it

From Ari's book review of
Looking for Alaska

Once Pudge meets Alaska, everything changes. In the book, after just one glance, it is apparent Pudge has fallen in love with Alaska. Pudge is drawn to not only her physical beauty, but also to her personality. Alaska is confident and strong, but also acts depressed and self-conscious and Pudge is intrigued by her mysterious and unknown story. Alaska takes Pudge on wild adventures and shows him how to live life to the fullest, but with Alaska's reckless personality she can't even keep herself safe. Looking for Alaska [by John Green] is an exciting and emotionally gripping novel about one boy who knows everyone's last words, but will never know Alaska's.

might seem complicated to juggle so many students with so many different needs in so many different places in their writing, there are a few classroom conditions that make this kind of teaching possible.

Space and Time for Writing

First, and most important, students are actively engaged in writing. As you can see in the opening vignette, writing isn't an assignment students complete at home in isolation. Writing, in all its messiness, happens during class where students have resources at their fingertips, where they can immediately experiment with the techniques from that day's writing lesson, where they can get feedback from peers and confer with a teacher. After a little notebook time and a brief writing lesson, the rest of the class time is devoted to the work you see in the opening vignette—planning, drafting, revising, collaborating, conferring, and, of course, learning from mentor texts.

Most professional writers have very specific writing habits. They write at a certain time of day, in a certain place, with a certain pen or a certain drink in hand. This predictability helps them dive into the thinking and get into the flow of writing. The time we give to writing during class creates similar writing habits for our students. Nancie Atwell reminds us that "[w]riters need regular, frequent chunks of time they can count on, anticipate and plan for. Only when [we] make time for writing in school, designating it a high-priority activity of the English program, will [. . .] students develop the habits of mind of writers—and the compulsions" (1998, 91). We devote our time to this because writing is a high-priority activity for us, and our students need writing time they can depend on in order to "figure out how they will solve writing problems" (Graves 1994, 65).

Units of Study

Rather than organizing writing around works of literature, we organize our writing instruction into units of study—each unit focusing on a single genre or writing technique. In the vignette, the class is studying the genre of critical review. They had previously studied narratives, and, after critical reviews, they will study the technique of weaving evidence into their writing to support their purpose. Throughout the course of a school year, students write in a wide variety of forms and for a variety of purposes (Chapter 3 details many of these for you). This is how professional writers work, and this is how we want our students to work, too. We want them to develop authentic ideas and then find the forms that fit them. While our students do write about literature, it is just one of the genres they explore.

In each unit of study, students read like writers, diving deeply into mentor texts to uncover essentials of the genre. We teach writing lessons that hone in on techniques that will raise the level of every student's writing. We confer with students as they write to encourage them, nudge them, and lean into their needs as writers. The craft of writing is truly *studied*, not assigned, and we study it together.

Choices for Writers

While the whole class studies a single genre or technique together in each unit of study, students are given lots of room for choice. Donald Graves said that when students don't have any choice over their writing, their work becomes "dishonest" and removed from the true purposes of writing. As a consequence, "the student can even graduate without learning that writing is the medium through which our most intimate thoughts and feelings can be expressed" (Graves 1994, 62). By offering choices in topic, process, and mentor texts, we promote creativity and diversity in our student writers.

CHOICE OF TOPIC

In our classrooms, you won't find an entire class writing an essay on a single piece of literature. You won't find writing prompts. Instead, students are choosing their own topics so they are engaged and so they can "discover what moves them and what they think" (Graves 1994, 67). You can see this clearly at work in

From Cole's review of the video game *Elder Scrolls V*

The *Elder Scrolls V* begins with creating a character. The options of creation in this game are extremely detailed, but do take some time to complete. For example, do you want a 3 inch beard or a 9 inch beard, and do you want it to be brown or dark black? Some players were very pleased with the amount of customization options, but others were not as pleased due to the fact that it took some time to create the character. There are multiple races a player can choose to be. You could be anything from a giant cat with ferocious scars, tattoos, and piercings, to a giant lizard with scales and gizzards. Personally, I prefer the Khajjit, a giant cat species, due to the fact that it gives a better unarmed attack, better pickpocketing, lockpicking, archery, one-handed attack, and sneak.

From Jake's product review of KDV Elite basketball shoes

While the KDV Elite may be aesthetically pleasing and the signature shoe of basketball player Kevin Durant, it is not worth the demanding price of $180. What I will give the KDV Elite is exceptional traction. The traction features storytelling traction, a traction pattern that represents the player in a different way than the standard herringbone traction pattern. The traction seemed to work decently on clean courts at first but did not hold well on dusty courts. The more I played with the shoes, however, the better the traction got on both court surfaces. But you will need to wipe consistently. One thing I found out the hard way: when cutting or making moves, you will need to stay firmly planted on the ground because if you even slightly tilt your foot, you will slip badly and fall hard because of the carbon fiber siding. You must consistently wipe to ensure best available traction.

the vignette. While all students are studying and crafting critical reviews, and while all the teaching is focused on elements of critical reviews, students have chosen both the type of critical review they will write and the topic. Some have chosen to write reviews of books they love, while others write film reviews, restaurant reviews, and video game reviews. Students are engaged because they can pursue their passions, their interests, and their wonderings all within the framework of a whole-class unit of study that teaches them the skills of critical review they'll need for college and beyond.

Perhaps even more important than engagement, however, is the way choosing their own topics for writing helps students craft powerful personal identities at such a critical time in their lives. What they choose to write about makes students *known*—to themselves, their teachers, their classmates, and the larger world—in a way quite unlike anything else. Because of their choices, someday many years from now, students will be able to look back at the writing they did when they were sixteen and glimpse the people they used to be. And we all know, you don't get sixteen back, so what a gift this writing will be.

CHOICE OF PROCESS

In this kind of flexible, responsive, student-centered writing environment, students also work to "find their own process for each piece" (Kittle 2008, 12). While all students have a common due date, how each student gets there is largely up to him or her. Because we recognize that writers work in different ways, students are allowed to move at their own pace and make lots of choices about the process they will use to go from an idea to final publication. Notice in the vignette, some students are still brainstorming, while a few are in the thick of drafting, and one group is forging ahead toward publication. Regardless of where they are in the process, students are using mentor texts to support them, choosing the ones that are most germane to whatever they are working on at that moment.

When decisions about process are in students' hands, they have a chance to learn what does and doesn't work for them as writers. And no question about it, lots of them spend time learning what doesn't work, but it's their learning to own. All successful writers have to find a process that works for them. If students are simply checking off requirements from a predetermined process defined by someone else, there is no hope they will become the purposeful, independent writers we want them to be. So we let students choose how to move forward as writers, making sure their mentors are close by to guide them, and we're there to give them advice and teaching as well.

CHOICE OF MENTOR TEXTS

Because we use multiple mentor texts throughout a unit of study, students also make decisions about which mentors they want to guide them in their writing, and they do this in every phase of the process. You can see this clearly in the opening vignette where the class is working with mentor texts showing a range of critical reviews (see Figure 1.1). Notice that students choose their mentors for a variety of reasons, but they all have to do with *how* the reviews are written rather than *what* they are about.

For example, Ari studies John Green's review of *Eleanor & Park* because she is also reviewing a single book and is looking for a way to organize her thoughts and structure her writing. In another corner of the room, at Allison's suggestion, Niki studies the same Green review but for totally different reasons. She wants to see how he develops a particular kind of content (comparing and contrasting). Pete Wells' restaurant reviews help Reed, who's just started drafting, figure out how to develop his content, and another group who's mostly finished drafting consider how they might use hyperlinks. A few students who are ready to publish and want to create audio texts listen to Ken Tucker's podcast to get ideas for their own publications. Green, Wells, Tucker—together these writers show students many ways to write an excellent review and many different ways to get there.

When students choose the mentor texts they wish to learn from throughout the process of writing, their choices help them each develop an individual writing voice. Just as our individual speaking voices are tuned to the sounds, habits, and tendencies of the people we hear speaking around us, our students develop voice as writers by listening to the writing of the mentors around them, especially the ones they've chosen. One student might be drawn more to the witty, self-deprecating voice of David Sedaris, while another wants to sound more like the lyrical voice of Sandra Cisneros. Just as they so easily adopt the language of their peers, students take on the nuances of voice from the writers they most admire.

"Young Love, Complicated by Cancer" by A. O. Scott
A review of the American romantic comedy-drama film directed by Josh Boone, based on the novel of the same name.

Text 1.1 "Young Love, Complicated by Cancer" by A. O. Scott *http://www.nytimes .com/2014/06/06/movies/the-fault-in-our-stars-sets-out-to-make-you-cry.html?_r=0*

"*Titanfall* Supplants Its Ancestors with Speed and Scale" by Ryan Smith
A review of Respawn Entertainment's *Titanfall*, a multiplayer, first-person video game.

Text 1.2 "*Titanfall* Supplants Its Ancestors with Speed and Scale" by Ryan Smith *http://www.avclub.com/article/titanfall-supplants-its-ancestors-speed-and-scale-202272*

"A Farewell to Twang" by Jon Caramanica
A review of *1989*, the fifth studio album by American singer-songwriter Taylor Swift.

Text 1.3 "A Farewell to Twang" by Jon Caramanica *http://www.nytimes.com/2014/10 /26/arts/music/taylor-swift-1989-new-album-review.html*

"Fred and Barney Would Feel Right at Home" by Pete Wells
A review of the American steakhouse M. Wells in Long Island City, Queens.

Text 1.4 "Fred and Barney Would Feel Right at Home" by Pete Wells *http://www .nytimes.com/2014/01/29/dining/restaurant-review-m-wells-steakhouse-in-long-island -city-queens.html*

"Scary New World" by John Green
A review of young adult dystopian novels *The Hunger Games*, by Suzanne Collins, and *The Dead and the Gone*, by Susan Beth Pfeffer.

Text 1.5 "Scary New World" by John Green *http://www.nytimes.com/2008/11/09 /books/review/Green-t.html?pagewanted=all*

continues

"Two Against the World" by John Green

A review of the young adult novel *Eleanor & Park* by Rainbow Rowell.

Text 1.6 "Two Against the World" by John Green *http://www.nytimes.com/2013/03 /10/books/review/eleanor-park-by-rainbow-rowell.html*

"Pharrell Williams: Just Exhilaratingly Happy" by Ken Tucker

A review of *G I R L*, the second studio album by American recording artist and record producer Pharrell Williams.

Text 1.7 "Pharrell Williams: Just Exhilaratingly Happy" by Ken Tucker *http://www.npr .org/2014/03/06/286864627/pharrell-williams-new-album-is-as-happy-as-its-hit-single*

"*Modern Family*: 'A Hard Jay's Night': Wash That Man Right Outta Your Hair" by Joshua Alston

A review of *Modern Family* "A Hard Jay's Night," Season 5, Episode 19.

Text 1.8 "*Modern Family*: 'A Hard Jay's Night': Wash That Man Right Outta Your Hair" by Joshua Alston *http://www.avclub.com/tvclub/modern-family-hard-jays-night-203009*

Figure 1.1 Mentor Texts Students Used in a Study of Critical Reviews

Mentor Texts for All Phases of Writing

Mentor texts have the potential to inspire and teach students at every step of the writing process, from play and experimentation with words, to planning for writing, to crafting and revising, to publishing. As we explained earlier, throughout a unit of study, students are choosing mentor texts that will help them most in their writing at any given time. For example, the students studying Pete Wells' work are reviewing products or experiences with major visual components; a book review wouldn't really help. So they gather around Wells' review because it has numerous hyperlinks and a slideshow of pictures. Some of these same students, however, worked with John Green's *Eleanor & Park* review at another point in the study—when they were looking for ways to begin. As teachers, it's important we understand all the different ways mentors might support writers in different phases of the writing process so we can help students engage strategically with the mentors they choose. Figure 1.2 highlights some of the most common ways mentors support students in different phases of the writing process.

Writing Phase	Mentor texts can help writers . . .
Play	✳ dream up new topics ✳ complicate old ideas ✳ discover new sentence possibilities ✳ develop perspective on an issue ✳ discover a new approach to writing in a certain genre
Planning	✳ generate new ideas or give life to old ideas ✳ understand features/techniques of a genre ✳ find a structure to begin writing ✳ focus on tone and audience in a given genre ✳ narrow or expand ideas to include in a draft
Drafting	✳ keep the big picture (of the genre) in mind ✳ shape themes and purposes ✳ experiment with form ✳ troubleshoot writing struggles ✳ find additional examples of interesting craft beyond those shown in the writing lesson
Getting Writing Ready for Readers	✳ create multimedia publishing opportunities through hyperlinks, photos, and video ✳ discover different ways of publishing work ✳ learn formatting and citation rules of a genre ✳ create subsections and sections to organize their content ✳ identify mechanical and grammatical errors

Figure 1.2 Ways Students Use Mentor Texts Throughout the Writing Process

Space and time for writing, units of study, choices for writers—these conditions, when coupled with mentor texts, create classrooms where students can make decisions that maximize their creative potential and empower them as writers. Time and again when these conditions are present, we see students who feel supported and uplifted and encouraged to take risks. We see students who feel capable—equipped with the tools they need to write, prepared for any writing situation. Most important, they feel valued.

Through their work with mentor texts, these writers are ushered into a larger writing community where their ideas and words matter.

Closing Thoughts

Imagine what it would be like to be a student in the classroom in the opening vignette. To know that each day you will have the opportunity to learn from multiple mentors, each of whom will offer a different perspective. To know, as you open your writer's notebook, that today's class will be different from yesterday's because you are someplace new in your work, and your work shapes your daily experience. To know that you will be encouraged to make choices, think for yourself, exercise independence, learn about your world, and create. To believe, as you study the words of other writers, that the work you are doing is just as real and important and meaningful.

These are the outcomes that keep us teaching with mentor texts. We want nothing more than to help cultivate happy, productive, resourceful writers who see the value in what they are doing to their lives inside and outside of school. As you read on, we hope you'll return to this vignette and the others we've interwoven throughout the book as reminders of what's possible for you and your students.

CHAPTER TWO

Developing a Mentor Text Habit of Mind

I was at the intersection of Turner and Elkart when I heard it.

Pharrell's silky smooth croon, singing about being happy, followed by Ken Tucker's unmistakable voice. I turned the volume up:

"Pharrell Williams, who frequently goes by just his first name, is the sort of pop star whom many people would like to view as a friend. Emerging from hip-hop, he makes charming recordings that suggest a deep appreciation of pop, soul, and R&B . . ."

A few blocks from home, I listened to Ken Tucker's review of Pharrell's new album G I R L, spliced between excerpts of the songs themselves. The review was captivating, fun, and smart. And it just oozed with mentor text potential. I was excited. Pulling into my driveway, I dashed off a quick text message to a colleague: Just found a great mentor text on Fresh Air on drive home. Will show you tomorrow.

That night, I pulled up the transcript online, hoping to confirm that Tucker's review held the same kind of mentor text potential it seemed to have hours earlier. My eyes scanned the four-paragraph review, and I scribbled a few thoughts down in my notebook.

- *The title—simple and catchy and riffing on the title of Pharrell's number-one hit song*
- *His intentional use of second person—so engaging!*
- *Allusions draw on readers' background knowledge of soul music—Mimi will love this!*

- *He playfully scoffs at Pharrell's critics*
- *Figurative language goldmine—"a rubber-band rhythm that stretches and snaps with witty elasticity"—wish I had written that*
- *Only four paragraphs—students will appreciate!*
- *Students love Pharrell.*

A few minutes of scribbling yielded many, many possibilities for teaching and learning with students. All that was left was to make copies and start imagining the conversations we'd have when my students got their hands on this amazing text.

—Rebekah

Just like putting the right book in the hands of the right student at the right time, we can't overstate the important role of the teacher—one who knows her students, finds texts that engage and inspire them, and helps them discover the craft that will move their writing forward. The real power of mentor texts lies in the teacher whose habit of mind is tuned to the needs of student writers and searches for the mentor texts to meet those needs—during planning periods, in conversations with colleagues, even on the commute home.

This sounds daunting, right? Like the description of only the very best teachers, impossible for us mere mortal teachers. But this isn't impossible. This is us. This is *you*.

Think about why we all became English teachers in the first place. We were children who hid under our bedroom blankets to sneak in just one more chapter before we went to sleep. We feel a strange sense of possession over our very best, often fictional, friends. As a rule, we don't leave the house without a book. We have favorite bookmarks for our very best books and pens reserved for underlining and scrawling notes in their margins. We spend too much time arranging and rearranging our bookshelves. We read feverishly, some of us breaking the spines of our books, others leaving them pristine. We read for our own pleasure but also for the pleasure of gifting a friend with the perfect book. We tweet and share almost every article we read online, excited to share the joy of our discovery, the joy of the perfect sentence, the joy of good writing.

The joy we feel when we read and share good writing with others is why we became English teachers. And even though we've been told our personal passions don't have a place in our profession, it's actually these personal passions—the same passions that drove us into the classroom in the first place—that give life to our teaching and lead us to the texts that can ignite a similar passion in our students. Embracing this passion and excitement for writers and their writing is the key to how we teach with mentor texts.

In the opening vignette, Rebekah was driving home from work when she heard Tucker's review. For a minute, she stopped thinking about the slow driver in front of her and the grocery list taking shape in her mind. She listened. She knew instantly the review she was hearing had potential to be studied as a mentor text, which she confirmed later that night. Finding this mentor text was a combination of luck and good timing, but it happens more often than you'd think. In the natural course of our reading lives, we find mentor texts all around us, even when we're not searching for them.

On Saturdays, when Allison's alarm sounds and the coffee smell rises like heat up to her room, she knows it's going to be a good day. She takes her time on Saturdays. She drinks her coffee while browsing Feedly or reading through recent issues of *The New Yorker*. And even though she gives herself permission to relax and not think about school or writing instruction or her students, inevitably her eyes catch a line of beautiful prose, and she makes a mental note to add that sentence, that paragraph, that essay to her cache of mentor texts. She can't help it.

During a recent classroom visit, the teacher Rebekah was observing smartly used the first sentence of Vonnegut's "Harrison Bergeron" to teach the concept of tone: "The year was 2081, and everyone was finally equal." Pen in hand, poised to take notes on the teacher's instruction, she couldn't help but jot emphatically in her margins: *Use this as a mentor text*! The next day, playing with this sentence formed the foundation for notebook time in her classes (see more on this in Chapter 5).

The thing is, because we are teachers of writing, we can't help but read a little differently than other people. We read with the very real understanding that a great mentor text may be waiting just a page-turn away. We read with a sense of possibility because everything we teach is grounded in the writing we love. In many ways, our teaching lives and our reading lives are seamless because they feed each other and, in turn, feed our students—a recursive process that yields inspired, knowledgeable readers and writers.

Finding Mentor Texts

The first step in helping student writers learn from mentors is finding texts that will inspire students to want to write, expose them to the many possibilities of the written word, and show them craft moves for their own writing. This first chapter is devoted to helping you learn how to find good mentor texts for your teaching, and as we know from experience, selecting just-right texts is a teaching skill that develops over time.

We used to spend hours pulling books from our bookshelves, skimming old favorites, and praying something useful would jump out at us. Failing that, we would uselessly search the Internet, hoping to randomly strike mentor text gold. Invariably, we'd walk away exhausted, frustrated, and with a mentor text (or maybe two) that was typically humdrum but passable. We went through all the motions, but we weren't excited about the mentor texts; neither were our students.

Over time, however, as we've used mentor texts in our teaching and seen what has and hasn't had an impact on our students, we've become much more strategic and savvy about finding them. We've found better—and easier—ways of building a rich, dynamic storehouse of texts for teaching.

Engaging in the World (or When Mentor Texts Come to You)

As we explained earlier, in our daily interactions with the world of words, we find mentor texts everywhere. We find them when we read each day for fun, for knowledge, and for inspiration in our out-of-school lives. We find them in the articles that pop up in our Feedly account in the morning, the stories that catch our eye on the *New York Times* Twitter feed. When we hear something interesting on NPR during our commute, we make note of it and use it as a mentor text later. Post-It flags dot the pages of our pleasure reading, reminding us to return later and share with students: *Use this paragraph as a mentor text on dialogue.*

Finding mentor texts doesn't have to be laborious. What reading interests you? What do you pick up to read throughout the day? What are your favorite magazines, newspapers, and websites, and what elements of those might also inspire your students? The key is to realize mentor texts are all around you all the time, especially in the places you read every day.

You see, we read largely as we have always read—as readers, as lovers of literature, as passionate consumers of words. But as teachers whose work with student writers relies heavily on mentor texts, we read with two additional lenses—we also read as writers and as teachers of writers. These three lenses simultaneously illuminate each piece we read, and of course our own personal preferences as readers come into play as well.

Allison loves poetry, so she subscribes to Ted Kooser's *American Life in Poetry* and *The Writer's Almanac.* She looks forward to reading the daily poems that come to her inbox, and she often reserves them to be used as mentor texts later. Just the other day she discovered "Vernal Sentiment" by Theodore Roethke, and she might just pull the first stanza to demonstrate how writers move from concrete details to autobiographical significance.

Text 2.1 "Vernal Sentiment" by Theodore Roethke *http://writersalmanac.publicradio.org/index.php?date=2014/06/16*

How I Met Your Mother was a favorite television show in Rebekah's household for years. On the day of its series finale, she read an article about its run on *The A.V. Club*.

Text 2.2 "On the Eve of Its Finale, It's Time to Compare *How I Met Your Mother* to Itself" by Donna Bowman *http://www.avclub.com/article/eve-its-finale-its-time-compare -how-i-met-your-mot-202733*

A fan of the show, she was reading just for fun, but as she read she noticed the interesting and nuanced way the writer compares *How I Met Your Mother* to other popular television shows in history—sometimes explicitly and other times only through allusion. Her IB

A WAY IN

In your notebook, take a moment to consider the places where you are likely to find mentor texts in your daily life. Putting these ideas in writing now will make it easier to begin your search!

* Make a list of your usual reading haunts. Consider this reading a part of your daily planning time.
* Create your own chart of favorite websites and the types of writing you typically read there. This will help you when you need to search for a particular genre.
* What are you currently reading for pleasure? What passages might be evocative for students to study? Consider leaving a notebook or a stack of sticky notes next to your pleasure reading book for jotting down potential mentor texts as you read.
* What blogs do you follow? Add your favorite blogs to an RSS feed reader so you can easily keep up with them and access them quickly.
* Who are your favorite authors and journalists? What are your favorite news sites? Refine your Twitter feed, adding your favorite sites and writers. Who knows what inspiration they might share?

students needed this skill of nuanced comparison for their exam. With the article in hand the next day, she asked her students to study how the writer compares and contrasts *HI-MYM* with other shows. They annotated. The class discussed, and they developed a list of noticings about the qualities of effective comparison.

In addition to supporting our teaching, when we bring in mentor texts we've found in our out-of-school reading lives we see two other important benefits. First, these texts help us build relationships as they offer students glimpses into our authentic reading lives and our extracurricular passions. The writing that excites the teacher often says a lot about his personality. Second, using these hot-off-the-press texts also reinforces the idea we desperately try to share all year long: The world is full of writers who are alive and interacting with the world. Writers are not *just* novelists and journalists. They are people like you and me, who love to watch television—or play video games, or go to art galleries, or commune with nature—and write about it.

The Other Days (or When You Have to Go Mentor Text Hunting)

Yes, on the very best days, mentor texts just come to us organically. But what about the other days? What about the days when you are looking for a mentor text to address a very specific issue with an individual student? Or the days when you need to teach a certain technique? Or the days when your normal reading rhythms don't yield anything relevant to your workshop?

On those days, we search our go-to sources, which range from pop culture blogs to podcasts to weekly columns and cover a wide range of reading predilections and habits. Figure 2.1 offers a sampling of these sources and the kind of texts we find there.

Starting with a source you trust helps minimize the time spent reading bad writing and things that just won't work. Good writing is good writing, regardless of the genre, so you shouldn't have to look too far into these engaging sources to find what you need to teach any technique of good writing. As you gain experience looking for mentor texts, you'll find your own favorite go-to sources—writing that excites *you*, work that reflects *your* personality both in and out of the classroom.

Beyond searching through our favorite sources, we often find mentor texts when we ask our friends, families, colleagues, and our Twitter Personal Learning Network (PLN) what recent reading has excited them. And in desperate times, a cry for help, "Searching for a mentor text for . . ." on Twitter often yields remarkable results.

Source	If You're Looking For ...
The A.V. Club (avclub.com) AND *Vulture* (vulture.com)	Insightful analysis of TV, music, movies, games, books, and other pop culture phenomena
Grantland (grantland.com)	Sports and pop culture analysis
NPR (both via radio and NPR blogs)	A smorgasbord—every genre, every topic; these make for great mentor texts because they are short and easily digestible
American Life in Poetry (americanlifeinpoetry.org)	Contemporary poems with introductions by Ted Kooser
The New Yorker	Longer, more detailed analysis, book reviews, essays
The *New York Times*	Everything! These are also typically longer pieces of writing. The *New York Times* Learning Network is a particularly helpful resource for finding texts and other lesson plans; the "What We're Reading" column shares what *Times* writers are reading around the web
TED.com	Home of the TED Talk, TED.com offers talks on seemingly limitless topics; each talk comes with a printable transcript (the mentor text)
FiveThirtyEight.com	Smart, accessible writing on politics, economics, science, entertainment, and sports
The Paris Review	Interviews with authors among other smart articles and features
@dataisbeautiful	This Twitter handle pumps out a regular stream of fascinating graphs, charts, and other data that is perfect for notebook time
Feedly (or other RSS reader)	Feedly and other RSS readers provide a systematic way to add the consistent work of brilliant bloggers (whose work you enjoy) to your routine and ensure you don't miss anything
Twitter	The unpredictable array of articles and information tweeted and retweeted by those you follow; a great source for rounding up things you might otherwise miss

Figure 2.1 Sources for Finding Mentor Texts

A Brief Note on Finding Mentors for Teaching Literary Analysis

There is one genre that consistently presents a hurdle for us while searching for mentor texts: literary analysis. While it's not a genre native to the writing workshop, our high school students need to learn to write literary analysis in order to be prepared for the English courses ahead of them. And we don't want it to be perfunctory; like all of their writing, we want it to be inspired. But we struggle to find real-world examples of *literary* analysis (it doesn't really exist outside of the English classroom and academia). However, there is no shortage of analysis. It's everywhere. On blogs. In *The New Yorker*. On our favorite pop culture websites. With a little searching, we can find exciting, relevant examples of analysis, like a review of Lucie Brock-Broido's book of poems *Stay, Illusion* and a review of the remake of Stephen King's *Carrie*.

Text 2.3 "The Ghost Writer: Lucie Brock-Broido's 'Stay, Illusion'" by Dan Chiasson
http://www.newyorker.com/magazine/2013/10/28/the-ghost-writer-3

Text 2.4 *"Carrie"* by A. A. Dowd *http://www.avclub.com/review/carrie-104381*

Rather than using an entire mentor text in a study of literary analysis, we use excerpts (mini-mentor texts) that are relevant and specific to the genre. For example, students need to give textual evidence to support their claim in an analysis. Consider how the following excerpt (Figure 2.2) from a *Grantland* article about Stephen Curry, an American basketball player, shows what the skill of supplying evidence looks like. In this article, the writer, Zach Lowe, is arguing that the Warriors owe their 2013 postseason success to Curry.

Text 2.5 "The New Stephen Curry: How the Warriors' Super-Shooter Has Transformed His Game in the Playoffs" by Zach Lowe *http://grantland.com/the-triangle/the-new-stephen -curry-how-the-warriors-super-shooter-has-transformed-his-game-in-the-playoffs/*

In very simple terms, Golden State has taken Lee's touches and given them to Curry, unleashing him as something much closer to a full-time off-the-dribble force. And as it turns out, most standard NBA defenses are simply not equipped to deal with an off-the-dribble player who can shoot 45 percent from 3-point range. The change has crystallized against the Spurs, who haven't been as committed as Denver to trying to take the ball from Curry's hands with aggressive traps out toward midcourt; Curry dribbled the ball more in both Game 1 and Game 2 of this series than in any of the approximately 60 prior games recorded by SportVU data-tracking cameras installed at Golden State's home arena and 14 other arenas this season, per data provided exclusively to *Grantland*. He has held the ball for nearly three more full minutes per game over those two games than he did on average in the regular season, a massive change for a player who controlled the ball, on average, about 5:20 per game this season, according to the data.

Figure 2.2 Example of a Mini-Mentor Text

In this paragraph (the fifth paragraph in the article), Lowe builds toward his ultimate point by asserting that Curry is an excellent player, "a full-time off-the-dribble force." Here is the evidence he provides:

* "an off-the-dribble player who can shoot 45 percent from 3-point range"
* "Curry dribbled the ball more in both Game 1 and Game 2 of this series than in any of the approximately 60 prior games"
* "he has held the ball for nearly three more full minutes per game over those two games than he did on average in the regular season."

Lowe supplies evidence just like a writer of literary analysis. He cites at least four specific statistics, all supporting the idea that Curry is a tremendous offensive force. The main difference between this kind of analysis and literary analysis is that Lowe's "text" is an athlete, not a book, poem, or play, but the craft of the writing and what makes analysis *effective* analysis, is the same. As you help students understand the connections between sports (or pop culture, political, etc.) analysis and literary analysis, they will see that analysis is something real writers do and real readers react to—not a stuffy, irrelevant assignment useful only in English class.

Related to this, it's important to note the strong connection between this way of teaching—a writing pedagogy centered on mentor texts—and the teaching of analysis. Students practice analysis every time they read a mentor text and notice its craft, every time they read a text and break it into parts to study its structure, every time they decide which craft elements would strengthen their own writing. To put it simply, analysis is *the* tool used to study mentor texts in every phase of the writing process.

Building a Collection of Mentor Texts

As teachers, we know our students need to see more than one example of something to really understand how it works, so once you've found mentor texts you're excited about, the next step is to begin gathering multiple texts in the same genre or multiple texts that showcase the same writing technique. The more texts you have, the more likely you are to appeal to different writers with different sensibilities and the more possibilities you are able to explore. On the other hand, too many texts can overwhelm, so we aim to select a cluster of between three and six texts for whole-class teaching (with more we can pull for individual students or groups who might need them).

Once you've gathered a number of possibilities and are ready to narrow your selection, it's important to select texts for your teaching cluster that show a diverse range of topics, styles, and approaches to the writing. For example, with diversity as our goal, we selected these texts to create a cluster for a study of commentary.

> ### "Bullying: Why Zero-Tolerance Policies Don't Work" by Andrew Zack
> **Text 2.6** "Bullying: Why Zero-Tolerance Policies Don't Work" by Andrew Zack
> *http://www.huffingtonpost.com/andrew-zack/bullying-zero-tolerance_b_815231.html*

> ### "Social Media Can Be Deadly" by Leonard Pitts Jr.
> **Text 2.7** "Social Media Can Be Deadly" by Leonard Pitts Jr. *http://www.miamiherald .com/opinion/opn-columns-blogs/leonard-pitts-jr/article1956196.html*

> ### "It's Not Just the Guns, It's the Person" by Mitch Albom
> **Text 2.8** "It's Not Just the Guns, It's the Person" by Mitch Albom *http://mitchalbom .com/d/journalism/7800/its-not-just-guns-its-person*

While they are all commentaries, each of these pieces is also a unique essay that invites students to see the myriad possibilities in commentary writing. Zack uses rhetorical questions to engage readers and help them follow his line of thinking. As a former victim of bullying, his article relies heavily on anecdotes. Pitts introduces his subject by pointing out the twisted irony of it, uses second person to engage the reader, and incorporates interesting juxtapositions like "to be alone, together" and "Technology has trained us to look down . . . you need to look up." He then ends with a great one-liner. Albom opens with a scenario and dialogue. Many of his paragraphs are single sentences. He uses subtitles to break his commentary into various sections. He finds strategic places for the pronoun "we" to demonstrate a sense of solidarity.

What's important is that these texts are as individual as the writers who crafted them, and a diverse cluster is like a "choose your own adventure" lesson in writing. Students see the different paths writers can take, even within the same genre, and are able to begin imagining possibilities for their own writing. Clusters illustrate what single mentor texts cannot: No two texts—and no two writers—are alike.

Mentor Text Flexibility

When we were first-year teachers, we dreamed of that mythical file cabinet, of the days when all our instructional ducks would be in a row, our planning periods would not be filled with frenzied panic, and we could just pull the perfect text out of the drawer and dazzle students *every* time. We learned along the way, of course, this isn't the way it really works. Let's be honest—the *How I Met Your Mother* article Rebekah used to teach meaningful comparison is already outdated. Next year, it will be every bit as irrelevant to her students as the lesson plans she made her very first year as a teacher.

When teaching hinges on dynamic, hot-off-the-press mentor texts, you have to be willing, as authors like Faulkner have said, to "kill all your darlings." So while on occasion we do dig out a perennial favorite (like Gary Soto's memoir "The Jacket"), in truth we have found few mentor texts that are actually timeless or connect with every group of students. Instead of demanding our students fit one text, we find texts to fit our students, and even when we loved a text the year before, we often find something different for a new year.

The real key to selecting mentor texts effectively is not the mythical file cabinet: It's flexibility. While we certainly have specific plans for a new school year or a new study, we live on the edge a bit, waiting to see what comes alive in the weeks and days immediately before we teach. In fact, the mentor texts we'll use probably haven't even been written when we sit down with our planners in August to map out the year. For instance, we know we'll study editorials with our ninth graders in the winter. We know we'll explicitly teach skills such as developing a claim and supporting it with evidence, structuring an argument, and acknowledging and responding to the other side. We know this study will take us about three weeks.

What we don't know is which mentor texts we will use. In fact, we *can't* know what will be happening next winter, what hot topics newspapers and pundits will be discussing, which professional editorials will best connect with the students who'll be sitting in front of us. So, we wait. With our other plans in place, we spend the weeks and days before we begin our study finding relevant, compelling editorials to mentor our students.

For those of us who love having a firm plan in place, this letting go takes some getting used to. This is why the structure of our planning and our classes doesn't change. Keeping these routines constant makes it easier to be flexible when it comes to finding mentor texts. Ultimately, we've found that relinquishing some advance planning in favor of the best organic planning accomplishes something wonderful, not just for our students but also for us. While our students receive instruction and inspiration from fresh, current texts, they also receive instruction and inspiration from a fresh, current *teacher*. Our teaching lives and breathes and stretches when our plans wait and we lean in to the new texts and ideas we find around us as we teach.

Selecting Mentor Texts to Teach Writers

Do you remember Captain's Choice? Those moments standing on the field during gym as classmates carefully selected players for their teams? We can still see their eyes darting back and forth as they sized up their potential teammates. For some of them it was—and still is—serious business. They had real selection criteria. *How fast is she? How much experience does he have? How many goals did she score last week?* For some of us, it was a painful experience. But looking back, we don't begrudge them. We realize now they were simply trying to build the best possible team.

We think about these boys with a smile now as we select texts to support a study. Like them, we mean business. In a world full of mentor texts, we have to choose those that will best engage and inspire our students, give them vision for the writing they're about to do, and propel them forward through the process. We can't risk choosing poorly and losing our students along the way, so we search with clear selection criteria in mind. We ask a series of questions of all potential texts we're considering as mentors.

"Question Flooding" Potential Mentor Texts

To help us explore the criteria of text selection, we've reprinted Ken Tucker's review of Pharrell Williams' album *G I R L* (Figure 2.3) below and followed it with a "question flood"

Pharrell Williams, who frequently goes by just his first name, is the sort of pop star whom many people would like to view as a friend. Emerging from hip-hop, he makes charming recordings that suggest a deep appreciation of pop, soul and R&B music extending at least as far back as the 1960s. To hear Pharrell on his new album *G I R L*, you'd think his world consisted of grooving on catchy beats and flirting with women. It's a lightweight image that draws gravitas from his prolific work ethic and a shrewd deployment of those influences.

"Brand New" is a song that dares you to think of it as brand new, as opposed to a canny recasting of riffs reminiscent of the Jackson 5. Pharrell is so confident in his ability to beguile you as producer, songwriter and singer, he all but buries the major guest star on that track: Justin. Even when Pharrell dares to come off as slightly predatory, as in "Hunter"—about tracking a woman—it's all done in the mildest manner possible. "Hunter" is also one of the high points of this album, with a rubber-band rhythm that stretches and snaps with witty elasticity. His high voice can remind you of Smokey Robinson and Marvin Gaye, as can a few of his musical hooks, but his tone is also pleasantly ghostly, wafting in and out of a melody with sinuousness that can be sly or sexy or serene.

Pharrell Williams began his career as half of a production duo called The Neptunes, providing material for acts as various as Nelly, Clipse and Jay Z. He was glancingly involved in a little pop scandal last year as a producer of (and video guest star in) "Blurred Lines," Robin Thicke's appropriation of Marvin Gaye. Pharrell can even confer fame upon inanimate objects: The Vivienne Westwood–designed hat he wore to the Grammy Awards achieved such fame; it was conscripted to help out again during the Oscars. In the new "Come Get It Bae" he says, "I can do anything you like," and it barely registers as boasting.

Pharrell has come in for some criticism recently as being merely a glossy pop hitmaker; for lacking edge. I find that this sort of critique is really code for his declining to revel in irony, sarcasm, or a bleak view of the world. And that is, in turn, why I find Pharrell Williams—and particularly the Pharrell on display throughout *G I R L*—an exhilarating performer. His big hat can barely contain his radiant braininess.

Figure 2.3 "Pharrell Williams: Just Exhilaratingly Happy" by Ken Tucker

(Gallagher 2006) explaining how we selected the review to use with students (Figure 2.4). As you read, note the things that strike you in the text, and try to name them as best you can. Don't spend too much time searching for the perfect label; use words that make sense to you and help you describe what you're noticing on the page.

WILL THE TEXT ENGAGE OUR CURRENT STUDENTS?

After we have been engaged by a text—and only after—the next thing we ask is, "Will it engage our students?" We thought Tucker's review of Pharrell's album would certainly

Primary Questions	Follow-Up Questions
Will the text engage my current students?	✳ Is the topic relevant to their lives? ✳ How much background knowledge do they already have? ✳ Do I have any experts in my class on this topic? ✳ How many of my students will express an interest in this text?
Does the text pass the highlighter test?	✳ Is it well crafted? Can I find lines I love? ✳ Can I find lines I think my students will love?
Is the text accessible to my students? How much scaffolding will the reading require?	✳ What unfamiliar or challenging vocabulary does this text contain? ✳ Can students use context clues to determine the meaning of unfamiliar words? ✳ Are there allusions students might not grasp? ✳ How much scaffolding will the reading require?
How long is the text? How might the length affect how we use it?	✳ Can it be read in a single class period? Will students have to take it home? ✳ Is the length challenging? How might the length affect how I use it? ✳ Should I use the whole thing or excerpted lines and sections?
Is it mentor text gold?	✳ Does the writer have a strong digital footprint? ✳ Can I find other texts by this writer?

Figure 2.4 Questions to Ask of Potential Mentor Texts

engage our students. *G I R L* had just been released, and many of our students were listening to it and also favored many of the musicians Tucker alludes to in the piece: Justin Timberlake, Nelly, Clipse, Jay Z, and Robin Thicke. Also, Pharrell had won a Grammy just a few short months prior to the publication of the article, so even if a student didn't care for his music, he might be interested in the bit of pop culture that it offered.

What's key is to select texts based on your *current* students' hobbies, interests, passions, and beliefs. We teach in a school where sports rule, so we are always on the lookout for great mentor texts about sports. In any given year, we have football players, soccer players, baseball players, softball players, runners, lacrosse players, field hockey players, basketball players, tennis players, and golfers in our classes, but even the sports change from year to year. When wrestling was added at our school two years ago, we looked for mentors who write about wrestling. Last year, we had a concentration of football and baseball players. This year we have a lot of runners, several dancers, two gymnasts, and a horseback rider.

Two years ago, finding a lot of Stephen Curry fanatics in our classes, we brought in the article about him mentioned earlier in this chapter. This year we used a new article about him, "Splash Engineering: A Look at the Science Behind Golden State's Sublime Shooters" (2014), but we quickly discovered many students didn't know much about him or seem to care. (2012–2013 was a breakout season for Curry, so he was on the news a lot more.) This flop taught us something important: We can't assume the texts we used with last year's students will have the same resonance with this year's. We have to know our students and listen to them carefully, pay attention to what they're reading, and ask them what they do outside school, what interests them. Then we have to go in search of texts that will engage them and teach them something about writing.

To ensure you're choosing mentor texts that will interest this year's students, try to envision a specific group of students (or even one student) you know will be excited about the text you've selected. Consider asking a student or a small group of students to read a mentor text before bringing it to class. Then ask, "Is this interesting to you? Do you think it's worth studying as a whole class?" Ultimately, the texts you select have to match the fluctuating, diverse interests of *your* students.

DOES THE TEXT PASS THE HIGHLIGHTER TEST?

The fact that the topic is engaging, however, is not enough to select a text as a mentor. It also has to pass the "highlighter test" and make us long for a marker in our hands so we can start noting the teaching possibilities immediately. It needs to move us to call one another and say, "Listen to this . . ." Texts that pass the highlighter test have a certain *I-wish-I-had-written-that* quality that excites us as readers, writers, and teachers. By nature this criterion is a bit subjective, but texts that bear this mark have certain qualities in common.

* They have a wonderful "way with words"—the writing is thoughtful, intentional, human.
* They have a strong sense of voice—the author seems to be talking directly to you.
* They have a sense of music—the writing is rhythmic, alliterative, and generally pleasing to the ear.

* They use words in surprising or playful ways.
* They have a meaningful structure and strong progression of ideas.
* They are highly imaginative or fresh.
* They contain persuasive, engaging, moving ideas.
* They present new ways of seeing or thinking about a topic or idea.

Needless to say, Tucker's review passed the highlighter test with its showy display of meticulous crafting. Any writer who can craft a phrase like *a rubber-band rhythm that stretches and snaps with witty elasticity* makes a reader (and a teacher) long for a highlighter! This is by far one of the most fun and most alliterative sentences we've ever read.

Highlighting the teaching possibilities in potential mentor texts is one of the most enjoyable parts of text selection because you get to do what you love to do: revel in words. You'll learn to notice and name the things in texts that strike you as well crafted, and everything you notice has teaching potential. And if you're having trouble finding anything to highlight, you'll know the text is probably not worthy of your and your students' attention.

IS THE TEXT ACCESSIBLE TO OUR STUDENTS? HOW MUCH SCAFFOLDING WILL THE READING REQUIRE?

While we knew our students might need help with some vocabulary (*gravitas, prolific, shrewd, canny, beguile*) and might be unfamiliar with some references (Jackson 5, Smokey Robinson, Marvin Gaye), we felt the basic message of Tucker's review—Pharrell is an "exhilarating performer"—was accessible. We also believed our students' interest in the review would make them want to make sense of it and thereby make it even more accessible.

In general, if you think the reading effort required of students outweighs the instructional value of a mentor text, you should think twice about using it. For example, some of the pieces in *The New Yorker*—one of our favorite sources—are just too challenging. Our students would have to read them multiple times before even getting to the reading-as-writers part. On the other hand, elevating students' writing inevitably means raising the level of their reading, so rarely do we throw a text out because it seems too challenging. You can always scaffold the study of a challenging text more, but if making sense of it is going to require so much effort students lose interest before they even get to read it as writers, it's probably best to put it aside. You might also consider excerpting longer, more challenging texts as mini-mentor texts. It's really important to show students whole mentor texts during a genre study (they need examples of how these texts work from beginning to end), but if you're trying to illustrate a specific technique, an excerpt will do just fine.

HOW LONG IS THE TEXT? HOW MIGHT THE LENGTH AFFECT HOW WE USE IT?

At four paragraphs long, Tucker's review is a perfect length for a mentor text. It's not that "short" is a quality of writing we look for in particular—in fact, students should be able to read and write papers of varying lengths—but shorter texts are often more accessible to students. For the same reasons a student (or adult!) may resist reading a 500-page book, students who are confronted with lengthy articles of five or more pages can feel defeated before they even begin. The brevity of Tucker's piece is one of its most appealing features as he manages to say so much about Pharrell in so few words. It's an exemplar of concise, smart writing. We also knew we'd be able to read it out loud—more than once—in a class period and still have time for discussion.

Depending on what you're looking for, you'll find that you have very little control over length. Most op-eds are very short, while memoir and commentary tend to run several pages. But we do not give priority to short texts. We favor engaging, moving texts, and if they happen to be short and conducive to reading within a short, forty-five-minute class period, we consider ourselves very lucky. So why talk about length at all then? While length does not determine whether we use a mentor text, it informs how we introduce it to students. For very long mentor texts (more than three pages), we ask students to complete the "first draft reading" (Gallagher 2006) at home. They are expected to come in with marked-up drafts indicating anything that caught their attention and intrigued them as writers. Then, during class the next day, we use our collective notes to determine which passages we reread together as a class.

Sometimes length determines if we choose to use a text as a mini-mentor or a whole mentor text. If we find a lengthy text and there's one section with interesting crafting work, we may choose to use just an excerpt rather than the entire text. In sum, while length never determines whether or not we select an excellent text as a mentor, it often influences how we present it to our writers.

IS IT MENTOR TEXT GOLD?

Finding mentor texts that are engaging in both content and form is a major success. However, some mentors deliver even more, providing little bonuses that can both simplify and enrich their study. We do a little happy dance when we strike mentor text gold and find a writer who

* uses the social mediums of the day (Twitter, Tumblr, etc.). Students respect writers who have the digital savvy to get their writing across both old and new mediums. As teachers, we like digital texts because they are easier to find and because using them shows students that looking to mentors is not

school work (textbooks), it's life work (everything we read anyway). Using digital texts also makes it more likely students will continue to look at texts in this way on their own.

∗ publishes on a regular (weekly, monthly) basis in newspapers, magazines, or blogs. We can study the patterns and interests of these writers over time.

∗ is knowable beyond his writing. When we find author interviews (printed or audio), pictures, or quotes about the writing process, they humanize writers and writing in important ways for students.

Lucky for us, Ken Tucker has a big digital footprint! In addition to his own website (kentucker.net), he is very active on Twitter (@kentucker). In fact, when we first tweeted his review of *GIRL* as a possible mentor text, he "liked" our tweet. A simple search for him will also reveal an NPR page, listing all his recent articles and stories, a Wikipedia page, and a few articles describing his past work at *Entertainment Weekly*.

Throwing Out the File Cabinet: Methods of Mentor Text Organization and Storage

One thing is for sure, without a strategy for organizing the mentor texts you collect, all of your reading and uncovering won't actually work for you or your students. There is no one right strategy, but there are specific questions you'll need to think about, such as where the texts will be stored, who will have access to them, and how you will label them so you can easily find them when you need them. Luckily, we have a lot of trial-and-error experience in organizing mentor texts and can share what we've learned and offer you some good ideas about how to get started.

Storage Options for Mentor Texts

We dabbled in paper storage in our early years of teaching with mentor texts. We kept giant binders behind our desks, organized by genre, where we would print, hole-punch, and store each mentor text we thought had potential for our students. We kept duplicates of these mentor texts in a crate of hanging files accessible for students to use during writing time. And, for the most part, this system worked. Except that it was bulky, unwieldy, and nontransportable. The texts weren't searchable for the teacher—except by hand and by skimming. And students had only limited access to them.

You might not be surprised to hear that we have since found that digital storage is the way to go.

There are many online digital curation platforms these days—so many, in fact, that we'll not presume to cover all of the tools you could use to keep track of your mentor texts. Troy Hicks, Sara Kajder, Catlin Tucker, and other leaders in digital literacy are more qualified to speak about the breadth and depth of online curation. In our experience, these platforms fall into three main categories: visual curation, social bookmarking, and digital storage. Here are four free options we have explored and think have potential for teachers as they find and store mentor texts for future use. We'll explore how students can use these tools in their own journey toward mentor text independence in the final chapter.

VISUAL CURATION

Visual curation relies on images to organize and store links to other websites. Rather than directly viewing your link, you first see an image thumbnail with a brief description of the site's content. One user or multiple users can post links to the various boards you create. Boards can be made public or privately shared with select users. The biggest advantage of this kind of curation is that it's visually attractive and appealing.

Learnist, the more educational cousin of Pinterest, is a popular curation site allowing you to build virtual bulletin boards to store information. While still highly visual, Learnist has a more professional (and less recipe-filled) feeling to it than Pinterest does. It also has the added benefit of allowing you to directly upload video in addition to website URLs. Learnist requires students to create an account in order to follow your mentor text boards. However, this platform is highly appealing to students for their own mentor text curation since tools like these are widely popular and look great.

SOCIAL BOOKMARKING

Diigo is a great social bookmarking tool, allowing you to quickly mark and easily retrieve saved websites from any computer. Though it doesn't have the visual impact of Pinterest or Learnist, it is cleanly organized and easy to access. Students can find you on Diigo and follow your library, or you can email specific texts or folders directly. Best of all, Diigo allows you to highlight and annotate a text online (and stores your markings), making it perfect for mentor text study, even when you're not with your students! You can use this feature to point out techniques of interest or leave questions for students to ponder as they consider the author's craft. Additionally, students can set up a Diigo account and annotate articles on their own (or in writing groups) and save those notes.

DIGITAL STORAGE AND ORGANIZATION

Our absolute favorite way of managing mentor texts is through Google Drive (Figures 2.5 and 2.6). Google Drive is an online hard drive, storing 30 GB of documents, spreadsheets,

Google and the Google logo are registered trademarks of Google Inc. Used with permission.

Figure 2.5 Mentor Text Organization in Google Drive

presentations, and images for each user for free. Basically it's your computer's hard drive, instantly accessible from any Internet-connected device and instantly shareable. Since all our other class materials in our nearly paper-free classrooms are linked directly to students on the drive, students already know how to use it, and all class resources are neatly housed in one place. There are no additional account setup or sharing logistics; it's easy and flexible, and we love it.

Our mentor text dropbox, as we call it, is a shared folder within our Google Drive where we have subfolders organized by genre, technique, topic, and purpose, and mentors for notebook time, which we'll discuss in Chapter 5. Google Drive not only makes these texts easy to categorize through our folders, but it also has a search bar that allows us to quickly search for a specific text in our subfolders.

Evernote, a note-taking and archiving app, is rapidly gaining popularity in the education world for its incredible flexibility. Just like Google Drive, information stored in Evernote can be accessed from any Internet-ready device (with the free Evernote app), and you can organize documents into folders and subfolders that are searchable. We mention Evernote because it has one big advantage over Google Drive. In Evernote, you can tag documents. We typically tag mentor texts by genre, technique, purpose, and topic. Later, we can view all our tags for all our notes to find articles that cluster together to form mentor text collections.

Notebooks in Evernote can be shared with individuals who, if they also have the app, can contribute to the notebook. This is ideal for collaborative gathering of mentor texts.

Evernote also allows you to create a public URL for your notebook so students can access the mentor texts in your current study.

Considerations When Collecting and Organizing Mentor Texts

Regardless of which storage platform you choose, you will need to consider a few things about your system of organization.

HOW WILL YOU GROUP YOUR MENTOR TEXTS?

Rather than having one, giant, overflowing file of mentor texts, we've found it helpful to categorize them for easy access. Because the units we teach vary slightly from year to year, it doesn't make sense for us to put them into folders by unit of study. Instead, we place mentor texts into more flexible groupings that allow us to easily pull texts to fit a variety of teachable moments. Over time, we have found we can group our mentor texts in at least four distinct ways: genre, writing technique, topic, and purpose. Figure 2.6 shows how we might categorize a few texts we used last school year.

Text	Genre	Writing Technique	Topic	Purpose
"Better with Age" by Chris. B. Brown **Text 2.9** *"Better with Age" by Chris. B. Brown http://grantland.com/features/peyton-manning-denver-broncos-offense/*	Sports Analysis	Using evidence to support an argument	Football; Peyton Manning	To analyze the cause of Manning's success
"Repetition" by Phil Kaye **Text 2.10** *"Repetition" by Phil Kaye http://youtu.be/EILQTDBqhPA*	Poetry	Seeking inspiration from outside sources	Divorce; separation; family stories	To cope with memories, to make peace with the past
"Save Us from the SAT" by Jennifer Finney Boylan **Text 2.11** *"Save Us from the SAT" by Jennifer Finney Boylan http://www.nytimes.com/2014/03/07/opinion/save-us-from-the-sat.html*	Op-ed	Weaving together narrative and argument	SATs; student stress	To persuade

Figure 2.6 Ways of Categorizing Mentor Texts

Does every text end up in four different folders? No. When a text beckons to us, it typically does so for one dominant reason. When Rebekah found "Better with Age," she was not looking for sports analysis; she needed something powerful to help students better understand how to support an argument with concrete evidence. Thus, she first stored this text in a folder for the writing technique "Using Evidence." However, many of Rebekah's students are interested in football, so she also placed it in a topic folder labeled "Football," as it might prove useful when conferring with these students. In short, we store texts where we are most likely to use them. Since we frequently alternate between genre-based and technique-based workshops, these are the folders we use most often.

Your system might be different, and it's important to consider the writing in your classroom. For a course in which students primarily write in a single genre (like AP or IB English courses in which the majority of students' writing is analytical), grouping by genre, topic, or purpose may not be helpful for you. In this situation, grouping texts by technique would likely be the way to go. For example, your folders might include: writing a strong claim, writing about characters, comparing and contrasting, writing about symbols. The mentor texts in these folders would exemplify these techniques. If you teach writing based solely on genre, that might be the only way you choose to group your mentor texts. If you teach by theme, then grouping texts by theme makes sense (relationships, heroes, quests). The bottom line is, what will make your life easiest? What will you reach for most often as you plan?

HOW WILL STUDENTS ACCESS YOUR MENTOR TEXTS?

Once you have figured out how you will store and access your own texts, you need to determine how students will access them. While we have scads of texts stored away digitally for future use, our students don't have access to all these texts at once. We use hard copies of mentor texts for instruction because we believe many of our students, especially those generally challenged by reading, need to see the words on paper where they can highlight and annotate. But we also want students to have digital access for revisiting these texts, so we add them to a folder in Google Drive. That folder, organized by genre or technique unit (Narrative Workshop, Literary Analysis Workshop, Evidence Workshop, etc.), also contains all the minilessons and handouts from that unit. Even though our students have all of this information in their writer's notebooks, this is a one-stop online shop of every resource a student might need as he or she writes. This hub is invaluable for students who lose or misplace notebooks, take incomplete notes during class, or have accommodations providing copies of class notes. It can also be used by parents or administrators who want to see what we're doing in class or by tutors who are working with our students.

However your students access your collection of mentor texts (perhaps through your Learnist board or Diigo library), depending on their experiences with writing, you might consider giving them more freedom to roam around your collection. Especially with the guidance that comes from conferring, students might use these texts in all kinds of ways to move their own writing forward. Ultimately, the goal is for students to use mentor texts the same way real writers do, with the independence and confidence to pull what they need when they need it. With plenty of scaffolding and modeling, we expect students to integrate these texts into their writing routines by the end of the year.

HOW CAN YOU MAKE MENTOR TEXT COLLECTION MORE COLLABORATIVE?

Throughout this section, you might have noticed we've referred to "our mentor texts" and "our Google Drive." While we each have our own classrooms and frequently chat about planning and instructional strategies, the collection and organization of mentor texts is something we truly do in tandem for this simple reason: It's richer, more useful, more productive, easier, and much more fun. In Chapter 9, we'll discuss getting students involved in the search for mentor texts. But there is no substitute for a group of like-minded, supportive colleagues to share the work of finding inspiring texts and the enjoyment of watching students discover their riches. Grab some colleagues—in your school or through your PLN—and devise a way to pool your mentor text resources!

Closing Thoughts

Being a teacher who puts mentor texts at the center of the classroom is a rich and exciting way of life. It means running to your computer to scan your Twitter feed in the morning as you look for mentor text treasures for your students. It means tapping into your writing sensibilities every time you read and enjoying it doubly—as a reader and as a teacher of writing. It means learning beside your students and keeping their interests at the helm. It means finding an organizational system that works for you and your students and puts the mentor texts at everyone's fingertips for the moments when they will be needed in the throes of writing. It means finding texts and mining them for lessons because there is no better way to honor your teaching and increase the repertoire of what you can offer students.

CHAPTER THREE

Moving from Mentor Texts to Writing Lessons

"**W**hat would you still like to do as writers that you have not had a chance to do?"

It was May, and my students were staring out the large courtyard-facing window, watching the lawn mower kick up fresh grass.

We had explored multiple genres together that year—memoir, critical review, and profile, among others—and I was curious about the vision these writers had for their next piece of writing. It would take some prodding, though.

"Jimmy, what's on your Feedly right now? What are you reading?" I asked, hoping to engage him.

"Um, stuff from The Onion, I guess," he said nonchalantly. I jumped on it.

"OK! So satire! How do we feel about satire?" He nodded, looking up from his notebook.

That night I spent a lot of time on theonion.com. My lack of knowledge about satire both daunted and exhilarated me. So I set to work, trying to figure out this thing called satire. I read dozens of news articles. I read The Onion cofounder Tim Keck's five-step guide to writing an Onion article. I researched humor writing and spent some time surfing The New Yorker's Daily Cartoon Archive. I watched a few Colbert Report skits. I laughed so hard my stomach ached.

And in just a few hours' time, a new genre study was born.

—Allison

When Allison decided to teach a unit of study in satire, she found mentor texts, figured out the components of effective satire, and developed lessons around those elements. From start to finish—teacher planning to student publication—her entire study was built on a strong foundation of mentor texts. And while satire was a very new genre for her to explore as a teacher, the process she used to plan and implement the unit of study was very familiar. It's the same process we follow every time we set out to plan a study:

1. Decide on a writing unit.
2. Collect mentor texts.
3. Study patterns to create lessons.
4. Arrange lessons into a unit.
5. Teach.
6. Confer, study patterns in student writing, and return to mentor texts.

You may be wondering how this happens—how an entire study can be formed around a set of mentor texts, how to find techniques to teach, and how to build lessons from those techniques. In this chapter, we'll unpack all those wonderings as we walk you through the different phases of planning with mentor texts. For each phase of planning and implementation, you'll find anchor questions to help guide your thinking. We'll begin by looking at how to decide on a writing unit to teach.

Step 1: Decide on a Writing Unit

Anchor Question: What kinds of writing do my students need to study? What kinds of writing are my students interested in studying?

The best plans come from both the quiet, contemplative moments with your planner and the spur-of-the-moment revelations you have when you're reading or working with students. Some things you know you have to teach; other things you *want* to teach as they spring up more organically, like the satire study in Allison's class. The key is to work with a master plan that leaves room for both.

Typically, writing units are planned around one of four ideas: a genre, a writing technique, a student interest or need, or a mentor text. Most required curricula (the have-tos of our master plans) focus on genres or writing techniques. Writing arguments, informational articles, and narratives, or studying the support of an argument or the use of concrete detail are the foundations of all competent writing. They are also written into state and Common Core standards, so most all of us have to plan to address them in our teaching. But even with prescribed studies, hopefully you can still be a decision maker in your own classroom. In a previous school where Rebekah taught, the writing genres were dictated by quarter. Rebekah couldn't choose when she taught argument writing, for example, but she could choose *how* to teach it. Rather than pulling rote prompts from a suggested list, Rebekah's students learned the same skills through writing reviews of books, television shows, video games, films, iPhones, or restaurants.

To imagine a year filled with interesting writing units, it's useful to think about possibilities for study within each of the four frames. We'll start with genre, since it's the most common.

Starting with Genre

Exposure to a variety of kinds of writing and experience working with those genres is fundamental to learning to write at increasing levels of depth, sophistication, and effect. Because genre is about fulfilling different purposes with writing, it increases a writer's agency to make a difference in the world when she has confidence writing in different genres.

The genres we teach change slightly each year as curricular considerations change, as our student populations change, and as our interests change. But year to year, one thing remains nonnegotiable: All genres must be *real* to make it into the curriculum. We must be able to find examples of the genre, written by professional writers, in the world outside school. This includes academic writing like literary analysis. After all, if we are teaching our students to be writers, we must justify to them that the writing they are doing is life writing, not just school writing. To this end, we connect students with argument writing through the op-ed section of the newspaper; we introduce literary analysis to our students by first working through film analysis; students create informational texts and learn to sort facts using infographics; narrative is folded into larger memoirs and profiles.

Each year, we teach six to eight different genres to expose students to many different kinds of real-world writing. Here are some genres we have recently taught:

* critical review (film, book, album, television, products)
* memoir
* narrative scene
* extended narrative
* This I Believe essay
* editorial
* interview/profile
* infographic

 * poetry
 * film analysis
 * literary analysis.

In selecting genres, it's important to find balance between the kinds of writing students will need to be successful for their academic future and the kinds of writing you are reading through your Twitter feed—the real-world writing being produced every day. Remember, students won't be in school forever, so they need to see purposes for writing beyond school. Genre studies not only give students a good foundation for writing, they also help them see what writing is really used for and what writers can accomplish when they settle on a form that best serves their purpose.

Starting with Techniques

Another kind of study you might plan is one focused on a writerly technique that transcends genre and is important to all types of writing. Luckily, the qualities of good writing aren't easily boxed in by genre, so sometimes it makes sense to study specific techniques that help students make more sophisticated, informed choices in their writing. In a technique study, you show students mentor texts in a *variety* of genres, each text displaying a different element of the same technique. For example, rather than planning a genre study of editorials, you might decide to teach a technique study focused on author's purpose. You then might examine how the author's purpose is revealed in a poem, in a news report, in a narrative scene, and in a book review. To show what they've learned from the study, students choose the genre they want to write and incorporate the technique into their writing. Students choosing their own genres is one of the real benefits of technique study, as well as their being exposed to even more different genres of writing.

Other possibilities for technique studies that cross genres include

 * **story:** the narrative a piece of writing tells; the way it's plotted; its beginning, middle, and end
 * **evidence:** the way a writer supports the point of the piece
 * **argument:** the writer's claim or purpose and how it is developed
 * **voice:** the writer's personality expressed on paper
 * **observation:** how writers closely describe events, people, places, objects
 * **research:** the way a writer weaves in pieces of outside information to support the purpose
 * **punctuation:** the punctuation a writer uses to create style and meaning.

When might a technique study make sense? You might consider this path to planning with students who are ready for a new challenge. Perhaps your students already have a lot of experience with different genres and are excellent writers. Technique study extends students' thinking about the qualities of good writing and encourages them to zoom in on craft. Conversely, technique study is also helpful when most of a class needs specific, focused instruction on a single technique. Later in the chapter, we'll show how Rebekah planned a technique study to help a group of students who were struggling with using evidence to support their arguments.

Technique studies can also be useful for teachers in courses that primarily focus on a single genre of writing, such as AP or IB courses where students principally write literary analysis. As we described in Chapter 2, because literary analysis is hard to find outside of school, we use mini-mentor texts for a variety of technique studies that support students in writing any kind of analysis. For example, in an AP/IB course, units of technique study might look like this:

* analyzing theme
* analyzing character
* analyzing symbol
* analyzing an entire text
* analyzing a short passage
* comparing and contrasting two texts.

While technique studies tend to be better suited for writers who have the foundation of genre study, they can help all students hone in on specific craft elements, pushing their writing forward into new territories.

Starting with Students' Interests and Needs

Looking at a yearlong planning calendar, you won't be able to tell which studies were planned in response to students' interests and needs because these studies are also focused on genres or techniques. What makes them different is *why* they are on the calendar at all—because your students wanted or needed them to be.

Remember Jimmy from the vignette at the beginning of the chapter? Jimmy was a voracious reader. He devoured war novels, outgrowing the history section of Allison's classroom library within the first month. He was also a fan of humor writing—sometimes she would catch him reading online articles from *The Onion* when he was supposed to be researching. He was a strong writer, too, but his enthusiasm for the written word stopped at the books he chose to read. Allison would often catch him cradling a book in his lap during writing lessons—or gazing longingly out the window during notebook time. She recalls brief flickers of engagement during class that year. For instance, during a critical review study, he reviewed the video game *DayZ* and used screenshots of himself playing the game to help illustrate the high quality of the graphics. But, in general, he was a passive writer. What might happen if Allison gave Jimmy some stake in the direction of his writing? What if she started with the thing he loved?

Allowing for this kind of flexibility in your year-at-glance planning can often have surprising and rewarding results. Jimmy's satire, "Putin and Obama Decide Fate of Ukraine in a 1v1, No-Holds-Barred Cage," was brilliant—his strongest piece by far. And all Allison had to do was ask him what he was reading for him to learn that the stuff he reads for fun could be the stuff of his writing life.

Sports analysis, graphic novels, fan fiction, fantasy writing—these aren't our natural go-tos when planning writing instruction. Our students are interested in these genres, however, and incorporating them into our plans for writing can engage students like nothing else. Remember, also, that so many techniques for writing well are used across all genres, so students are learning the craft of writing, regardless of genre.

Starting with a Mentor Text

Sometimes a plan for a writing unit starts with a particularly spectacular mentor text or group of texts. While we normally plan "forward" by choosing a unit and then finding the mentor texts to fill it, we occasionally plan backward because *we* are so inspired by the texts we hope will also inspire our students. On the yearlong calendar, these units look just like other genre and technique studies, but they start in a very different place.

Last summer, Allison stumbled across an infographic titled "How Teens Read: The Kids Are All Right."

Text 3.1 "How Teens Read: The Kids Are All Right" by Delano Scott and Daniel Vecchitto *http://www.slideshare.net/PenguinRandomHouse/how-teens-read*

The bright and funky blue-and-yellow infographic grabbed Allison's attention as the content displayed results of surveys about how often teenagers read for fun, how much they have read in the last month, the popularity of eBooks, where students get book recommendations, and more. Her first thought: "I could share this in my reading work-shop. It's so visually appealing! It's so fun to read! My students will be captivated!"

The infographic stuck with her, and she found herself thinking about it again and again. She began searching: What other educational infographics could she find? What other topics do infographics explore? What do all infographics have in common? What are the necessary parts and pieces of a successful infographic? In short, she got sucked into the infographic craze, and what began as a personal interest in learning more about infographics quickly became a full-on search for ways to bring infographics into her writing classroom. She was truly starting from scratch; she couldn't yet articulate what an in-fographic was when she decided to plan an infographic study.

She began her study just as we begin with our students: by fully immersing herself in the literature of the genre. She googled "sports infographics," "reading infographics," "teen infographics," and other search terms she thought might yield student-friendly infograph-ics. She favorited infographics others were tweeting. She searched the website fivethirty eight.com. In short, she tried to get her hands on as many infographics as she could so she could begin to understand the genre: what it is, how it works, and what it enables writers to do.

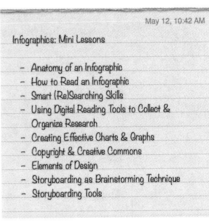

During the immersion period, she created a list of noticings, things like "combines visuals and text" and "in-corporates stats and facts." From that list of noticings, an informal curriculum began to emerge in the form of pos-sible lessons (Figure 3.1).

A whole study was born out of the passion for a single text. These studies are incredibly engaging because they al-ways lead us to new understandings, and our students en-joy seeing us learning alongside them. The next time you read something that's so compelling you can't stop think-ing about it, try imagining it into a study!

Figure 3.1 Allison's Noticings About Infographics

Units Across the Year

Writing studies should be planned so they build on one another across the year, allowing the techniques students learn early to be transferred to studies later in the year. In *Write Beside Them* (2008), Penny Kittle suggests a continuum for developing writing skills, be-ginning with familiar genres like narrative and expanding to analysis by the end of the year. Similarly, when we look at the yearlong calendar, we like to build our studies from the most fundamental to the most challenging, while still being flexible enough to look at our students and the writing around us and shift our game plan when needed. Because genre study is fundamental to all yearlong planning, it's important to consider it specifically.

When planning genre studies for a year, you might consider

* *Which genres are most accessible?* Plan these studies early in the year. We typically start with memoir. However, Nancie Atwell recommends beginning with poetry as it has the power to teach "every lesson . . . about effective writing" (2014, 66).
* *Which genres complement one another and share skills you can build on and from?* Plan these genre studies so they fall next to each other in the yearlong plan. For example, literary analysis is a tough starting point for many young writers, so we think it's best to study film analysis first, then literary. The skills they acquire studying films are the same skills they will need to tackle literature.
* *Which genres will require more practice and stamina?* Plan these genre studies later in the year. For us, this means critical, analytical writing at the end of the year because the students we teach move on to English classes that write analysis exclusively. We want to leave them with the skills they will need to access first in their upcoming English classes.

Figure 3.2 gives a snapshot of two different yearlong calendars we have used in our classrooms.

Genre Study	Genre and Technique Study
August/September—Intro to Writing Workshop and Book Review	**August/September**—GS: Memoir
October—Narrative Snapshot	**October**—GS: Feature Article
November—This I Believe	**November/December**—GS: Critical Review
December—Territory Writing	**January**—TS: Evidence Study
January—Editorial	**February**—GS: Editorial/Commentary
February—Film Analysis	**March**—GS: Poetry
March—Interview/Profile	**April**—TS: Research Study
April—Literary Analysis	**May/June**—TS: Punctuation w/ Multigenre Writing Project
May/June—Territory Writing/Portfolio	

Figure 3.2 Yearlong Calendar of Units

A WAY IN

We spend a lot of time thinking about our writing units because there is just so much to consider. What is required of us by our school? Our district? State and federal standards? What experiences have our students had with writing? Where do we need them to go as writers? What do they need to be prepared for the future? What is interesting and relevant to them? What are we inspired to teach? What is *best* for our students?

In your notebook, spend some time writing down the considerations *you* will have to make in planning your units: What writing are you "required" to teach? What writing do your students really want or need you to teach? What writing would you be *excited* to teach?

Looking at these three lists, where is there overlap? Where is there opportunity to teach something your students need to learn in a way that will be relevant and engaging? Where is there opportunity to teach something that is required in a way that also inspires you as the teacher?

Step 2: Collect Mentor Texts

Anchor Question: How can I create a cluster of mentor texts to enhance students' understanding of a genre or technique while demonstrating a range of writing possibilities?

Chapter 2 was devoted entirely to the topic of finding mentor texts for teaching, so we don't need to say a whole lot more about it here other than a few reminders. Once you have chosen the study you want to plan, you'll need to select a cluster of mentor texts— three to six seems ideal—that you'll use for your whole-class teaching in the study. For individual texts, remember the criteria of engagement, accessibility, length, and, of course, the highlighter test to select the best possible mentor texts for your study. For the cluster of texts, remember that it's important the different selections show a range of topics, styles, and tones in writing. When you have found the cluster you feel will be successful, you are ready to plan your instruction.

Step 3: Study Patterns to Create Lessons

Anchor Question: What combination of skills would best serve my students in this study?

We know we will include three basic kinds of lessons in every writing study: author's purpose, content/organization/style, and grammar/usage. Early in the study, it's critical to explore author's purpose as it helps students understand why authors do the kinds of writing we are studying. The bulk of our lessons (four or five at least) will then focus on content/organization/style as this represents the heart of crafting and writerly decision making. And then based on the content of the study, we always choose a few grammar/usage lessons that make sense in the context of student work. These categories cover the basics of learning to write well.

With the mentor texts in front of us, we ask ourselves a series of questions about the texts in order to pinpoint teaching possibilities (Figure 3.3). We then list all the techniques that have potential for us. If a technique appears in multiple texts, we know it's important, and it moves to the top of our instructional priority list.

When you study a cluster of excellent mentor texts, you will find so many good writing techniques, each with the potential to make a fantastic lesson. We typically find eight to ten lesson ideas in *each* text. It would take far too long to teach them all, so selection is key.

Type of Skill	Questions We Ask of the Mentor Texts
Author's Purpose	∗ How is the author's purpose made clear in this text? ∗ How does the author support this purpose?
Content/Organization/Style	∗ How is this text organized and structured? How does it begin? How does it end? ∗ What are the parts of this text? What ideas/topics are explored? How are the shifts from one idea to the next marked? ∗ How does the writer make this writing compelling for the reader? ∗ Are there certain stylistic patterns that seem to be characteristic of this writer?
Grammar and Usage	∗ Are there grammatical structures that are particularly useful to this genre? ∗ What punctuation might be useful for establishing a student's voice within this genre? ∗ Does this mentor use a particular tone or jargon?

Figure 3.3 Questions We Ask of the Mentor Texts

Selecting Lessons to Teach

Of course, not every technique will be relevant to the unit you are developing or appropriate for your students, but many of them are. How then do you choose which techniques make the cut? Here are the questions we ask.

WHAT RECURRING PATTERNS ARE PRESENT IN THIS MENTOR TEXT?

We teach our close readers that repeated ideas are important in a story. They are also important in writing. If a mentor uses a particular technique, say figurative language, multiple times in a piece, we note this as an important aspect of that writer's style and possibly of that particular genre. Since we can easily point to different examples of the same technique at work in a single piece, that technique gets bumped to the top of our teaching list.

WHAT CAN THIS MENTOR TEXT TEACH THAT THE OTHERS IN THE CLUSTER CAN'T?

The reason we collect a cluster of mentor texts is to emphasize the different paths writers take to writing effectively in a specific genre or with a specific technique. When we consider how we will use a specific mentor text, we examine that text's unique qualities and focus on the techniques it can highlight that others cannot.

ARE THERE RECURRING PATTERNS IN MENTOR TEXTS ACROSS THE CLUSTER?

Recurring patterns and connections between texts often help us see what really makes a genre, a genre. For example, when planning her satire unit, Allison noticed that every mentor text she was considering began with a very short "get to the point" sentence that was jam-packed with information and funny details. With a little research, she discovered that these sentences are called ledes, and ledes are also one of the essential features of news articles. The lede became an important concept in their study, and students were able to grasp it because they saw it working in multiple mentor texts, not just one.

While each mentor text in a cluster highlights different facets of a single genre or technique, what's similar across the texts is equally important, and these overlapping lessons also move to the top of the teaching list.

WHAT CAN OUR STUDENTS HANDLE? IS THIS TECHNIQUE TIMELY IN THE BROADER SEQUENCE OF LESSONS?

In all our planning, we think about what our students need to learn, but we also think about what our students are *ready* to learn. Our mentors often use brilliant, sophisticated crafting techniques, but our student writers just aren't ready to learn them. We teach only those skills that are developmentally appropriate and timely in the broader scope of the course. If our students haven't yet mastered using simple figurative language in a piece, it doesn't make sense to push them to craft extended metaphors. Our mentor texts and our lessons are only as strong as our knowledge of our students.

Step 4: Arrange Lessons into a Unit

Anchor Question: How can I sequence my lessons in a way that will support student writing and anticipate the needs of writers as they move through a study?

Once you've selected the lessons you think you'll teach, your calendar is wide open and you're ready to plan the study. How do you begin? The first thing you'll want to consider is time. How often you see your students and for how long will greatly impact the pace of your study. We see our students daily for about forty-five minutes. Chapters 5 through 8 are devoted to unpacking what the elements of our class look like in action. For now, Figure 3.4 shows in broad strokes what a class period looks like for us once we've settled into our routines. If you are lucky and have a longer class period, your students can have even more time for writing and conferring!

Class Element	Approximate Class Time	Purpose
Notebook Time	7–10 minutes	Stimulates thinking, writing, and play with words. Notebook time also provides opportunities to practice revision and to develop bigger pieces of writing down the road.
Writing Lesson	10–15 minutes	Provides explicit, direct instruction on a single technique for students to try in their own writing.
Writing and Conferring	As much time as possible	Gives students the gift of time—time to practice, time to use the skills they have just been taught, time to marinate in ideas, time to have questions answered, time to share and have writing shared with them. In short, this is the time students need to write and become writers.

Figure 3.4 Overview of One Class Period

How long a study might last depends on many factors—your students, your class schedule, your personal preferences. Linda Rief (2014) asks her eighth graders to bring two pieces of writing to final draft every four weeks; Nancie Atwell (1998), two pieces every six weeks. Given our class length, asking students to bring one piece to final copy every three to four weeks seems appropriate to us. Some studies may take longer, however. A commentary unit with research, for example, might span four to five weeks. We like to use the month as our basic unit of time with the understanding that some studies may take more or less time.

We estimate that we can teach between twelve and fifteen lessons in any given study—one per class period. Some of these lessons are procedural—how to submit an essay to your Google Folder, how to hold a peer conference. In other lessons, we roll up our sleeves, put our notebooks under the document camera, and write in front of our students. But the bulk of our lessons target specific techniques gleaned from our mentors that students need to write successfully in the study.

When arranging lessons into a unit, consider a few guidelines.

* *Frontload content and craft lessons.* Writers will need these first. Without ideas, without a way with words, students will struggle to begin.
* *Follow with lessons on structure.* Once students have their ideas down, they will be ready to learn about ways to structure and organize their writing.
* *End with lessons that focus on the conventions of writing.* Writers won't be ready for these lessons until they are ready to take their writing to final copy anyway.
* *Build on the skills students have been taught in previous studies.* For example, description of people and places is often covered in a study of memoir. However, vivid description is equally important in satire as it engages the reader and is often what amplifies the hilarity. Students should have the opportunity to practice skills over multiple studies, not just one.
* *Introduce skills that might bridge one study and the next.* When planning, it's important to think about where your students have been and where they're headed, and how the skills you're teaching can lay the foundation for rich lessons ahead. When planning her satire study, Allison began with the skill of "getting to the point," a lesson in narrowing the scope of a piece that had helped her students at the end of their previous study of critical reviews.

With these guidelines in mind, it's important to take a flexible approach when arranging lessons into a unit. Students need things you don't plan for. Some lessons take more time than you originally planned. Your goal is to create a framework that will maximize writing practice and allow the unanticipated, real writerly needs of your students to emerge.

Step 5: Teach

Anchor Question: How can I use mentor texts in writing lessons to engage students and teach them something about writing?

When it comes to teaching lessons, mentor texts remain front and center. While every lesson does not necessarily include a mentor text, the majority do because mentor texts help you "show" your writers what you "tell" them about during the instruction. If lessons create powerful frames of reference, then mentor texts extend these frames, showing writers different ways of achieving a desired effect in their writing. Depending on the technique and the number of examples you have, each lesson will be a little different but will follow a predictable format.

The Anatomy of a Writing Lesson

A solid lesson has the following components:

1. **Introduction:** Tell students in clear terms what technique they will be learning.
2. **Purpose:** Explain why writers use this technique.
3. **Plentiful examples:** Show mentor texts that illustrate the technique.
4. **Invitation:** Ask students to think about how this technique might benefit them and to look for strategic places in their writing where this technique might prove useful.

Present the techniques as a "choice to consider" (Atwell 1998, 66), inviting students to play and experiment with them in their writing that day. A good lesson adds a tool to each writer's toolbox.

Although most lessons follow this format, you might consider two alternatives. Occasionally you might start with step three, showing examples of mentor texts and asking students to deduce the technique through observation. For example, you might highlight three or four sentences from mentor texts that illustrate the technique you want students to learn. Read these sentences aloud and ask students to jot down what they notice. As students talk about what they noticed, nudge them to "make a theory about why a writer might use this craft" and "give the craft a name" (Ray 1999, 233).

For a change in routine or for students who are ready to be challenged, you might consider giving students a mentor text and letting them decide what they think is worth zooming in to study. A lot of the things we know about writing we learned this way because students notice things in texts we had never thought to notice. Sometimes students are so excited about what they want to study in a text that you can extend this teaching over several days if you have time.

Step 6: Confer and Study Patterns in Student Writing

Anchor Question: How can I use mentor texts to clarify, reteach, and push student writing forward?

Ah, but the planning is not over. As students begin to write, we enter a more responsive phase of planning, moving around the room, pausing to sit beside students, check in, ask questions, and see how the work is going. And we are learning. We often have aha moments during these conferences, suddenly realizing we haven't taught something fundamental, or that students desperately need a specific technique that's not in their toolbox, or that something we have previously taught needs clarification.

Allison learned this only too well in her study of satire after she taught a lesson on ledes. A lede is the first paragraph of any news story, and it gives the who, what, where, when, and why of the story to follow. In satire, ledes incorporate small, absurd details. As she conferred in the days after her lesson, she noticed many students struggling to identify the main points of the news story they were satirizing—a skill she hadn't anticipated them needing and hadn't planned into her unit. So she pushed the pause button and planned a lesson on identifying the main parts of a news story and weaving them into a compelling lede. Over the next few days, it was clear the extra lesson helped her students as their ledes were so much more concise, relevant, and clever.

Just as you studied the patterns in your mentor texts to identify lessons for teaching, now you will study the patterns you see in students' writing. If the whole class is struggling to incorporate concrete details, or five students really need clarification on writing a clear claim, or a single student's writing is ready for a next-level challenge, head back to the plan book and consider what additional lessons you need to teach and which mentor texts you'll use to teach them.

As you plan to reteach, or just teach some more, you may find just what you need in your cluster of mentor texts. If you initially used a restaurant review to teach the skill of making a claim, for instance, you might use a different text in your cluster to revisit this same skill. Alternatively, you might search for new mentor texts to add to the cluster. This often happens when a student masters the skills of the study and is waiting for the rest of the class to catch up. A more sophisticated mentor text in the same genre may be just the thing to nudge this student toward more sophistication in her own writing.

Planning—just like every aspect of teaching, just like every aspect of writing—is recursive. It is almost never finished, and it is certainly never perfect. Even as students are submitting their polished papers, we are thinking, "Ugh, why didn't I state that more clearly?" and "I am definitely going to do that better next time." As long as students are still drafting and revising, we are still searching for ways that mentor texts can instruct and inspire them.

Allison and Rebekah Each Plan a Unit

The consistent, intentional use of mentor texts in our writing classrooms has both grounded and lifted our instruction in ways we never imagined. While we share the same structure for planning, and sometimes even the same texts, our classes often look very different, reflecting our different students and our different planning processes.

Last year, we each planned writing units using Ken Tucker's review of *G I R L*, Pharrell's new album (the same review you saw in Chapter 2). What follows is a snapshot of each unit. As you read through each snapshot, consider how individual our planning and teaching are even though we're both using the same process (described earlier) to plan. Consider, also, the versatility of a single mentor text.

A Genre Study in Allison's Class

The first snapshot describes a genre study of critical reviews (of restaurants, music, books, and video games) in Allison's classroom.

DECIDE ON A WRITING UNIT

The idea for Allison's study started with a desire to study critical reviews. At the time, her mixed-grade writing workshop (9–12) had just finished a study of concept essays—essays that explain a concept, phenomenon, or theory (kind of like the writing you see in *Time* or *Scientific American*). Students used Storify, a social network service that lets users create stories using social media, to embed relevant media bytes into their writing. She wanted to continue exploring multimedia writing, and it seemed critical reviews would offer an opportunity to do this with her students.

COLLECT MENTOR TEXTS

Allison remembered a mentor text Rebekah had told her about recently—a review of Pharrell's new album. She knew her students were listening to his music, so she went in search of it on the dropbox. Reading through it, she instantly liked the brevity of the piece, Tucker's creative metaphors, and the embedded sound clips. She was confident her students would find this review enjoyable and relevant.

From there, Allison began thinking about other topics that might engage her students. Her mind wandered to food—something all students like—so Allison cued up the *New York Times* food section on her computer and read several reviews by food critic Pete Wells. She chose his review of a steakhouse for two reasons: She thought it would appeal to her students, and she wanted a review of a restaurant that would be accessible, not stuffy and over the top.

Next she thought of the morning conversations that filled her room and knew immediately what she had to find: a review of a video game. Did they exist? And if so, were they any good? Were people writing intelligently about video games? A quick visit to *The A.V. Club* gave Allison just what she needed. To round out her collection, Allison searched for a book review and landed on a review of Kevin Powers' new book of poems. Jimmy had just finished reading *The Yellow Birds*, and her secret agenda was to turn him on to some of Powers' poetry. She also chose a television review of *Modern Family*, a show she knew her students were watching. She confirmed the quality and readability of these texts, and she was ready to begin.

"With Poetic Intensity, Kevin Powers Tackles the Terror of War"
by Abigail Deutsch

Text 3.2 "With Poetic Intensity, Kevin Powers Tackles the Terror of War" by Abigail Deutsch *http://www.npr.org/2014/04/02/295828579/with-poetic-intensity-kevin-powers -tackles-the-terror-of-war*

"*Modern Family*: 'A Hard Jay's Night'" by Joshua Alston

Text 3.3 "*Modern Family*: 'A Hard Jay's Night'" by Joshua Alston *http://www.avclub .com/tvclub/modern-family-hard-jays-night-203009*

continues

"*Titanfall* Supplants Its Ancestors with Speed and Scale" by Ryan Smith

Text 3.4 "*Titanfall* Supplants Its Ancestors with Speed and Scale" by Ryan Smith *http://www.avclub.com/article/titanfall-supplants-its-ancestors-speed-and-scale-202272*

"Fred and Barney Would Feel Right At Home" by Pete Wells

Text 3.5 "Fred and Barney Would Feel Right At Home" by Pete Wells *http://www .nytimes.com/2014/01/29/dining/restaurant-review-m-wells-steakhouse-in-long-island-city -queens.html*

"Pharrell Williams: Just Exhilaratingly Happy" by Ken Tucker

Text 3.6 "Pharrell Williams: Just Exhilaratingly Happy" by Ken Tucker *http://www.npr .org/2014/03/06/286864627/pharrell-williams-new-album-is-as-happy-as-its-hit-single*

STUDY PATTERNS IN THE MENTOR TEXTS TO CREATE LESSONS

When Allison studied her cluster to identify possible lessons for the unit, she was look-ing for broad, sweeping noticings that would help her students understand the genre of review writing, as well as "on the line" craft moves that might excite her students and give them a sense of possibility for their own work. She read each mentor text carefully, making note of possible craft techniques for teaching. Figure 3.5 shows her notes for Tucker's review.

ARRANGE LESSONS INTO A UNIT

Allison first thought about what her students needed and how the mentor texts might help them address those needs. Coming out of the concept essay unit, some needed more practice with multimedia writing. Many of the reviews she had collected incorporated hyperlinks, images, and audio/video. Additionally, her class struggled with the crafting of complex sentences, and Tucker's serpentine sentences provided excellent models. But these felt like "later lessons."

Looking at her list of noticings, she wondered what would make a good first les-son. Her mind drifted to an interview she had recently read in which Sam Tanenhaus,

Pharrell Williams: Just Exhilaratingly Happy
by Ken Tucker, NPR

Pharrell Williams, who frequently goes by just his first name, is the sort of pop star whom many people would like to view as a friend. Emerging from hip-hop, he makes charming recordings that suggest a deep appreciation of pop, soul and R&B music extending at least as far back as the 1960s. To hear Pharrell on his new album *G I R L*, you'd think his world consisted of grooving on catchy beats and flirting with women. It's a lightweight image that draws gravitas from his prolific work ethic and a shrewd deployment of those influences.

"Brand New" is a song that dares you to think of it as brand new, as opposed to a canny recasting of riffs reminiscent of the Jackson 5. Pharrell is so confident in his ability to beguile you as producer, songwriter and singer, he all but buries the major guest star on that track: Justin. Even when Pharrell dares to come off as slightly predatory, as in "Hunter" — about tracking a woman — it's all done in the mildest manner possible. "Hunter" is also one of the high points of this album, with a rubber-band rhythm that stretches and snaps with witty elasticity. His high voice can remind you of Smokey Robinson and Marvin Gaye, as can a few of his musical hooks, but his tone is also pleasantly ghostly, wafting in and out of a melody with sinuousness that can be sly or sexy or serene.

Pharrell Williams began his career as half of a production duo called The Neptunes, providing material for acts as various as Nelly, Clipse and Jay Z. He was glancingly involved in a little pop scandal last year as a producer of (and video guest star in) "Blurred Lines,"Robin Thicke's appropriation of Marvin Gaye. Pharrell can even confer fame upon inanimate objects: The Vivienne Westwood-designed hat he wore to the Grammy Awards achieved such fame, it was conscripted to help out again during the Oscars. In the new "Come Get It Bae" he says, "I can do anything you like," and it barely registers as boasting.

Pharrell has come in for some criticism recently as being merely a glossy pop hitmaker; for lacking edge. I find that this sort of critique is really code for his declining to revel in irony, sarcasm or a bleak view of the world. And that is, in turn, why I find Pharrell Williams — and particularly the Pharrell on display throughout *G I R L* — an exhilarating performer. His big hat can barely contain his radiant braininess.

Author
Comment [1]: Playful Title

Author
Comment [2]: Intentional use of second person

Author
Comment [3]: Argument-Description pattern

Author
Comment [4]: A thesis statement

Author
Comment [5]: Using a colon to introduce an important topic

Author
Comment [6]: Em dashes and/or parentheticals to add emphasis

Author
Comment [7]: Using figurative language to support his claim

Author
Comment [8]: Argument-Description pattern

Author
Comment [9]: Figurative Language to support claim

Author
Comment [10]: Using background to establish the subject's credibility

Author
Comment [11]: Argument description pattern

Author
Comment [12]: Using a counter-argument to contradict a popular opinion.

Author
Comment [13]: A strong conclusion that pushes forward but also circles back to the title

Figure 3.5 Allison's Noticings About Tucker's Review

former *New York Times* book review editor, talked about the argument-description pattern germane to review writing. She decided to place this lesson first because the skill of integrating an argument with specific, supporting details seemed fundamental to how students would construct a critical review. This skill would then lead nicely into a lesson on strong paragraphing, and she wanted to show her students how Tucker manages a four-paragraph review bursting with information. A lesson on figurative language as evidence (borrowed from Rebekah's unit) and a study of titles seemed like appropriate "middle study" lessons, followed by a lesson on how to wrap up a review with a conclusion that reflects the topic. Allison's thinking led her to this roadmap of lessons:

1. Weave description and argument together.
2. Write strong paragraphs that pack a lot of punch.
3. Use figurative language to convey a vivid picture of the product.
4. Include a title that intrigues the reader and forecasts the review.
5. Provide a conclusion that follows from and reflects on the topic.
6. Combine sentences without comma splices.
7. Provide hyperlink, photos, or videos to enhance information.

Text 3.7 Sam Tanenhaus Interview *http://www.thedailybeast.com/articles/2012/08/08 /inside-the-nyt-book-review-how-i-write-interviews-sam-tanenhaus.html*

Next, we'll walk through just one of these lessons—weaving description and argument together—to show you the predictable way Allison moved from noticing to teaching.

TEACH

To begin the lesson, Allison showed her students a picture of Sam Tanenhaus and talked a little about his background as a newspaper editor. She then read bits of the interview aloud, pausing to comment on his advice. Next, Allison asked her students to underline the following sentence in the second paragraph of the Tucker review: "His high voice can remind you of Smokey Robinson and Marvin Gaye, as can a few of his musical hooks, but his tone is also pleasantly ghostly, wafting in and out of a melody with sinuousness that can be sly or sexy or serene." She asked them to consider how this sentence demonstrated the concept of weaving together argument and description.

As they talked about the sentence, students noted Tucker's "show don't tell" method of arguing his point that Pharrell's voice is versatile and classic: "voice . . . of Smokey Robinson and Marvin Gaye," and "his tone . . . wafting in and out of a melody with sinuousness . . ." They repeated this process with sentences from two other mentor texts in the cluster, exploring how each one demonstrated the argument-description technique.

After this whole-group conversation, students worked in small groups to find both where and *how* writers used this same technique in the remaining mentor texts. Here's what they found.

* Writers use figurative language to enhance their argument.
* Writers use well-placed, specific adjectives to describe a product.
* Writers combine details and argument in the same sentence rather than writing an opinion sentence, followed by a sentence with details.
* To support their opinion, writers incorporate details that the average player/user/wearer/listener and so on might overlook—this is a writer's job.
* Writers follow a description with questions that propel them into the argument, "Does it, though?"
* Writers use both nouns and verbs to show their opinion.

Most of the lessons Allison taught in this unit followed a similar pattern: She discussed the technique or shared something about it, she offered a few examples from about half the mentor texts, she asked students to search for more examples in the remaining mentor texts, and then she invited students to try the work of the lesson in their writing.

CONFER AND STUDY PATTERNS IN STUDENT WRITING

Over the next few weeks, as Allison continued to teach lessons with the mentor texts and confer with writers about their work, she noticed a wide variety of writing needs. Most of these could easily be addressed in one-on-one conferences. However, she also noticed several writers still struggling to use complex sentences in their writing without making comma splice errors. She adjusted the sequence of lessons to accommodate this need and planned another lesson on complex sentences so the class could probe the phrases, commas, and clauses that made up each sentence.

A Technique Study in Rebekah's Class

The following snapshot describes a technique study of evidence across multiple genres (editorial, review, narrative, and This I Believe) in Rebekah's classroom.

DECIDE ON A WRITING UNIT

In early spring as she reflected on her students' progress, Rebekah observed that students consistently struggled to use evidence to support their point in multiple genre studies. Time after time, this was their glaring weak spot, and it was too important to go unaddressed. Her students were stuck and prone to view evidence only in its driest iterations—for them, statistics, quotes from the text, and expert testimony were evidence. And that was it. Rebekah wanted them to see that evidence is *anything* that illustrates or supports the point the writer is trying to make or his perspective. Evidence is both the logical facts we present and the playful way we mold our language. Her students needed a greater command of this skill, so she decided to plan an evidence study.

COLLECT MENTOR TEXTS

Rebekah collected mentor texts in four different genres previously studied in the first semester (editorial, review, narrative, and This I Believe). Because these were familiar genres, students were able to apply a new reading lens and jump into the study more quickly. The mentor texts had two things in common: Each was written about snowboarding (it was still cold outside, and she was trying to engage a group of young snowboarders), and each used evidence to support its point. Her aim was this: Show a single topic being explored in a variety of genres, then show how each genre uses evidence to support its point.

Around this time, Rebekah first encountered Ken Tucker's review of *G I R L*. Tucker's use of figurative language immediately struck her as she listened to the review on her commute. When writers use figurative language—making comparisons, using idioms, engaging in hyperbole—they are supporting their point in a very different way by helping the reader make connections. Tucker's review wasn't a lilting narrative; his was a critical review using figurative language to illustrate its point to incredible effect. Even though it wasn't about snowboarding, this review reinforced some other ways of looking at evidence and also opened new possibilities, so she added it to the cluster.

STUDY PATTERNS IN THE MENTOR TEXTS TO CREATE LESSONS

Rebekah studied the mentor texts as she decided which types of evidence she would focus on in her lessons. She had already addressed evidence earlier in the year when she taught narrative, editorial, and critical review, but she knew she would need to review and reinforce those skills. She also wanted to broaden students' definition and understanding of evidence through this unit.

Specifically, when Rebekah sat down with "Pharrell Williams: Just Exhilaratingly 'Happy,'" she looked at every technique she could possibly teach using this text. We sometimes reuse an already-familiar mentor text in a new way in a later unit, so she wanted to make sure she examined the text from every angle, even though she knew evidence would be the focus for this study. Rebekah annotated the review with her observations in her notebook (Figure 3.6).

Pharrell Williams: Just Exhilaratingly Happy
by Ken Tucker, NPR

Pharrell Williams, who frequently goes by just his first name, is the sort of pop star whom many people would like to view as a friend. Emerging from hip-hop, he makes charming recordings that suggest a deep appreciation of pop, soul and R&B music extending at least as far back as the 1960s. To hear Pharrell on his new album *G I R L*, you'd think his world consisted of grooving on catchy beats and flirting with women. It's a lightweight image that draws gravitas from his prolific work ethic and a shrewd deployment of those influences.

Comment [1]: STRUCTURE: Introduction

Comment [2]: Providing brief, useful context for the reader

"Brand New" is a song that dares you to think of it as brand new, as opposed to a canny recasting of riffs reminiscent of the Jackson 5. Pharrell is so confident in his ability to beguile you as producer, songwriter and singer, he all but buries the major guest star on that track: Justin. Even when Pharrell dares to come off as slightly predatory, as in "Hunter" — about tracking a woman — it's all done in the mildest manner possible. "Hunter" is also one of the high points of this album, with a rubber-band rhythm that stretches and snaps with witty elasticity. His high voice can remind you of Smokey Robinson and Marvin Gaye, as can a few of his musical hooks, but his tone is also pleasantly ghostly, wafting in and out of a melody with sinuousness that can be sly or sexy or serene.

Comment [3]: STRUCTURE: Specific Examples

Comment [4]: Using textual examples as evidence

Comment [5]: Using textual examples as evidence

Comment [6]: Using figurative language to support analytical writing

Comment [7]: Using allusion to help readers make connections

Comment [8]: Using figurative language to support analytical writing

Pharrell Williams began his career as half of a production duo called The Neptunes, providing material for acts as various as Nelly, Clipse and Jay Z. He was glancingly involved in a little pop scandal last year as a producer of (and video guest star in) "Blurred Lines,"Robin Thicke's appropriation of Marvin Gaye. Pharrell can even confer fame upon inanimate objects: The Vivienne Westwood-designed hat he wore to the Grammy Awards achieved such fame, it was conscripted to help out again during the Oscars. In the new "Come Get It Bae" he says, "I can do anything you like," and it barely registers as boasting.

Comment [9]: STRUCTURE: Additional background/ context

Comment [10]: Connecting the artist's persona to his work

Comment [11]: Using textual examples as evidence

Pharrell has come in for some criticism recently as being merely a glossy pop hitmaker; for lacking edge. I find that this sort of critique is really code for his declining to revel in irony, sarcasm or a bleak view of the world. And that is, in turn, why I find Pharrell Williams — and particularly the Pharrell on display throughout *G I R L* — an exhilarating performer. His big hat can barely contain his radiant braininess.

Comment [12]: STRUCTURE: Presenting and refuting a contrasting point of view

Comment [13]: Presenting a contrast in order to reinforce a claim

Comment [14]: STRUCTURE: Conclusion

Figure 3.6 Rebekah's Noticings About Tucker's Review

Now that she had some lesson options, it was time to make some choices. Using specific textual examples (quotes from a text, lyrics from a song, etc.) as evidence was a technique she could aptly address using other mentor texts in the collection. Presenting a contrast to reinforce a claim could be an interesting approach to using evidence. However, her students were still struggling with the basics, so this seemed like a stretch. She made note of this technique and set it aside for a student who needed an extra challenge. Since she noticed the use of figurative language multiple times in Tucker's work, she prioritized that as a "must teach" from this mentor.

ARRANGE LESSONS INTO A UNIT

Once she had studied all the texts and selected which lessons to teach, Rebekah knew she would begin by reviewing lessons she'd taught earlier in the year. Rather than repeating the same lessons, however, she would focus on showing students how writers use these techniques *across* multiple genres. From there, Rebekah organized the new skills from most universal to least universal, ending with the technique she thought the fewest students would find applicable to their writing. Her final unit looked like this:

1. Showing-not-telling (review).
2. Using anecdotes, facts, stats, and testimonies (review).
3. Using text evidence (review).
4. Using concrete, specific details.
5. Using figurative language.
6. Using ethos, pathos, and logos.

TEACH

Using examples from a few of the mentor texts, Rebekah taught the first four lessons before arriving at "Using Figurative Language" and the Tucker review. Ultimately, Rebekah used Tucker's review very simply. She gave students a definition of figurative language—language that is not literal; in other words, it doesn't mean *exactly* what it says—and five kinds to look for:

✳ **simile:** a comparison between two unlike things using *like* or *as*
✳ **metaphor:** a comparison between two unlike things without using like or as
✳ **personification:** giving human qualities to an inhuman object
✳ **hyperbole:** extreme exaggeration used for effect
✳ **idiom:** common, local sayings that don't have a literal meaning.

The class chatted about these types of figurative language, sharing examples and copying them into their notebooks. Rebekah then asked students where they expected to see figurative language. Naturally, they expected to see it predominantly in narrative or poetry. And that's true. But her goal was to show them how this technique can work in genres *other* than narrative.

She pulled up Ken Tucker's review. After a bit of searching, the students found:

✳ "buries the major guest star"
✳ "rubber-band rhythm that stretches and snaps with witty elasticity"
✳ "his tone is also pleasantly ghostly, wafting in and out of a melody . . ."

The class talked about the connotation of each example—what it made them think, how readers connected to it, and what it made them understand about music they had never heard (most had not heard the newly released songs mentioned in the review). Students concluded that while figurative language is not your standard kind of evidence, its well-placed use can help the reader see a new perspective, understand a new topic, or "hear" a new album in a way the reader couldn't otherwise. And it's the cumulative effect of this language that adds up across a piece. The reader is often unaware he's being swayed by language like this, but without a doubt, the language is framing a particular stance the writer has on his topic.

CONFER AND STUDY PATTERNS IN STUDENT WRITING

As Rebekah conferred, she noticed a particular weakness in her students' ability to incorporate concrete, specific details. This surprised her, as she had predicted this would be one of the easiest techniques for them to master. Rebekah thought another mentor text might help, so later that week, she pulled an excerpt from *Charlotte's Web* by E. B. White to demonstrate the effect of concrete details in a passage (Figure 3.7). Notice White's brilliant, specific focus on smell in this paragraph.

One Mentor Text, Two Studies: A Debrief

Take a minute to reflect on these two different writing studies. How did each of us use the Pharrell review? What were our different approaches to planning and teaching with mentor texts? Figure 3.8 compares the two studies.

> The barn was very large. It was very old. It smelled of hay and it smelled of manure. It smelled of the perspiration of tired horses and the wonderful sweet breath of patient cows. It often had a sort of peaceful smell—as though nothing bad could happen ever again in the world. It smelled of grain and of harness dressing and of axle grease and of rubber boots and of new rope. And whenever the cat was given a fish-head to eat, the barn would smell of fish. But mostly it smelled of hay, for there was always hay in the great loft up overhead. And there was always hay being pitched down to the cows and the horses and the sheep.

Figure 3.7 Concrete Details Passage in *Charlotte's Web*

Allison's Study	Rebekah's Study
Began with a desire to study a specific genre	Began with a desire to teach into students' needs
Found her mentor texts through a combination of recommendations and intentional searching for engaging topics	Found her mentor texts through a combination of intentional searching (snowboarding) and happenstance (heard Tucker's review on NPR)
Utilized multiple mentor texts in the lesson, among them, Tucker's review	Used Tucker's review to anchor her entire lesson
Noticings: focused on point of view, punctuation, and argument	Noticings: focused mainly on structure and evidence
Had a general goal in mind while making noticings: to figure out what makes review writing, review writing	Had a specific goal in mind while making noticings: to find examples of evidence

Figure 3.8 Comparison of Allison's and Rebekah's Studies

Closing Thoughts

In this chapter, we have shared a six-step process for planning a writing study that is infused with mentor texts from top to bottom. Take heart—as you practice this process it becomes fluid, recursive, and instinctual. In fact, one of the many joys we have found in structuring our teaching around mentor texts is that it has made our planning process easier and a lot more fun. No longer do we search our own brains wondering, "What is important to teach here?" The mentor texts tell us what's important. The mentor texts reveal the teaching points.

As mentor texts have increasingly formed the backbone of our writing instruction, our understanding of good writing has become simultaneously grounded and expanded. We know more than we have ever known about writing because we study the work of real writers, not just academic exercises in writing. We feel empowered to teach techniques we were previously afraid to teach because we worried we didn't have the language for it, that we just didn't know how. Mentor texts have become the communal language for teaching the elements of good writing, both for us and for our students.

CHAPTER FOUR

Introducing Students to Mentor Texts

I have never been so quiet on the second day of school. My new students, very fresh freshmen, were busily drawing images from their lives and adding artful captions. Every so often, a question would punctuate the silence.

"Mrs. O'Dell, how many pictures do we need?" Ben asked.

"Look at your mentor texts," I gently reminded him. Ben dug through his backpack, pulling out a few sheets of paper and placing them on his desk.

"Should my author introduction be colored, or is pencil okay?" Katie queried.

"Does the mentor text have color?" She looked down, searching for the answer.

"Yeah, they all have one or two colors."

"Okay. Well, if the mentor text uses one or two colors, you should take that into consideration when you are finishing your own piece."

The questions were simple. The assignment was simple: a low-stakes, creative way to introduce ourselves to one another. But, unbeknownst to them, the students were engaged in more than simply meeting one another—they were meeting mentor texts for the very first time.

—Rebekah

Chances are, like the students in this vignette, most students entering your classroom will not be familiar with mentor texts. They may have had English teachers in the past who shared an exemplar paper from a former student, but they will almost certainly not be acquainted with the regular rhythms of moving through myriad mentor texts, extracting implicit lessons on craft, and using them as inspiration for their own writing. They probably won't be conversant in the language of craft. In short, they won't arrive in your classroom ready for the rich and immersive experience you are about to offer them. You will need to introduce your students to mentor texts.

Right from the start, students need to spend time with mentor texts and see the role they can play in their writing lives. They need to understand they can consciously infuse their writing with the techniques of successful writers and recognize the value that adds to their work. Because students need time to intentionally learn *how to learn* from other writers, we teachers also have to give students time to breathe, to fiddle, to play, to figure it out. In the opening vignette, Rebekah describes just how quiet she was on the second day of school. This is hard at the beginning of the school year when there is so much to do and we want to jump into everything at once. This chapter is about resisting that temptation, about lingering a while to give students the skills and practice with mentor texts that will carry them through the rest of their writing experiences.

We spend nearly the entire first month of school introducing our student writers to mentor texts. Figure 4.1 gives you an overview of how we spend those days in three clear phases. How long you spend acquainting your students with mentor texts will depend on your teaching context: how many days per week you are devoting to writing study, how long your class periods are, if you see your students every day or every other day.

Phase One: Getting to Know Each Other *and* Mentor Texts	2–3 class periods
Phase Two: Learning to Read Like Writers	1–2 class periods
Phase Three: Using Mentor Texts as Writers for the First Time	10–12 class periods
	Total of 13–17 class periods

Figure 4.1 Overview of Introducing Students to Mentor Texts

In this chapter, we will walk you through these phases, from acquainting students with mentor texts to facilitating their first attempts at using these texts as inspiration and instruction for their own writing. Although we'll share some mentor texts that have been successful for us and teachers we admire, the goal here is not to give you a rigid plan to follow. Instead, we want to explain our goals for each phase of introduction and then show you how they have played out in our classrooms. This chapter is also not intended to be a prescriptive set of steps. You might spend more or less time in phase one or phase two. You know your students, and you will know how long they need before they are ready to move into subsequent writing studies.

That said, please hear this: It's never too late to get started. While we weave mentor texts into the curriculum from the first day of school through the last, you can get your students started with mentor texts at any point in the year. You can get started with mentor texts tomorrow. Let us show you how.

Getting to Know Each Other *and* Mentor Texts—Phase One

At the beginning of the year, we want to get to know our students, give our students opportunities to know one another, and introduce the routines of our classrooms. We want to dive into the work and set the tone for the year. Believe it or not, we've found we can accomplish all these goals with a well-chosen mentor text.

We set out with a few interrelated goals to guide us.

* Introduce students to our classrooms and to one another.
* Begin using the term "mentor text" with students.
* Use a mentor text in the context of a serious-but-fun activity.
* Promote student independence by continually directing students to the mentor texts for answers.

Take a minute to scan the opening vignette again. Rebekah is able to accomplish so much in the first two days of school using the mentor texts as introduction, inspiration, and teaching tool. When Rebekah continuously redirects her students' attention to the mentor texts, she is establishing the expectation that students will use the resources around them to find answers to their writing questions. She is establishing a climate of inquiry—one in which the teacher and students are working together with the in-print mentor to figure out what writing is and how it's done. Every time she asks students to check a mentor text, she is asking them to read it again, notice more, and learn something new. This will be the rhythm of the class all year long. This kind of serious-but-fun mentor text work in the first few days sets the tone for the rest of the year: We will read to become better writers. And we will have fun while we do it!

When you introduce students to mentor texts on the first day, you start building confidence and independence in your writers, and, more important, you are steeping them in powerful, memorable writing.

Choosing Introductory Mentor Texts

As always, when we set out to find a great introductory mentor text, we are looking for something really engaging and well-crafted to teach and inspire right out of the gate because we want our students to *be* great writers. We never want to show them subpar work or teach down to them, and we want them to adapt to the caliber of writing we'll be studying throughout the year.

With the secondary purpose of introducing students to one another, we also go in search of texts with autobiographical themes. We find these in our usual haunts; we just read with a very specific filter, favoring memoir, personal essays, and any other writing we can find that addresses issues of self and identity.

We also look for texts that are primarily visual or involve only tiny bits of writing. While this may seem counterintuitive, our goal in the *very* first few days of school is to introduce students to the tool (mentor texts) that will inspire writing and make better writing possible down the road. Writing-heavy assignments can actually undercut this goal because students become preoccupied with length requirements, time, and expectations. We want to inspire and instruct, not create anxiety.

This is a lot to look for—something engaging, well crafted, autobiographical, and light on writing. While we will make some suggestions in this chapter for mentor texts that fit the bill, we find that these mentor texts are difficult to search for. These are mentor texts we most often stumble upon in our reading and teaching. When we find a mentor text that meets these criteria, we file it away as an introductory mentor text that we can return to later.

Mentor Texts on Day One: A Possibility

Our ninth-grade students have been enthralled with Robin Bowman's book *It's Complicated: The American Teenager* (2007) when we have used it as an introductory mentor text. In this book, Bowman presents over 200 "collaborative portraits" of teenagers across America. Each page contains a black-and-white photograph of the teen and excerpts from an interview covering a wide range of topics from earliest memories to biggest fears to the most difficult thing about being a teen. Students love the candid nature of these interviews and the diversity of teens represented within the pages of the book.

The process we use in this introductory mentor text work is the same process we use with all mentor text work, so we're introducing students to three things: one another, mentor texts, and the process we use to approach them.

GIVE STUDENTS A CLUSTER OF MENTOR TEXTS

Just like the beginning of any writing study, students are given a cluster of mentor texts. While we don't often give students an entire cluster at once (this can be overwhelming in a study with several very different, word-heavy texts), we do give students the entire cluster for this introduction to mentor texts: six portraits from *It's Complicated*. Depending on what texts you choose for your introduction, you'll have to decide how many to give students on the first day.

For students who have never encountered mentor texts, it takes time to understand the power they have to inspire their own writing. They may, at first, see the texts you give them as yet another "handout," and that's okay. One of the goals of this introduction is for students to learn by doing—to learn about mentor texts by being mentored. Don't feel pressured to spend a lot of time defining mentor texts or unpacking the concept of mentors. Keep it simple and say, "These are mentor texts. A mentor text is anything that inspires and teaches us about writing." And then begin reading through the cluster.

READ AS READERS FIRST

It's important to take time to enjoy and connect with the mentor texts as readers before thinking about what you might learn from them as writers (Ray 1999). Exploring the texts as readers can happen in different ways. We often choose to read the texts aloud to students to evoke the pleasures of story time and allow students to hear the rhythms of good writing. Sometimes we start by reading aloud and ask students to complete the reading on their own. How you choose to explore the texts will depend on the length of the texts and the amount of initial support students may need.

After reading, students might respond in a variety of ways, from just turning and talking about what they're thinking, to jotting down responses in notebooks. This response might be totally open-ended, or you might frame it in some way. With *It's Complicated*, we asked students to respond to the following questions:

    ✳ What do you notice about these teens? Are there any common themes?
    ✳ What surprises you about the interviews?
    ✳ What do you connect with? Where do you see yourself in these teenagers?

Exploring the texts as readers first helps students not only understand the content, it also gives them a chance to enjoy and appreciate the mentor text before beginning to analyze it for its craft.

THEN, READ LIKE WRITERS

While we're not yet explicitly teaching the concept of reading like writers, our goal is to help students read this way before they even know exactly what it means and before we've even named it. We want students to get a feel for reading through a writer's lens, not articulate the difference between reading like a reader and reading like a writer (at least not yet). To this end, we feel it serves students better to scaffold this new way of reading with teacher-directed questions without spending too much time talking about what we're doing or why. We ask students to do a second reading of the mentor texts—sometimes as a homework assignment and sometimes during class, depending on time and the level of support they need. With *It's Complicated*, we asked students to read with the following questions in mind:

* How do you think the writer, Robin Bowman, chose what to include?
* How do you think she chose what to leave out?
* What makes the responses compelling?
* What do you want to know more about?

With whatever texts you are using, ask questions that point students to specific examples of craft you'd like them to think about. Then later, when you more explicitly introduce the concept of reading like a writer, you can refer back to this early reading experience.

STUDENTS CRAFT

After you've spent some time talking about what students notice about the writing in the mentor texts, it's time to get them crafting some writing on their own. What they write should somehow be connected to the mentor texts you've chosen. With *It's Complicated*, we have students use Bowman's interview questions to interview one another. To keep the focus on asking good follow-up questions, students film their interviews using phones or tablets and then take their time to transcribe them, take pictures of one another, and craft their collaborative portraits.

Throughout the process, the mentor texts serve as anchor pieces that help focus the work. When students aren't sure what to include and what to leave out in their partner's interview, they go back to Bowman's texts. When students aren't sure how to show pauses in their partner's speech, they go back to the texts. When students aren't sure how long their final portraits should be, they go back to the texts. In these very first days of class, students establish a vital connection to the guidance mentor texts provide.

STUDENTS REFLECT

For this introductory activity, there's no need to labor over the definition of mentor texts or their importance, but you will want to ask students to reflect on the experience and what they've learned from it. After students have written on their own, consider circling back and asking them to reflect specifically on what the mentor texts enabled them to do. Either through a class discussion or a written reflection, we always ask students these questions:

* Having used mentor texts to complete your own writing project, give your own, new definition of *mentor text*.
* What questions did the mentor texts answer for you?
* What did the mentor texts encourage you to try in your own work that you might not have tried otherwise?
* How do you envision yourself using mentor texts in the future?

Prompting students to spend a few minutes considering the impact of mentor texts on their work will lay a firm foundation for the more intensive work they will do with these texts down the road.

Introductory Mentor Texts: More Possibilities

With the goal of introducing students to one another and the routines of mentor text study, creating expectations that foster independence and students who are attuned to the craft of writing, there are a number of texts you might consider using. Below are a few mentor texts we've either used in the past or are excited about using in the future. Like *It's Complicated*, each one is actually a collection of short texts within a broad frame, offering multiple mentor texts in a single source. Some of these texts you will work with over a few days, while others, like six-word memoirs or haikus, can be completed more quickly. Regardless of the text you choose, you can use the same basic steps outlined in the lesson above: read like readers, read like writers, craft, and reflect.

ARTISTS, WRITERS, THINKERS, AND DREAMERS: PORTRAITS OF 50 FAMOUS FOLKS & ALL THEIR WEIRD STUFF (2014) BY JAMES GULLIVER HANCOCK

In this chapter's opening vignette, Rebekah is using this mentor text with her students. Hancock's "author introduction art" works on the premise that you can learn a lot about a person by looking at what he chooses to surround himself with. Each piece of art places a sketch of the author in the center and uses quirky drawings and hand-written captions to introduce the person through her "stuff." As students introduce themselves as authors, the class bands together. The scholars boast stick figures with books and math tests with red A-plusses. The athletes spot one another from across the room: Bright orange basketballs and lacrosse sticks dot the pages of their author intros. Students share their origins, their histories, and their passions.

ENCYCLOPEDIA OF AN ORDINARY LIFE (2004) BY AMY KROUSE ROSENTHAL

A collection of autobiographical vignettes and musings from A to Z, this book presents an opportunity for students to think about the objects, stories, and people that define their lives. Consider asking your students to create pages for their own encyclopedia. This could even be a project students add to throughout the year.

"SIX WORD MEMOIRS" FROM *SMITH* MAGAZINE

Started by *Smith* magazine, six-word memoirs have really taken off and garnered the attention of professional writers and amateurs alike. A six-word memoir is the story of your life—or a part of your life—told in exactly six words. Not only do these texts allow students to introduce themselves, they also invite conversations about compression in writing and "cutting to the bone" (Atwell 1998). *Smith* collects scores of six-word memoirs on their website, through their Twitter handle (@sixwords), and in printed collections that can be purchased through their site.

"NEW YORK CITY IN 17 SYLLABLES" ON NYTIMES.COM

Our colleague Betsy Reid uses the *New York Times* haiku contest as a way to encourage students to write about the landscapes that are important to them. In the original contest, writers were asked to stick to a few subjects: the island, strangers, solitude, commuting, 6 AM, and kindness. You might brainstorm common subjects with your students and have them write about themselves through the lens of landscape—their

Text 4.1 "New York City in 17 Syllables" *http://www.nytimes.com/interactive/2014/04 /27/nyregion/new-york-city-in-haiku.html?_r=0*

school, the field, the basketball court, the stage, the kitchen. A study of these mentor texts might lead to discussions about interesting punctuation, stanza and line breaks, and concrete imagery.

Learning to Read Like Writers—Phase Two

After the initial introduction, students will need a more structured approach to this kind of work and a shared understanding of why we use mentor texts. Here, we build on students' first exposure to mentor texts to achieve these goals.

* Help students develop the reading habits that uncover a writer's craft.
* Define the difference between reading like readers and reading like writers.
* Show students how to isolate and describe the techniques writers use in familiar texts.
* Encourage students to think with a sense of possibility about their own work.

No doubt there are countless ways to introduce students to this new way of reading, but we have been successful with a very simple approach: We try to create a reading experience for our students like we've had on countless Saturday mornings, mug of coffee in hand, when our eyes catch a phrase in the morning paper, and suddenly we're reading in a different way: as writers, as teachers of writing. We try to build in our students the same habits of mind we recommended for teachers in Chapter 2, habits of mind that transform readers' sensibilities and allow them to see the writing beneath the writing.

Choosing Texts to Help Students Begin Reading Like Writers

Just as we have specific criteria for choosing introductory mentor texts, we have an additional criterion for selecting texts to teach students how to read like writers: We search for the old and familiar texts our students knew as children or young teenagers. Picture books, popular young adult novels, and poetry for children work beautifully here. Students enter familiar texts more easily, and they require less support and scaffolding. Familiar texts also help draw a clear line in the sand between reading like readers, the way students have always read these texts before, and using the new lens of reading like writers. Reading like readers bridges into reading like writers.

Introducing Reading Like a Writer: A Possibility

Reading like writers is something you will practice with your students all year long, every time you study a mentor text. No single lesson teaches this skill once and for all; it's cultivated over time. The lesson we share here is meant to provide a snapshot of the initial conversation we have with students about the differences between reading like a reader and reading like a writer. Regardless of the text we use, these ways of talking about the two kinds of reading remain fairly consistent.

A text we and many, many other teachers love to use to teach a variety of crafting techniques is Cynthia Rylant's picture book *When I Was Young in the Mountains*. In fact, the widespread popularity of this book is one of the reasons it's such an ideal text to formally introduce the skill of reading like writers. There's a good chance many of your students have encountered this text before, and, if not, the picture book format makes it easily accessible to students.

GATHER STUDENTS TO READ LIKE READERS

Our high school students love stickers and story time—anything that reminds them of the wonder of their elementary school years. We play with this in our introduction to reading like writers. We gather students to sit around us on the floor (believe it or not, they love this!). We show them *When I Was Young in the Mountains* and ask them to share memories of the book if they know it, or make predictions based on the title and the cover if they don't (farm life, sibling stories, an older time). They listen as we read, pausing every now and then to invite them to make connections to the text as the memoir unfolds.

Afterward, we explain that they have enjoyed reading like readers, activating prior knowledge and making connections. They have paid attention to the plot and the illustrations—the "what" of the story. But we hint that there is another kind of reading to be done here, a kind of reading that considers the "how" of the story. We let them think about that as they return to their seats where they find a copy of the text waiting for them.

DEMONSTRATE READING LIKE WRITERS THROUGH A TEACH ALOUD

The best way to teach students how to read like writers is to show them how we do it—let them watch us read a text like writers and talk about what we notice. So we fire up the document camera and do just that.

Here is a snippet from one such teach aloud in Allison's classroom.

I can't help but notice this repeating phrase that Rylant uses—"when I was young in the mountains." She doesn't say how old but that she was young and where she was. I'm guessing that this sense of place is very important to her and to her telling of this story, so she decided to write it over and over again. In fact, repetition is found in lots of different kinds of writing. I feel like she wants to go back there. And as my eyes wander, I'm sort of wondering now about this sentence that begins with the word only. *It feels strange to me, that ordering.*

Usually we say "his lips were the only clean thing," and my sense is that she's started the sentence with the word only *because she wants us to understand just how clean his lips were and just how dirty and soot-covered everything else was. I like how she did that—used a surprising word order to really get my attention. I wonder if I might be able to experiment with that technique in my memoir. Now I'm thinking of this place in my memoir where I...*

And as we talk aloud, we demonstrate the habits of mind of a person who reads like a writer.

* Writers look for the writing beneath the writing—the writer's moves. They try to figure out how the writing was put together.
* Writers learn as much as they can about these moves so they can describe what they're seeing. They use words they've learned before or make up new words that fit what they're noticing.
* Writers are a little bit selfish when they read, always thinking about how they might bring what they're seeing in the writing back to their own work.
* Writers keep track of their noticings in a notebook.
* Writers may begin to develop preferences for certain writers and certain genres that appeal to their own writerly sensibilities.

INVITE STUDENTS TO ADD THEIR OBSERVATIONS

Once we've talked through a good bit of the text, we invite students to chime in and practice using their writer's lenses. When they first try to read like writers, many students will still read like readers. They'll say things like, "She used a lot of imagery. I can really picture it," or "There is a lot of good description in this text." We have to nudge these students toward a different kind of reading and help them see the writing beneath the description—the actual words that make the description "good." How to do this?

We ask students to provide text evidence for what they notice—to point to the very words in the text that make the description "good," for example. Reading like a writer is the ultimate form of close reading. Some students will grasp this concept sooner than others: Bring them up and have them walk their peers through their craft noticings. Let students talk about the possibilities uncovered by their peers, and they will begin to see more in the text. For example, a student may identify this line as an example of good description: "Afterward we stood in front of the old black stove, shivering and giggling, while Grandmother heated cocoa on top." When asked to provide textual evidence, she may cite the adjectives "old" and "black." Another student may point to the phrase "in front of" which makes the description more precise, and some students may even know this is a prepositional phrase. Someone may comment that the phrase "shivering and giggling" describes the "we" at the beginning of the sentence. Zooming out, the class may now be able to see that sometimes writers put descriptive words and phrases *after* the subject, not just before. As students begin to read with writers' eyes and share their observations, the energy and facility for this new kind of reading will spread.

STUDENTS REFLECT

After students' first foray into reading like a writer, ask them to reflect on what they have learned. These reflections are important for students' synthesis, but they also help teachers know where clarification or reteaching might be needed the next time the class practices this skill. Consider asking students the following:

* In your own words, what is the difference between reading like a reader and reading like a writer?
* What are some of the craft elements you want to be sure to look for the next time you read a text like a writer?
* How do you think reading like a writer might help you in your own writing?

EXTEND THE PRACTICE

This is not a one-and-done lesson—your students will need practice over time. After an introductory lesson like this one, you might want to spend a couple of additional class periods engaging with familiar texts in order to practice reading like writers. Students can practice reading for writer's craft in small groups or pairs. As you listen to groups work and to the discussions as the class shares their findings, you should notice that their eyes and ears have become attuned to writer's craft and, more important, to a sense of opportunity in their own work. If you're not noticing this, you can back up and explicitly demonstrate how to read like a writer again.

Practice will continue in your classroom all year through notebook time and the study of mentor texts in writing studies. Students' habits of mind will begin to shift as reading like writers becomes second nature. It's not enough to teach students to analyze the rhetorical and literary features of a text. This is only half the purpose. To read like a writer is to be encouraged and supported in bringing the craft into your own work—in short, to read like the writer you are becoming. Later in this chapter we will discuss how we make these reading-writing connections more explicit as students begin to take their findings back to their own work.

Beginning Mentor Texts: More Possibilities

Here are a handful of ideas for texts to help your students begin to read like writers.

POETRY FOR CHILDREN

Children's poetry provides lyrical, bite-sized opportunities for students to read for craft. Even if they are not familiar with a specific poet, they will be familiar with its themes of imagination, wonder, and discovery, with the rhythms of poetry for the very young. Small poems invite line-by-line readings that promote thoughtful writerly reading. We love Robert Louis Stevenson's *A Child's Garden of Verses* and Nancy Willard's *A Visit to William Blake's Inn*.

PICTURE BOOKS

Like a poem, a children's book does more with less space; we want students to be able to find beautiful craft without having to wade through pages of text. These texts are also highly visual. With children's books, students can enjoy a rich reading-like-a-reader experience before moving into a study of craft. Not just any children's book will do, though. These texts have to be word-rich in order to have potential for these kinds of conversations. In addition to *When I Was Young in the Mountains*, another picture book we love for this purpose is *Owl Moon* by Jane Yolen.

EXCERPTS OF POPULAR YOUNG ADULT NOVELS

Tremendously popular young adult novels (such as *Harry Potter* and *The Hunger Games*) make for great reading-like-a-writer mentor texts because students have read them like readers (often more than once) and they are very familiar. The characters, the plot, and the conflicts are all fresh in students' minds. But when you introduce a different kind of reading, students are amazed to learn about the thoughtful crafting in their beloved teen picks. To introduce and practice reading like a writer, almost any passage will do. Students will find craft to notice, and they will get excited to take a deeper, more analytical look at the texts they love. To find a good excerpt, pull from the most popular books students are reading for pleasure. Skimming the first few chapters will usually yield several good options for text study.

Using Mentor Texts as Writers for the First Time—Phase Three

By the time you reach this phase, your students will have become familiar with your class, played with an introductory mentor text or two, and started to use the skill of reading like a writer. Before you launch into the first full writing study, your students need practice taking their new skills to the next level and using what they have learned from mentor texts in a piece of their own writing. Students need focused, explicit practice studying and using mentor texts before we can expect this process to become a regular part of the writing routine they use.

As the culmination of students' introduction to mentor texts and as a prelude to other studies that will follow, the goals of the mentor text unit of study are for students to gain experience

* reading like writers with mentor texts
* discussing the moves writers make in their writing
* experimenting and playing with different techniques in their own writing
* moving the techniques they've chosen into an original piece of writing.

In a mentor text unit of study, the focus isn't the final written product but rather the process of studying mentor texts, finding inspiration and writing techniques in the texts, and then incorporating them into a piece of writing. Because this study is about process rather than product, we offer students the ultimate choice in this study and allow them to write anything they want. Students might find ideas from heart maps (Heard 1998, 100) or writing territories they have developed (Atwell 1998, 120), from play or previous writing in their writer's notebooks, from the mentor texts they study in this cluster, or from a piece of writing from a previous class. No matter what kind of writing they are trying, this study—practicing the process of using mentor texts—sets students up for the work we will do in every study to come while also allowing us to troubleshoot questions and misconceptions about using mentor texts in the future (Figure 4.2).

Read Like a Reader, Read Like a Writer	1–2 class periods
Share Craft Noticings	1 class period
Zoom In and Dig Deeper	2–3 class periods
Write with Mentor Texts	5–7 class periods
Students Reflect	1 class period

Figure 4.2 Time Line of Mentor Text Study

Choosing Texts for a Mentor Text Study

In general we recommend three to six mentor texts as the ideal number for a cluster, but we tend to include more here to show students a variety of styles and genres. As far as selecting these mentors, pick your favorites—the best short memoir, the best op-ed, the best poem, the best critical review. Really any kind of writing will do. If you decide you want to use a favorite text again down the road—say your favorite op-ed in your op-ed study— that's fine. Students only benefit from rereading and additional study of a text. Aim for quality and diversity in this cluster, and if you're looking for a starting point, the texts we mention in this book constitute some of our favorites.

Read Like a Reader, Read Like a Writer

This first step in the study, reading mentor texts like readers and then like writers, is probably starting to sound familiar. That's good! You want your students to internalize this familiar rhythm and routine as you will approach all mentor texts this way from here on out. Begin by introducing your students to five to six mentor texts, showing them lots of different genres, techniques, purposes, and options for writing. Read through the cluster as readers, considering the genre (What kind of writing is this?) and the author's purpose (What is the writer saying? And why?). Then, invite students to go back to the mentor texts as writers. Because this is part of students' introduction to mentor texts, let them spend a little time looking at the craft of each text. In small groups or with a partner, have students choose just two or three craft elements from each text and consider the following:

* Can you name what the writer is doing?
* Why is the writer doing this? What is it adding to the writing?

Share Craft Noticings

After students have studied a little of the craft of each mentor text in a small group, take time to share what they've found as a whole class. Project a text using a document camera or LCD projector, and walk through it with students, adding their observations as you move through the passage. As students share, everyone in the class has a chance to work together and hone vocabulary for discussing writers' choices.

When students are less than precise in their description of a technique, "He uses the same word a lot," you can jump in and offer a more concise and useful term, "You're absolutely right! When we talk about writing, we call that 'repetition.'" Students also tend to jump in, helping one another zoom in on just the right word to define the technique they are seeing. While you might suggest useful terms to help students name the techniques they are seeing, we don't recommend spending a lot of time or energy trying to move students toward a standard list of terms. In later writing studies, you can help students develop a more standardized writerly vocabulary, but at this point, you don't want to stop the momentum you've built by stopping to give rhetorical terms. As long as students understand what they are seeing and give it a name that works for them, they are owning the craft, the first step toward making it their own.

For students who are still reading like readers, it can be helpful to ask them to phrase their noticings as rules for good writers. For example, if students notice repetition in a passage, have them write it as, "Writers use repetition to emphasize important ideas or images." This helps remind students of the task at hand—to think about writing rather than reading—and it also provides them with a to-do list when they begin to transfer these noticings to their own writing.

Sharing these initial findings, with partners, with small groups, and with the whole class, is absolutely crucial to building confidence with mentor texts. Students need practice describing writing techniques in terms that make sense to them. This isn't easy—particularly for our students who have less experience and enthusiasm. In fact, this naming of writing techniques makes us teachers nervous sometimes. Just like our students, we want to say the "right" thing. But we all learn by trying, so while students' first attempts at reading like writers will likely be clunky, vague, and imperfect, their facility for describing what they see will grow as they gain experience and talk about writing with their teacher and peers.

There's also this: As the class annotates and discusses, students expand their view of the kinds of moves writers make, and this helps them see more. A student who at first notices only obvious punctuation moves and concrete details in texts will be exposed to richer and more varied techniques—maybe some repetition, interesting structural choices, nuanced word choice. Over time, what that student notices collaboratively will become what she notices independently.

Reinforce the "Why"

In these conversations, teachers must constantly repeat, "But why?" There is little purpose in studying what writers do if their technique is divorced from their purpose. We want the "what" and "why" to become inextricably linked for our students so that they cannot ask the first question without answering the second. *This* is the key to ultimately putting the writers' moves to work in students' writing. Our students love generalities, and left to their own devices, they would say that every move a writer makes is "for emphasis" and leave it at that. They need nudging here in order to get to the heart of the choices writers make and the choices *they* will make when they sit in the writer's seat. You might probe:

* Why would the writer want to place emphasis here?
* How does this technique affect the reader's experience?
* How might the piece be different without this technique?
* How might the writer have written it differently here?

These questions are challenging. They are not one-time or even one-study discussions. You'll need to ask these questions all year long as you study new texts together and as you confer. And, of course, eventually you want students to be able to answer these questions about their own writing, not just the writing of their mentors.

Zoom In and Dig Deeper

Your students should be getting used to the process of working with mentor texts, but you want them to do more than just go through the motions. You want your students' interactions with mentor texts to begin from a place of inspiration as yours do and then move to a place of learning. To that end, after students have briefly looked at the craft in each text, ask them to select the two or three mentor texts in the cluster that most excite them. These will be their touchstone texts for the study. You might invite students who are ready or who already have authors they are eager to study to find their own mentor texts. In Chapter 9, we'll share the steps we take to move *all* students to a place of independence in finding and using mentor texts, but at this point, we think it's best to leave this as an option.

Once students have selected their touchstone texts, they will dig in and study them more deeply, looking for as many craft possibilities as they can find. Students who need additional support can work in small groups with others who have selected the same mentor texts. After students annotate their touchstone texts, they should begin thinking about how these mentors might impact their own original writing, and they'll ask more writerly questions.

* What topics or genres could be inspired by this mentor text?
* Which crafting techniques are most interesting?
* Which would you like to try?
* Where could you use the craft moves you have identified in your own writing?

We put these questions in a chart that students complete as they work through the texts. They then have all of their ideas about the texts at the ready as they write.

Write with Mentor Texts

Now students begin the work of using the inspiration and techniques they have noted and incorporating them into their own work. Again, in this study, a perfectly crafted, brilliantly written final product isn't the goal—you will spend months and months focusing your energies there. What's important here is for students to simply practice transferring the thinking they are doing about craft into their writing.

Students choose the genre they will write and the topic, and they spend one class period flash-drafting the piece (Fletcher 1992, 63), writing quickly to simply get their ideas down on paper. While this isn't usually enough time to write a complete first draft, it does give students a foundation to work from. Rather than spend time teaching craft lessons as you would in a genre or technique study, students work directly with the mentor texts, examining their features and culling ideas for revising their flash drafts. Ultimately, the goals of this study are play, experimentation, making writerly choices, and trying things in writing students have never tried before.

Students are making lots of choices, but there are requirements for their work. Here's what we require in this study: regardless of what they have written, we ask students to make a certain number of mentor text moves and to reflect on how those moves have impacted their writing. As a means of encouraging students to try lots of different writing techniques, we ask them to make two or three of each of the following moves.

* *Structure moves.* Focus on how the pieces of the text work together. For instance, does it have strictly or more loosely defined sections? How does it move from one paragraph to the next? Is there a clear lead and ending?
* *Idea and detail moves.* Focus on the content of the piece, large and small. For instance, do unexpected details pop up in the writing? Are topics included that you had not previously considered?
* *Sentence moves.* Focus on the syntax, punctuation, and patterns that create striking sentences. For instance, does the writer use interesting syntax or repetition that you could mimic? Is there unique punctuation?
* *Word choice or tone moves.* Focus on the specific words and attitude employed by the writer. For instance, does the writer use interesting word combinations? What in the writing signals the attitude of the writer toward the subject? How could it help you sharpen your own attitude in your writing?

We decided on two to three moves per group because we wanted students to play around a bit and incorporate different techniques rather than stopping after their first attempt in any given category. You know your students, however, and what they're ready for.

You might consider requiring more or fewer moves in each category, or you might focus on just one or two kinds of moves this first time. Whatever you decide is best, your students will still benefit from time dedicated solely to practice with mentor texts in their own work.

Our students write in Google Docs, adding comments throughout the paper to show us where and how a mentor text was used. Your students could also add digital comments in Word or even add sticky notes to paper. What follows are examples from our students showing how they transformed their writing with the help of mentors.

A STRUCTURE MOVE

The opening of Caroline's original narrative about a memorable church mission trip (Figure 4.3), "The Night of the Fire," read

It was a warm, July day in the summer of 2011. Everything on the mission trip had gone as planned, just as it was supposed to. All 70 of us gathered at the entrance of the New York City subway, so that we would arrive at the same time.

Figure 4.3 Caroline's Original Lead

One of Caroline's touchstone texts was Reeves Wiedeman's essay "Child's Play" from *The New Yorker*, a profile of Venus and Serena Williams' father, Richard. Caroline is a tennis player, so she was drawn to the topic of the piece. Caroline observed, "In this mentor text, I noticed how the author used a collection of quotations and dialogue throughout the text. Also, the author went back and forth between the present and past, in a flashback type of way. I tried to use these things in my own piece by using both dialogue and by opening with flashback." Using these techniques, Caroline rewrote the opening of her narrative (Figure 4.4).

Text 4.2 "Child's Play" by Reeves Wiedeman *http://www.newyorker.com/magazine /2014/06/02/childs-play-6*

Substituting flashback and dialogue for description not only radically changed the structure of Caroline's narrative but also created an engaging lead to draw readers in.

"Run! Just get as far away as possible!" a man yelled, frantically waving his arms around while he ushered people out of the building. I was scared. Terrified. Nervous. Alone.

Thick, heavy, black smoke filled the tiny spaces between the tall, scattered buildings that covered New York City. Debris fell from the sky, coating everything it touched. White, blanket-like ash, like that of snow, had soon covered everything. Miniscule bits of debris flew threw the air, landing delicately in its path. Nervous eyes glanced around, unsure of what to do or where to go. Tears were shed, hugs were shared. Most of the cowering crowd had never experienced anything like that dark night.

Figure 4.4 Caroline's Rewritten Lead

The light was fading, creating light shadows and dark patches around me. As it became dark, only the sound of crickets chirping and leaves rustling could be heard. The trees stood tall and still, like statues in a museum where no leaf dared to fall. The full, yellow moon watched from above as we tried to find our way through the forest.

Figure 4.5 Allie's Work with Personification

AN IDEA AND DETAIL MOVE

When invited to choose her own mentors, Allie pulled straight from her real reading life and immediately went to her favorite blog: *Beyond the Edge*, the National Geographic adventure blog. Hiker Cameron Martindell used personification to describe his journey into the Grand Canyon: "The morning sun crept down along the walls, displacing the dark pooled in the canyon as we packed up our car camp and got on the rocky trail taking us down" (Martindell 2014). Allie liked how Martindell's use of personification drew her in and connected the reader to the lengthy descriptions of setting. She decided to personify the moon in her own original horror story (Figure 4.5).

After trying the technique, Allie made the clever connection between personification and tone. She reflected, "Describing the moon as watching from above made my story feel even creepier—like a person was stalking the characters as they moved through the forest. It was a little change, but I really like what it added to my story." Using personification as a detail deepened Allie's writing and helped her make important connections to other elements of her writing.

A SENTENCE MOVE

Students often look to the writers of their favorite stories, novels, and magazines as mentors. Theresa's favorite text from her previous English class was Kate Chopin's "The Story of an Hour." Theresa scoured the story, attempting to figure out why she liked it so much. She reasoned that if she could employ the best of Chopin's techniques in her own piece, she might be able to create something she liked nearly as much. She says, "There was one line in this story that caught my attention, 'And yet she loved him—sometimes.' Not only does this sentence make a reader think, but I love the way it is worded. I wanted to have a sentence like that in my story."

Theresa concluded that the thing she liked best, the reason the sentence resonated with her, was because of its beginning, "And yet." She searched her own story to find the perfect spot for her sentence: "And yet neither peaceful conversation nor civil discourse took place."

A WORD CHOICE AND TONE MOVE

Jamey flash-drafted a spirited editorial about a lack of transparency in the Obama administration. One of his expressed goals before writing was to use mentor texts to "find the perfect word" to convey his ideas.

Jamey wrote, "Obama was confronted several times and asked by several people to talk about the situation in Benghazi, but he was reluctant and refused to talk to the media about it." As he revised his draft, he felt that "talk about" wasn't quite right. In his mentor text reading, Jamey noticed the word "acknowledge" in multiple sources. The word jumped out at him. After a brief conference with Rebekah to discuss the connotation of "talk about" versus "acknowledge," Jamey made the switch.

He also noticed that Robert Mays, a sports writer he admires, often uses italics to emphasize key words in his articles. Jamey felt that some strategic italicizing would help him achieve a stronger, more pointed tone. Figure 4.6 shows his revised sentence.

Jamey was pleased with the result and felt that his new word choice and intentional tone more accurately reflected his message.

Obama was confronted several times and asked by several people to acknowledge the situation in Benghazi, but he was reluctant and *refused* to talk to the media about it.

Figure 4.6 Jamey's Revision

Reflecting

Stepping back to reflect on the process and the tangible effect of mentor texts on each student's final product is supremely important as students complete their mentor text study. Ask students to consider the following:

* How would you now define "mentor text" for someone unfamiliar with the concept?
* How has reading like a writer changed the way you read?

* How has the use of mentor texts changed your writing?

* When you read a mentor text, do you naturally look for ideas, mentor sentences, word choices, or structure? What naturally stands out to you as a writer?

* How do you envision using mentor texts the next time you write?

Students' responses to these questions will help you plan as you move forward into genre and technique studies, and you'll see where you need to clarify and reteach. For instance, last year a handful of our students expressed hesitance to fully engage with mentor texts because they were afraid they were plagiarizing. We realized we needed to go back and reteach the difference between homage and plagiarism. Your students' responses will guide you as you help them find new mentors and look at texts as writers, and they will

> Before learning about mentor texts, I hadn't thought of actually taking style choices that the author had made and transmitting it to my own work. Now, if I see a piece of writing that I enjoy, I can take a writer's technique and channel it into my own writing.
>
> —Oriana
>
> Reading like a writer has changed the way I read by helping me appreciate how a writer's tone comes across, how hard it is to develop a character, and how wonderful it is to create a scene, and how amazing it is when inspiration strikes. I love looking into a writer's ideas, and to evaluate it as a writer is a privilege. . . . Mentor texts showed me how to take their words and turn them into something new, something that is powerful and beautiful.
>
> —Collette
>
> It has helped me to realize there are so many other ways of writing than the conventional way of just putting down what comes to mind. I have found many mentor texts that will help me further beyond this project into college or even my future jobs. I will always know there are different ways to convey my opinion or tell an interesting story.
>
> —Sam

Figure 4.7 Student Reflections on the Process

help you identify the inevitable few students who haven't bought in and are just going through the motions. Be sure to confer with these students early in your first writing study and try to help them set a new course.

Students' responses to the questions also help the students. They provide them with a starting point for working with mentor texts in future pieces and are a tangible reminder of the before and the after of their writing lives. They give students a touchstone down the road for why and how mentor texts are important—not just in broad terms but how they are important *to them* as writers.

A WAY IN

It might be difficult to imagine how you will make all the pieces and parts of this work fit into your beginning-of-the-year instruction.

Take a moment and use the blank planning calendar (Figure 4.8) to sketch out what an introduction to mentor texts might look like in your classroom. We have given you room for one month, but your introductory lessons may take more or less time. Think about:

* Are your students going to move through all three phases? Just one? Two?
* Where might your students need more or less time than we have allotted in our time line?
* How often will you see your students? How many class periods, or parts of class periods, can you devote to writing instruction?
* What beginning mentor texts might you use that will inspire both you and your students in this work?

Monday	Tuesday	Wednesday	Thursday	Friday

Figure 4.8 Blank Planning Calendar

Closing Thoughts

Getting started with mentor texts is an exhilarating game changer. As we introduce our students to mentor texts, we connect their personal histories and interests with their experience as readers. And then we drive this connection forward into their writing lives. We give our time to the things we value, and from the very first day of school, our students know that the inspiration and instruction of other writers is highly valued in our classrooms. The more time we spend upfront teaching students to use mentor texts, the sooner their minds will be tuned to the craft of powerful writing and the sooner their writing will be transformed.

CHAPTER FIVE

Mentors Show Students How to Play

O n a Monday morning in September, I projected an image of a map of the United States, divided and color-coded according to dominant football fandoms. The map displays Facebook fans of NFL teams across the country in 2014. Counties are assigned colors based on the number of "likes" residents gave official team pages. The Midwest is painted with orange, showing its affinity for the Denver Broncos. Loyalty to the Dallas Cowboys is shown in navy all across Texas and bordering states. Different shades of blue, pink, yellow, cream, and purple dot the rest of the map, displaying different counties' loyalty to the Seattle Seahawks, the Minnesota Vikings, the Carolina Panthers, and many other teams in the NFL.

Text 5.1 Facebook Fandom Map 2014 *http://www.cbssports.com/nfl/eye-on-football /24697058/facebook-releases-nfl-fan-map-of-us-jets-have-no-fans*

When the bell rang, students opened their notebooks. They stared at the map on the board and began writing. Some moved out of their seats to get a closer look, balancing their notebooks in one hand as they recorded their observations. After four minutes, we reconvened.

"Okay, what did you see? What did you think about? What did you write about?" I asked.

George raised his hand. "There are a lot of Cowboys fans."

"Yes. Thank you, George. What else?"

"It looks like the Broncos are almost as popular as the Cowboys," Caroline offered.

"But wait," Luke jumped in quickly, "think about population. Yeah, that's a lot of space, but is it really as many people?"

I smiled. Now we were getting somewhere. "Interesting. What else do we notice? What did this make you wonder about?"

"It made me wonder how accurate this map is. I mean, this is based on Facebook likes. This map shows that no one likes the New York Jets the best. That can't actually be true," Zach argued.

"Yeah, and I wonder what the 2013 map looked like. Was anything different last year?" Ciara asked.

The students were getting excited now, buzzing among themselves, hands shooting up into the air. They were no longer just looking at the map, they were looking into the map. They were making meaning.

—Rebekah

Regardless of the powerful mentor texts we share with students, older students are often reluctant to take risks and play in a piece of work that will be graded. Somewhere along the way they have become afraid of "doing it wrong," afraid of doing anything other than what is explicitly set forth on a rubric. In order to grow as writers, students need safe places to *play* with writing—places that aren't assessed or evaluated or given a grade. They need places where their work can be messy, where thinking outside the box and being wild with ideas is encouraged. This is why we have daily notebook time, a time where mentors show students how to play.

The primary goal of notebook time is to inspire students. When students have outlets through which they can experiment with ideas, language, and craft on a regular basis, they become bolder in their writing. The experiments they have enjoyed begin to find a way into their processed, polished pieces. Their work is enlivened and charged with possibility.

Notebook Time: A Powerful Tool for Instruction

Notebook time also presents an opportunity for powerful instruction as students listen to one another's responses, discuss the craft moves they tried, or tease out possible meanings of a piece of data. The students in the opening vignette, in just a few minutes time, were able to move from a basic observation—there are lots of Cowboys' fans—to a much more sophisticated line of thinking: Maps can deceive us. There is so much positive potential during notebook time for students to become critical, thoughtful readers of text, data, and imagery.

This is why we devote an entire chapter to notebook time—an activity that constitutes only 20 percent of our daily class time. The skills and habits students develop here carry over into everything else we teach and into every other way we use mentor texts. Simply put, notebook time is an opportunity for students to learn about and play with different ideas, information, and genres inspired by mentor texts in the first few minutes of class. It's an amped-up, mentor-text-based bell-ringer that changes the way students write. The stakes are low. The sense of possibility is high.

While we have used quickwrites to open class, Penny Kittle encouraged us to expand the vision of notebook time to incorporate mentor texts. In addition to responding to prompts and provocative questions, Kittle uses notebook time to help kids think and write from information. "If you bring in really interesting information," she says, "kids want to write from it" (Kittle in a workshop, 2013). So we began to offer students a new kind of mentor text—statistics, charts, and graphics—to inspire their critical thinking and writing. We also have found even more ways for students to play and explore using mentor sentences, mentor poems and poets, and mentor images. What we've found is, if we put good stuff out there, our students bring good stuff back, and not just in their notebook play but also in their more processed, finished pieces of writing.

We use the same criteria for selecting mentor texts for notebook time as we use for selecting mentor texts for study. The only difference is that we look for very short texts that can be read in just a few moments so students can jump into the writing as quickly as possible. Figure 5.1 gives examples of some of our favorite mentor texts for notebook time.

In this chapter, we will introduce you to the rules and rhythms of notebook time as well as the different types of mentor texts we offer to inspire our students and encourage risk taking. For each kind of mentor text, we will give you an example from our classrooms, demonstrating a possibility for using it. Finally, we will explore how to push this writerly play into more substantial, polished pieces of writing down the road.

1. Sentence: "I get the urge" by Anna Quindlen: "Every year about this time I get the urge to buy a copybook. And some of those little rectangular pink erasers that look good enough to eat. And a whole lot of those round reinforcements, which were supposed to be pasted around the holes in your loose-leaf paper but were more often made into designs on the inside cover of your loose leaf binder" (Quindlen 1987).

> **Text 5.2** "Life in the 30's" by Anna Quindlen *http://www.nytimes.com/1987/09/09/garden/life-in-the-30-s.html*

2. Poem: "Solitudes" by Margaret Gibson

> **Text 5.3** "Solitudes" by Margaret Gibson *http://writersalmanac.publicradio.org/index.php?date=2014/09/11*

3. Raw Data: "How Much Snow It Typically Takes to Cancel School in the U.S."

> **Text 5.4** "How Much Snow It Typically Takes to Cancel School in the U.S." by Eleanor Barkhorn *http://www.theatlantic.com/education/archive/2014/01/map-how-much-snow-it-typically-takes-to-cancel-school-in-the-us/283470/*

4. Image: "What Kids Around the World Eat for Breakfast"

> **Text 5.5** "Rise and Shine: What Kids Around the World Eat for Breakfast" by Hannah Whitaker and Malia Wollen *http://www.nytimes.com/interactive/2014/10/08/magazine/eaters-all-over.html*

Figure 5.1 Examples of Favorite Mentor Texts for Notebook Time

Using Mentor Texts for Play and Exploration During Notebook Time

There are four main kinds of mentor texts we use for notebook time: sentences, poems, raw data, and images. Each type of text offers qualitatively different opportunities for students to hone their craft as writers, so understanding the potential of each mentor text type is important.

Sentences

We have all watched students struggle to put ideas into sentences. Exploring a writer's syntax and word choice within a single sentence has offered our students a way through this struggle. Sentence study takes the pressure off students to produce a sustained piece of writing and instead invites them to do something more manageable: write a sentence using the craft they noticed a mentor using. When students imitate another writer's work, they are engaging in a genre called pastiche—a literary or artistic genre that is a hodge-podge or imitation.

The best sentences for notebook time are those with imitable craft that can be easily identified and mimicked. Figure 5.2 shows an example of an excellent passage for notebook time from John Green, author of *The Fault in Our Stars*, *Looking for Alaska*, *Paper Towns*, and a number of other novels your students are most likely devouring.

The second sentence clearly has imitable craft and even students who struggle to read like writers pick up on the repetition of "I didn't want" and the string of *ands* at the end of the sentence. This particular mentor sentence helped one student, John, eloquently express his passion for hunting during notebook time one day. John was inspired not only by Green's repetition but also by the details Green used to bring life to each item in his list (Figure 5.3).

I really didn't want to go. I didn't want to see them lower him into the ground in the spot he'd picked out with his dad, and I didn't want to see his parents sink to their knees in the dew-wet grass and moan in pain, and I didn't want to see Peter Van Houten's alcoholic belly stretched against his linen jacket, and I didn't want to cry in front of a bunch of people, and I didn't want to toss a handful of dirt onto his grave, and I didn't want my parents to have to stand there beneath the clear blue sky with its certain slant of afternoon light, thinking about their day and their kid and my plot and my casket and my dirt.

Figure 5.2 Example of Sentence for Notebook Time from *The Fault in Our Stars* by John Green

> I waited for the sun to rise bringing shooting time closer, and I waited for the turkeys to awake from the rising of the sun and exit the roosting trees, and I waited for the sound of the gobbler to respond to my slate call, and I waited for the turkey to ignore its natural instincts and come toward the female, and I waited all year for this moment, the beginning of spring turkey season.

Figure 5.3 John's Imitation of John Green's Sentence

The Lizard

Summer mornings
biking past
I'd see these lizards
laying out tanning
on the scratchy grass
in front of the beach stairs
waiting for people to come by,
three lizards of green and brown
huddled beside the old, wooden boards
protected from the wispy wind.

This morning
I slowed to glance
and the greenest one
with brightly colored scales
and a pin for a head
huddled with his friends,
crawled towards me,
put his tiny feet
on my warm, tan skin
and walked up
my bare arm.

Figure 5.4 Mary's Poem Written Off First Line of "Back Road" by Bruce Guernsey

Studying the craft of a single sentence helps students more as writers than any lesson on sentence structure or variety we have ever taught. When students try crafting on their own and then share their attempts with each other, it builds curiosity in sentence work and gives them confidence to try something new.

Poems

Students respond to poems during notebook time in a variety of ways. Some write poems with the same number of lines or a similar structure, while others use a specific crafting move they noticed in the poem in a bit of prose. Students may simply write a response to the topic of the poem, or they may use the first line (or a favorite line) as a jumping-off point for their own writing. Figure 5.4 shows a poem in which a student riffed off the first line of the poem "Back Road" by Bruce Guernsey, a creative writing professor at Eastern Illinois University. In the first stanza, the speaker describes a winter morning ritual. In the second, he recounts a specific winter morning.

Text 5.6 "Back Road" by Bruce Guernsey *http://www.poetryfoundation.org/poetrymagazine/poem/23632*

A fun variation of "writing off a line" is using a favorite line as the last line of their writing. Students select a line from the mentor poem, write it at the bottom of their notebook page and begin writing on a topic of their choice. With one minute left, students try to connect whatever it is they are writing about to the line they've copied at the bottom of the page. Figure 5.5 shows one student's notebook time response using a line from the poem "Ross: Children of the Ghetto" by George Szirtes. The line taken from this poem is in italics.

Text 5.7 "Ross: Children of the Ghetto" by George Szirtes *http://www.poetryfoundation.org/poetrymagazine/poem/181102*

I slipped between the logs and toppled trunks, dropping into the cool shelter of our little hollow. Gladwell and BT were already waiting, holding their Moleskine notebooks. We chatted, laughing and joking for a while, before sitting down and flipping open our books. We started with Gladwell. As he read from the pages of his notebook, we were transported to an 18th century British naval boat, in the midst of a deadly battle between the crewmen, and the vicious pirates trying to board. When we moved to BT, she took us to a spaceship floating through the inky black darkness. When it was my turn, I brought us to a decrepit old mansion on the top of an abandoned hill. As the sun sank, we said our goodbyes and headed home for dinner. *Our knees were filthy with our secret places.*

Figure 5.5 Henry's Response Using a Favorite Line as the Last Line

Sometimes students will simply be inspired by the topic of a poem. Figure 5.6 shows a student response to the poem "The snow's/feet slip," a tiny twenty-five-line poem about snow by Maine poet Marty Walsh.

Text 5.8 "The snow's/feet slip" by Marty Walsh *http://www.americanlifeinpoetry.org /columns/503.html*

The ashes fell like snow. It was almost beautiful to watch the bodies catch the air and float around us. You stumbled forward, kicking up a cloud of someone's sister, aunt, mother, daughter. The embers had long grown cold, but I could taste the fire in the wind, hear their screams in every crunch of my boots. Nothing lived here anymore. Even the trees whispered, like God Himself was ashamed of what had happened.

Figure 5.6 Kate's Prose Inspired by "The snow's/ feet slip"

Students are invited to respond to the mentor poems however they like, and they frequently come up with responses we could not anticipate or assign.

Raw Data

Data initially seemed to us like the domain of other content area teachers. Certainly, charts and graphs and statistics don't fall under *English*, right? However, college professors note that freshmen are grossly lacking in the ability to interpret and make meaning out of raw data (Kittle 2013). Making meaning and finding the words to express it is what we do as English teachers. Along with our students, we have discovered that timely, relevant, challenging data can inspire flurried writing, spirited class discussions, and impassioned writing projects down the road. Raw data is the least familiar type of mentor text when we start notebook time, but it quickly becomes students' absolute favorite.

Harper's Index is an excellent source for stimulating statistics that are perfect for engaging students in critical thinking and writing. Sometimes we choose one statistic for notebook time, and other times we offer students a handful of statistics and ask them to write about a favorite. One such favorite comes from the December 2013 issue:

Number of Chicken McNuggets Usain Bolt ate during the 2008 Beijing Olympics, according to his autobiography: 1,000.

After students had a chance to respond in writing, we invited them to share something the statistic made them wonder. They postulated

* Are Chicken McNuggets actually athletic power food?
* How many McNuggets did Bolt eat in the 2012 Olympics?
* Did Bolt perform better in the 2012 London Olympics because he ate too many McNuggets in Beijing?
* Was Bolt sponsored by McDonalds? Who were Bolt's sponsors? Whom did McDonald's sponsor?
* How much did Chicken McNuggets cost in 2008, and in what quantities were they sold?
* Does McDonald's provide free food to athletes in the athlete's village?

Given a few minutes alone with the data and the encouragement to write their observations, questions, and inspired prose, students' responses yielded so many interesting thoughts and questions that a flurry of cell phone research began during the sharing portion of notebook time. Students didn't just ask these questions, they wanted to know the answers, and they wanted to know what those answers really meant. This powerful and immediate need to know something leads many students back to their notebooks to further pursue their questions in writing. There's really nothing quite like data, whether it's presented as a simple statistic or captured in a showy infographic (like the NFL fan map), to help students develop curiosity, a critical habit of mind for writers of any genre.

Images

Sometimes the mentor texts we offer our students don't include any text at all. Thought-provoking images also inspire students and open up imaginative pathways for their writing. The images we use during notebook time range from fine art to photojournalism. We simply grab pictures and photographs with striking visual power. Our usual haunts often yield useful images, particularly Twitter, and we also look to print magazines, specifically *National Geographic* and *The New Yorker*.

Sometimes the images contain bits of text that increase the possibilities for creative writing. We're crazy about James Mollison's art and photography book *Where Children Sleep*, a photo essay that beautifully and evocatively depicts portraits of young people from around the world side by side in the rooms in which they sleep. While the images are collected in a book you can purchase, most of them are also found on Mollison's website for free. Sharing a handful of these with students immediately reveals the incredible diversity of experience around the world and starkly depicts how little we know about how others live.

Text 5.9 "Where Children Sleep" by Jane Mollison *http://jamesmollison.com/books /where-children-sleep/*

Creative writing teachers have long known that images provide useful writing prompts—write a story from the perspective of the person in the picture, or write a story using what you see in the photo as your setting. Invitations like these encourage students to practice narrative writing, but when you let students choose how they respond to an image, they surprise you again and again with the range of possibilities for writing they explore.

For example, in Mollison's book there is a photograph of Bilal, a six-year-old living in the West Bank. In his portrait, Bilal, dressed in a button-down shirt, looks like he has gone a few days without a bath. A small black-and-white goat is draped across his shoulders as he confidently stares at the camera. His bedroom is a small, outdoor lean-to; his bed is a rug covering the dirt.

As we've shown this photograph to students over time, we've seen such a range of interesting responses. Students have written about the life they imagine Bilal leads. They've written about the similarities and differences they notice in Bilal's world and their own and careful, detailed descriptions of what they observe in the portrait. They've written mock *National Geographic* articles and short poems from the boy's perspective. They've written about their wonderings—how was this young man selected for the project? In what ways is he representative of others his age? In this city? What did the photographer think about Bilal's lifestyle? Is the photographer biased?

Figure 5.7 shows a few different student responses to the portrait of Bilal. Images tend to produce the widest range of responses of any mentor text, and students enjoy listening to their peers' diverse perspectives.

The beginnings of a short story by Jordan:

They kicked me and Arshy, my goat, out of the town. And within seconds, I was running, climbing over the chainlink fence, but still carrying the goat on my shoulders. Thirty minutes later, I stopped, gasping for breath. There was a little puddle of water, mixed with mud, though. But I was thirsty and so was Arshy. I stared into the muddy water, knowing that I could have gotten very sick. But I drank it anyway. I cupped my hands and slowly put them in the water, trapping it. I quickly brought my hands up to my mouth. The moment the water made contact with the back of my throat, I jumped, not pleased with the taste. But it was cold, felt good. I did it again. And again and again.

A haiku by Alex:

Sleeping on the ground
looking up at the city
But am I safe here?

The beginnings of an editorial by Julia:

In this day and age, especially where I live and in the U.S. in general, a lot of kids aren't grateful for what they have and don't realize how much worse other people have it. I think it's important to educate kids about current events and issues close to them to give them a better perspective. There is the stereotype of kids starving in Africa, but I can't do anything about it. There could be a starving child living a few blocks away from you and you wouldn't even think of it.

Figure 5.7 Student Responses to Portrait of Bilal and His Bedroom

Establishing Routines and Rules for Notebook Time

In our classrooms, notebook time occurs at the beginning of class before the lesson and the writing and conferring that happen later. It lasts about ten minutes (Figure 5.8), leaving five to fifteen minutes for the writing lesson and twenty or more minutes for writing and conferring in our forty-six minute block.

Share and introduce mentor text	1 minute
Give students time to jot down noticings and write	4 minutes
Give students time to revise and proofread (optional)	2 minutes
Share student responses	1–3 minutes

Figure 5.8 Notebook Time

While we use notebook time as a way to begin every class, you might decide to incorporate it just a few days a week. Regardless of the timing you choose, what's important is that notebook time becomes a regular practice your students can depend on. Katie Wood Ray writes, "When teaching has a predictable rhythm to it, students recognize what's happening and can engage with the whole process of teaching and learning much more intentionally because it is so familiar" (2006, 110). The predictable rhythms of notebook time, coupled with the invitation to take risks and explore with writing, allow students to be playful and flex their writing muscles regularly.

Share and Introduce the Mentor Text

Mentor texts can be shared during notebook time in a few different ways. They can be photocopied and given to students to glue or tape into their notebooks or file into their binders. If the mentor text is a sentence or passage from one of the texts you are currently studying, you can simply ask students to turn to that piece and mark the sentence you want them to study. In the opening vignette, Rebekah projected her mentor text onto the whiteboard directly from theatlantic.com; students came up to the board for a better look. Additionally, you might consider typing or cutting and pasting your mentor texts onto PowerPoint slides. An advantage to sharing mentor texts this way is that you'll create a running slideshow of mentor texts that students can access at any point in the year. What matters is that students can see the text clearly for the whole of notebook time so they can reread it as they write and talk.

The next step is to introduce the mentor text; if it's a written text, this usually means reading it aloud twice. The first reading is for students to get a feel for the mentor text and what it's about. With the second reading, students are listening and looking more closely for the craft moves in the text. In our experience, asking a student to do the second reading tunes our ears in different ways: Everyone hears things the second time we didn't hear the first. We may also briefly share about the author and his or her published works.

If the mentor text is visual (raw data or an image), we read the title of the piece and provide a very brief introduction. With data the introduction may include the source, when it was published, and whether it's part of a larger study. With an image, we might say where we found it, but sometimes we don't say anything because we want students to respond to the raw power of the image. We can always talk about the source later.

Give Students Time to Write

Students write for about four minutes during notebook time. This usually yields anywhere from half a page to a page, depending on the student. If students do this every day, they will easily fill a composition notebook and possibly two by the end of the year. It truly gives them a sense of accomplishment to flip through a notebook of their own writing in June, pages dense with words.

While students are free to discover their own process with most of the writing they do in our classrooms, we do have some rules for the four minutes of writing they do during notebook time. These rules aren't ours—they have been adapted from other writing teachers we respect like Natalie Goldberg in *Writing Down the Bones* (1986) and Donald Graves and Penny Kittle in *Inside Writing* (2005). Figure 5.9 lists the rules we post in our classrooms.

While the rules are simple, they are incredibly important in liberating students from self-consciousness and helping them begin exploring where their words and ideas can take them.

As students write, consider writing along with them, modeling the good habits you're trying to instill in them. Some teachers prefer to walk around and monitor their students' efforts. Depending on what you and your students are comfortable with, you might do a

* Keep your hand moving the whole time.

* Don't think too much. Try to write fast enough that you "outrun the censor" in your head.

* Don't worry about grammar or punctuation. Let your ideas lead.

* If you don't know what to write, write *I don't know what to write* or take to sketching until other words come to you.

* Let the writing take you where it takes you—that is, don't feel you have to "stay on topic."

Figure 5.9 Rules for Moments When Students Are Responding on Paper

little over-the-shoulder reading to identify a strong sentence or passage you will later ask a student to share.

Give Students Time to Revise and Proofread (Optional)

A few times a week, we give students two to three minutes to revise and proofread what they've written. We encourage students to extend their ideas, add detail, combine sentences, add punctuation, fix spelling, and so on. The rule is that they're not to think about grammar and punctuation as they are writing, and they're not. But once they've stopped writing and are rereading, this changes. We want students to know most writers don't wait until the end to correct mistakes. When they stop to reread, if they see things that need fixing, most writers correct them in the process of composing. This invitation to quickly reread helps us reinforce this recursive habit we're always trying to teach and helps students develop a habit of rereading to revise and proofread as they draft.

Share Student Responses

One of the joys of notebook time is the after party when students share from their work. Sharing can happen in a number of ways. Students might turn to a partner and read an excerpt or describe what they've written. They might form a circle and each read a line from their response. Volunteers can read entire responses aloud, or the class might share what they noticed about the day's mentor text. *How* you share doesn't matter as much as *that* you share. Students learn so much from hearing the different ways their peers have responded.

Scaffolding Notebook Time in the First Few Weeks of School

The kind of seamless, almost automatic work you see students doing during notebook time later in the year has to start somewhere, of course. In the first few weeks of school, when students are just getting accustomed to reading like writers and writing spontaneously, we may devote up to 15 minutes to notebook time each day. We use the extra time to provide scaffolds that show students how to do the different work of notebook time and learn the routines. We work with scaffolds until we see students can move independently through the process of notebook time. Students are, of course, also getting practice looking at mentor texts and reading like writers in their other class time. What follows are some of the ways we scaffold the new work of notebook time at the beginning of the year.

Give Students Guiding Questions

Students need to understand the kinds of thinking we want them to do during notebook time, so we share some guiding questions to help direct them when they're just getting started. We'll think about these questions all year long, and they will eventually become habits of mind. We want students to do three distinct kinds of thinking, depending on the type of mentor text we're using. Figure 5.10 lists the guiding questions for sentences and poems, images, and raw data. It's ideal to have a poster-sized copy of these questions in your room, as well as a copy for each student's binder or notebook.

Model the Thinking

While it's helpful to have questions like these that name the kinds of thinking we want students to do, the danger is that students will think of them in a checklist sort of way rather than as an integrated way of thinking and looking at texts. This is why it's so important when students are just getting started to model the thinking that comes from questions

Questions for Written Mentor Texts (sentences and poems)

＊ What do you notice?

＊ How is the writing put together?

＊ What craft moves can you identify?

＊ What do you see that you might want to try?

Questions for Visual Mentor Texts (images)

＊ What do you notice?

＊ What is the big picture? What are the small parts of the picture?

＊ How does the text (if there is any) relate to the picture?

＊ What story does the picture tell?

＊ What writing might emerge from this picture?

Questions for Raw Data

＊ What do you notice?

＊ What does this data say?

＊ What does this data *not* say?

＊ What does it mean?

＊ What writing might emerge from this data?

Figure 5.10 Guiding Questions for Notebook Time

like these. Most students have never encountered the kinds of texts we are asking them to consider, much less this way of thinking about them. For these notebook invitations to push students' thinking and writing beyond their routine boundaries, we need to show students what this thinking looks like in action.

When we model the thinking we want students to do in response to texts, it sounds a lot like the modeling we showed you in Chapter 4 when we introduce reading like a writer. For example, if Rebekah were using the Facebook fandom 2014 graphic from the opening vignette in the very first days of school, she might demonstrate her thinking like this:

> *The first thing I notice about this graphic is that the biggest fandoms are Cowboys and Broncos. It looks like the Vikings and Seahawks are also much larger than the others, which kind of surprises me.* [As Rebekah talks, she writes in her notebook: Cowboys & Broncos—biggest fandom]
>
> *Hmm . . . what else do I notice?*
>
> *I wonder why all of Alaska is in the Seahawks' fandom and all of Hawaii is for the 49ers?* [in notebook: surprised by AK and Hawaii] *That's another surprise for me. I obviously want to see where the Redskins rank, since they are my favorite team. Seems like they are pretty much only in Virginia. Redskins and Cowboys are in Virginia. That's kind of funny because all of my family are Redskins fans except for my brother who is a Cowboys fan! When we were little, he had a Dallas Cowboys bedroom—my parents even let him put Cowboys wallpaper up!* [in notebook: Brother's Cowboys bedroom] *Once, we were fighting over his Cowboys helmet and broke the stereo in my room. We hid it from my parents for years.* [in notebook: broken stereo secret]
>
> *I guess it could be interesting that South Carolina has so many different groups represented—it looks like Florida and South Carolina are the most diverse states. South Carolina doesn't have a pro team, but Florida does. I wonder if Florida has a higher population of people who have moved from other states and brought their favorite team with them?* [in notebook: does loyalty travel?]

By listening to Rebekah and watching her jot down ideas, students see a model of the kind of generative thinking notebook time elicits. They also see that the point is not to tick off answers to questions but to let their thinking take them wherever it will. Over time, as students become more practiced with notebook time, their own thinking will come more quickly and easily and they won't need the scaffolds of questions or models any more.

Model the Writing

In the early days of notebook time, students also benefit from seeing what it looks like to write in response to thinking about a text, so modeling the actual writing is another helpful scaffold. In the example above, Rebekah reviewed her jottings and then selected one idea to write about: her brother's Cowboys room and the trouble they would get into there. She set a timer and wrote for four minutes while her students watched silently, noting observations about her process. The students noted Rebekah ignored typos when she wrote, wrote the words "I don't know what to write" when she was stuck, and veered off topic at one point—all part of the rules!

Over several early days you will probably need to offer a demonstration of writing in response to each different kind of text you plan to use during notebook time.

Move Students into the Work of Notebook Time

When students are ready to try looking at a text and noticing on their own, scaffold their first tries by reminding them to look back at their guiding questions and remember the demonstrations you've offered. Explain that their noticings can take the form of bulleted notes, words and phrases, or pictures—anything that helps them generate ideas for writing. Then give them two minutes to jot down their first noticings about a fresh mentor text they haven't seen. It's critical with these early, first attempts that you ask students to turn and talk to one another about what they noticed. This talk should add new ideas to their own lists, see new ways of thinking about a text, and double their writing possibilities.

After a bit of noticing and talk, students should be ready to select something they've jotted and try writing in response to it for four minutes as they've watched you do on multiple occasions. Again, sharing this writing—in pairs, small groups, or with the whole class—provides critical scaffolding when students are first getting started. They need to hear and see what other students are doing to extend their ideas about what's possible with this new work.

Pushing Past Play into Projects That Matter

Sometimes notebook time is just notebook time. And that's fine. Students grow and mature as writers with this daily practice. It is a worthy end in itself.

But sometimes notebook time becomes something more.

One of the guiding questions for notebook time asks students to consider what kind of writing might emerge from the mentor text. This is actually one of the most important questions students ask. The students studying the NFL fandom map in the opening vignette brainstormed several possibilities:

* a research paper about the real number of fans in each county
* an informational paper about how the popularity of different teams has changed over time

* an argument paper about which team is the best
* a story about a player who leaves a really popular team to go to an unpopular team—like the Jets!—or the other way around
* a poem written from the perspective of one of those players.

As students share writing possibilities, we encourage everyone to take the ideas down in their notebooks so they see the range of genres and topics that can emerge from a single, common inspiration point. Even if students don't use any of the ideas generated in their own writing, the exercise of moving from an inspiration source to new writing ideas is an important one. With experience, students will begin to internalize this exercise and will suddenly be finding new ideas for writing everywhere.

In addition to inspiring new writing projects, notebook time can also breathe life into a piece of writing a student is currently working on. As teachers, we listen to students' work with a sense of possibility. For example, during notebook time one day, Allison shared the following sentence from slate.com writer Eliza Berman's personal essay "My Mother's Death Cured My Anxiety": By day, I am restless legs and nervous habits: picking the skin on my lips, peeling back my nails (Berman 2014). After students wrote in response, Grayson volunteered to share a sentence from his writing: "I am a swinging golf club, trying to find my place in the game." Allison encouraged him to consider it as a potential lead for the golf memoir he was currently writing. Figures 5.11 and 5.12 show the first paragraph of Grayson's memoir before and after this conversation.

Text 5.10 "My Mother's Death Cured My Anxiety" by Eliza Berman
http://www.slate.com/articles/double_x/doublex/2014/08/how_my_mother_s_death_cured_my_anxiety.html

While Grayson found inspiration in a mentor sentence from a memoir during a study of memoir, other students may benefit from playing with mentor texts outside the current genre study. For this reason, it's important to have mentor texts for notebook time that represent a variety of genres, not just the one you are studying as a whole class. For example, during a study of memoir, Aubrey Scott was trying to find the heart of her piece about her relationship with her brother. Over the course of the study, the class wrote from

> I remember playing golf for the first time at the age of 4 or 5. Getting used to playing golf for the first time can be really challenging and tough because you have to learn the fundamentals of the game. I remember my dad teaching me how to swing the golf club and to have a good plane at impact of the ball. It was really hard at first at that young of an age, but I soon got the hang of it like Phil Mickelson or Tiger Woods hitting a great shot.

Figure 5.11 Grayson's Lead Before Notebook Time

> I'm a swinging golf club, trying to find my place in the game and hitting the ball. I remember playing golf for the first time at the young age of four or five. My dad would walk with me over to the range and teach me how to hit a ball. He would put his arms around me and turn my body, and I would swing the club. Once I had gotten used to hitting the ball, it turned into a rhythm, and it was consistent. My dad would tell me, "Good job kid, you're getting the hang of it!" I would keep on hitting and smile.

Figure 5.12 Grayson's Lead After Notebook Time

several mentor texts in different genres during notebook time, and several clicked with Aubrey Scott and helped her craft her memoir. Figure 5.13 shows the three mentor texts that helped shape the meaning in her piece. Figure 5.14 is an excerpt from her piece where you can see the impact of these mentor texts.

Poetry, fiction, personal essay—short excerpts from three different genres helped Aubrey Scott discover what she was trying to say about her relationship with her brother. It's often in the strange, in-between, out-of-study writing experiences during notebook time that students make discoveries that change and help reinvent their current writing projects in ways not possible without an opportunity to play, to imagine, to ask, "What if?"

And don't think the garden loses its ecstasy in winter. It's quiet, but the roots are down there riotous. (Rumi, "Form is Ecstatic," *The Soul of Rumi*)

When did creating a flawless facade become a more vital goal than learning to love the person who lives inside your skin? (Ellen Hopkins, *Perfect*)

Here he was, jumping off a boat into the Maine waters; here he was, as a child, larkily peeing from a cabin window with two young cousins; here he was, living in Italy and learning Italian by flirting; here he was, telling a great joke; here he was, an ebullient friend, laughing and filling the room with his presence. (James Wood, "Why? The Fictions of Life and Death," *The New Yorker*)

Figure 5.13 Poetry, Fiction, and Personal Essay Mentor Texts That Shaped Aubrey Scott's Memoir

"First place goes to . . . Peyton King!" Of course. Beat again. It was continuous, all the attention always on him. And I felt riotous, I felt the jealousy bubbling up inside me. I was quiet, but underneath I couldn't bare the fact that I had been beat once again.

Now at fifteen, my relationship with my brother remains the same. When did competition become a more vital goal than having a close bond with your sibling? We have our moments, times when he is my best friend, these moments don't come as often as they should though. Change is hard, I don't think either one of us can really imagine just all of a sudden always being nice to one another, and I think that is why we are never going to act that way. Maybe things will change, but I guess you could say having a little brother did not turn out how I had dreamed it would all those years ago.

This is me as a kid: I just scored my first basket ever in basketball. It was probably the most exciting moment of my life—fans cheering, teammates clapping. I couldn't have been more proud of myself. After I ran off the court, I jumped into my mom's arms.

"Mom! Did you see my basket? Did you see how good it was?"

"Aww, honey I missed it. I was on the phone with your father. Peyton took his first step! Isn't that so exciting?" my mother giddily replied. And here I was, in second place again; here I was tears hanging on to the edge of my eyes; here I was wondering if first place would ever be in my reach.

Figure 5.14 Excerpt from Aubrey Scott's Memoir

A WAY IN

Notebook time is one of our favorite and fastest times of the day to plan. Whenever we come across something that looks like fun, we save it in our Google dropbox and digitally load our queue for daily writing practice.

Try sitting at the computer, in front of a bookshelf, or at the kitchen table with a magazine or newspaper on the screen or spread out in front of you. Go in search of five mentor texts for notebook time. For an extra challenge, try to find one of each type: sentence, poem, raw data, and image. This activity will set you up for at least one week of daily writing inspiration with your students!

Closing Thoughts

The impact of notebook time extends far beyond the ten minutes of class time it encompasses. Many students turn the ideas marinating in their notebooks into larger writing projects. Davis, a junior, keeps circling back to a line graph showing the relationship between University of Alabama Athletic Department revenue and the costs of scholarships in between 2005 and 2013: "Something I'd like to work on that really intrigued me [during notebook time] was the scholarship-to-revenue ratio generated by colleges. It was pretty obvious that the schools were generating a significantly larger amount of revenue from the sports than they were putting out in scholarships. And I feel like, at that level at which the schools are generating revenue, they should either offer some form of compensation for the students or increase the amount of scholarships they give out for sports." Davis has a lot to say on this topic—a topic that made it onto his radar during notebook time one day. He hopes to write this piece soon.

Text 5.11 University of Alabama Sports Revenue http://www.businessinsider.com/university-alabama-athletics-revenue-scholarships-2014-10

It's okay if students don't use notebook time to launch into bigger writing, though. As we've said throughout this chapter, the play, experimentation, and critical thinking that take place during notebook time is a worthy end in itself. It builds writing muscles, making our writers stronger. And sometimes our students really do become so inspired during notebook time that they return to one of these ideas for a piece of longer writing. Real writers try new things and have plans, and notebook time gives our students an added opportunity every day to broaden their writing horizons and build on that writing plan for the future.

CHAPTER SIX

Mentors Show Students How to Plan

"I have no idea what to do," Gianna said, closing her notebook.

I admired her honesty. I could always count on Gianna to tell me exactly what she was thinking. But I also knew that she struggled to embrace uncertainty. Like many of her peers, Gianna wanted to know what the end result should look like, and she wanted a plan for getting there.

"Let's focus on what you do know," I said, balancing on my footstool. I pulled it closer to her desk and tapped gently on her notebook. "Show me what you've been working on."

Reluctantly, Gianna opened her notebook. A few half-finished sketches of horses dotted the page and a list of some kind filled the lower half.

"Tell me about this," I said, pointing to the list.

"Well, I'm thinking about comparing different kinds of horseback riding—like Western and English riding. But there's a lot I could say about it, and I don't even know where to begin."

"Have any of the mentor texts given you ideas for how you might compare two things?"

She thought for a moment. "I don't remember."

"Well, there's a mentor text I have in mind. Let's look at it together, and see if it jogs anything for you."

I instructed her to go to our class Learnist board where she could visit all of the infograph-ics I had uploaded for this study. We scrolled down to the infographic titled "The Price of Being Batman: Then and Now," which offers a side-by-side comparison of the cost of Batman's uniform and accoutrement in the past and present. Thick block letters spell out different elements of Bat-man's ensemble with smaller type and bright blue numbers detailing the exact cost of each item.

Text 6.1 "How Much Does It Cost to Be Batman in Real Life?" by Sarah Ang
http://mashable.com/2013/07/16/batman-price-infographic/

Gianna's eyes moved back and forth across the computer screen. "What do you see here that might be helpful to you?" I asked.

She paused to think. "Well, they're comparing two things just like I want to. And they have different categories, which helps keep all the information organized. Maybe I could do some-thing like that."

—Allison

We all have a natural tendency to want to know where we are going before we even get started. We look down the road; we hope for a map. Our students want this, too, as they embark upon a new writing study. Just like Gianna's struggle to begin her infographic, stu-dents want to know what to do and where to go in their writing. This is why at the begin-ning of every study, we put lots of roadmaps in their hands in the form of mentor texts.

Students need time to think and plan for writing. They need help finding topics, narrowing their focus, and arranging their ideas. There are many different ways to offer students support during this phase. Graphic organizers, feedback circles, process demon-strations—all of these things can be helpful. But some students need more than a Venn diagram or feedback to get started. And all students need strategies for moving forward that can be sustained on their own beyond the classroom walls. Using mentor texts is a lifetime skill that can provide inspiration and direction for the planning process that a graphic organizer alone cannot.

Planning is strongly linked to genre. Most writers approach the planning of a work of analysis very differently than they would when writing a novel or a poem. Essayists of-ten write their way to a greater discovery in their work. And editorialists have a very firm, logical structure planned from the start. Thus, the planning phase of writing and the les-sons you use to guide it will likely look different depending on the genre your students are writing. There will be times when you nudge students to develop a detailed plan up front. Other times, you might allow more freedom and fluidity in discovering a plan for writing. Regardless of how you approach the planning of a piece of writing, both mentor writers and the texts they create provide guidance and inspiration.

At the beginning of any new genre or technique study, mentor texts can support students as they plan and make the writerly decisions that will breathe life into their ideas. In this chapter, we will show you how to use mentor texts to introduce the elements of a new genre or technique so students can begin the planning process. We will also show how to follow up with whole-class and individual lessons as students begin drafting and how to use the wisdom of mentors—the writers behind the mentor texts—to model different modes of planning for your students.

Generating Ideas

Students can find ideas for writing everywhere—from the little bits of writing that pop up during notebook time, from the athletic field, from conversations at home, from their reading, from the movies they watch. Georgia Heard and Nancie Atwell help students become intentional about cultivating lists of potential writing ideas through heart maps and writing territories (Heard 1998, Atwell 2002). These running lists of ideas provide students with an at-the-ready source of individual, interesting topics when they are beginning a new piece of writing.

Mentor texts can also help students generate ideas for writing. New ideas and potential topics bubble up from students' interactions with the mentor texts we read in any given study. We don't approach this kind of planning in any kind of formal way. We don't devote a writing lesson to generating ideas based on mentor texts. We don't insist that students use mentor texts for ideas for writing topics. At the beginning of a new writing study, we simply remind students that their mentor texts (past and present) are one of the many resources that might help them come up with something they are excited to write about. When students do find potential topics in the mentor texts they're reading, we encourage them to jot them down in their notebooks and add them to their running list of ideas.

Introducing a Genre or Technique

Grounding students' initial planning in mentor texts will give them not only a focus for writing but also touchstones from which to seek inspiration and refer back to throughout the writing process. The introduction to a new writing study is students' first invitation to begin planning. As soon as students get hold of a set of mentor texts and begin to see the bones of the given genre or the footprint of the highlighted technique, the wheels in their heads begin turning. Before they even take pen to paper, they are mentally creating a plan for the piece of writing they will craft. We meet them here to provide the support they need as they get started.

To begin grounding students' understanding of a particular genre or technique of writer's craft, we share the mentor text cluster we have compiled for that study. As always, the class will read the texts with a reader's eye for understanding first, either individually or in small groups, and then the class will go back to read like writers. This is where the most intense mentor text work happens in a unit. As if approaching a puzzle, students untangle and identify the parts and pieces of writing—topic, structure, tone, style. They uncover the features of genre or track an element of craft through the texts in order to get a picture of all the directions their writing could go.

Over the course of a few class periods, each text in the cluster is introduced. At times, particularly with the very first mentor texts, we allow students free reign to observe craft features. We ask, "What do you see? What jumps out at you?" As a class, we collect their noticings and writerly interests (just as we do during notebook time). We type them and project them on a screen for students to transfer to their notebooks or compile them on large pieces of paper to post in the front of the room as anchor charts for the study. These noticings give students a starting place as they begin to consider the crafting of their own writing for that particular study. Their noticings also help us add to our existing plan of writing lessons, as students often notice features of texts we never even considered in our planning.

Our primary goal in the first few days of a study is to inspire students and show them several models of the writing they're about to do. So we place the best examples we can find into their hands and ask them to consider the following questions:

* Which mentor texts do you like?
* What other writers have written on the same topic?
* What writers do you admire who write in this genre?
* What have you read that might help you begin writing?
* What have you read that is like the writing you want to do?

Students can respond to these questions in a number of ways. You might suggest that they respond in their writer's notebooks so they can track their thinking over time. You might refer to these questions when conferring with students. Students might gather in small groups and discuss their answers to these questions with one another.

Using mentor texts to introduce students to the kind of writing they will do gives them sources of inspiration and lets them see plentiful options as they begin to lay out their plans for a new piece of writing. These mentor texts also give students confidence as they move forward and the feeling of firm ground under their feet as they plan. The mentors take the often scary and overwhelming work of getting started and provide something tangible—a place for students to return as often as they like as they figure out the parts and pieces of their own writing.

Planning for Drafts

Some lessons in planning and preparing to write are meant for the whole class because they address needs nearly all the students in your class will have. These are lessons about the fundamental elements of a genre, the crafting techniques you would like all your students to try, or lessons in grammar and punctuation that are important early in a study. Other instructional conversations are smaller, individual lessons that take place during writing conferences and help nudge a single student forward in his or her process. These conversations can focus on any planning topic—developing good writing habits, finding an idea, choosing a genre in a non-genre study, finding a structure. We would like to share a few of these kinds of conversations with you now to demonstrate how students use mentor texts to develop solid plans for their writing.

A Conversation with a Class of Writers

Even when students have an idea in mind for the current writing study, there are still those minutes—frightening for both them and us!—when they stare at the blank page in front of them. They wonder, *Where do I even begin? What comes first? Then, what's next? How will I get to the end?* Using mentor texts to help students choose a strong structure for their writing is often one of the most powerful planning lessons you will teach, and it's exactly the kind of conversation that should happen as a whole class. Students will need a structure for their writing, and once they've identified a framework for their ideas, they suddenly have a way to start drafting. While this structure can certainly change and develop as the writing itself changes and progresses, planning the frame of the writing gives students a starting place from which to work. How can mentor texts help students get there?

While the next example focuses on helping students find a meaningful structure for their writing, the framework of this lesson is incredibly versatile and is useful for planning virtually any lesson. In fact, you will almost certainly notice that this lesson follows the same framework you've seen in most all the lessons in the book so far. It's

the same framework you'll see us use in later lessons too. We plan lessons over and over
the same way because the structure of the lesson itself actually teaches students a critical habit of mind: *For any question you have about writing, always start with mentor texts.*
Want to help students think about the tone of their writing? Need to show students how
to elaborate on their initial ideas? Identify the elements of a specific genre? *Always start
with mentor texts.*

READ LIKE READERS, EXPLORING MANY POSSIBILITIES

As we've mentioned before, using a cluster of mentor texts is critically important in showing students a variety of ways to approach writing. Sure, we could hand them one master-
ful example and encourage them to mimic that structure, but then, when we sit down to
look at their work, that's the *only* thing we would see. Providing a single model would also
fail to move students toward independence with this work. Using a single mentor text
wouldn't enable students to do any decision making as writers because they would be
limited to following the moves we have given them to follow.

Instructing through a cluster of mentor texts reminds our students that there are end-
less "right" ways to be successful in a given genre or using a certain technique. We share
multiple mentor texts when studying structure so students can make the choices writers
make—selecting the best structure for their work, sometimes combining elements from
multiple mentor texts to create something new and specific to that writer. For example, in
a study of This I Believe essays, we provided students with six different mentor texts, each
excellently crafted but demonstrating different structures, topics, and tones. We used this
cluster for every phase of writing instruction throughout the study, and students returned
to the six texts independently as they crafted their own essays. (See Figure 6.1.)

In most studies, before we began reading the mentor texts, students spend some time
brainstorming ideas they might like to write about without committing to a topic. The students studying the This I Believe essays, for instance, considered the beliefs that mattered
most to them. Once we start reading the texts in the cluster, these ideas take shape and
solidify as students see the many different possibilities offered by their mentors. Sometimes, however, reading the mentor texts sends students in a whole new direction with
their ideas.

READ LIKE WRITERS, ZOOMING IN ON STRUCTURE

Before you teach a lesson in planning structure, students will be familiar with the mentor
texts and will have read through them and noticed features of the genre and elements of
craft. In fact, some of the craft elements students have already noticed may very well be

"Find a Good Frog" by Delia Motavalli

Text 6.2 "Find a Good Frog" by Delia Motavalli *http://thisibelieve.org/essay/101469/*

"The Triumph of Kindness" by Josh Stein

Text 6.3 "The Triumph of Kindness" by Josh Stein *http://thisibelieve.org/essay/83477/*

"Accomplishing Big Things in Small Pieces" by William Wissemann

Text 6.4 "Accomplishing Big Things in Small Pieces" by William Wissemann *http://thisibelieve.org/essay/39318/*

"The Beatles Live On" by Macklin Levine

Text 6.5 "The Beatles Live On" by Macklin Levine *http://thisibelieve.org/essay/46931/*

"Finding the Flexibility to Survive" by Brighton Earley

Text 6.6 "Finding the Flexibility to Survive" by Brighton Earley *http://thisibelieve.org/essay/31840/*

"Inner Strength from Desperate Times" by Jake Hovenden

Text 6.7 "Inner Strength from Desperate Times" by Jake Hovenden *http://thisibelieve.org/essay/269411/*

Figure 6.1 This I Believe Mentor Text Cluster

related to structure. This was certainly true in the This I Believe study as students were very aware of the repetition of the eponymous tagline in all the essays.

For this lesson, students should reread the mentor texts you are studying and think very specifically about structure. How does each writer order his or her ideas? How does each piece move from beginning to end? Are there unique structural features like sections or headings? We encourage students to label each paragraph as they read, giving it a category name that makes sense to them and describes the kind of information or ideas contained in each paragraph. For example, in the This I Believe study, students broke into small groups, and each group studied one text solely for its structure. Groups identified the sequential pattern of ideas in their assigned essay. Figure 6.2 shows the structure our students identified in each of the texts in their cluster.

"Find a Good Frog"	"The Triumph of Kindness"	"Accomplishing Big Things in Small Pieces"	"The Beatles Live On"	"Finding the Flexibility to Survive"	"Inner Strength from Desperate Times"
P1—Introduction + statement of belief **P2**—Narrative **P3**—Conclusion/wrap-up **P4**—Tagline	**P1**—Introduction + statement of belief **P2–P7**—Narrative **P8**—Belief restated	**P1**—Introduction + background **P2**—Belief #1 + how it came to be **P3**—Background narrative **P4**—Belief #2 + how it came to be **P5**—Belief #3 + how it came to be **P6**—Beliefs #4 and 5 + how they came to be **P7**—Summary of all beliefs **P8**—Tagline	**P1**—Statement of belief + background **P2–P7**—Narrative **P8**—"And now…" **P9**—Belief restated	**P1–P6**—Narrative **P7**—Statement of belief + "And now…"	**P1–P2**—Background **P3**—Statement of belief **P4–P5**—Narrative **P6**—"And now…" **P7**—Belief restated

Figure 6.2 Structure of Each Text in This I Believe Cluster

The kinds of information and ideas students are tracking will differ some depending on the genre of writing they are studying. An informational piece, for example, will no doubt have sections of examples, supporting evidence, and facts. Memoir and fiction will have passages of description and dialogue. The important thing is to teach students to look at a piece of writing and see the work each section of text is doing and how the writer moves from one section to the next.

SHARE NOTICINGS

At this point, whether students have studied the mentor texts independently or in groups, it is useful to share out as a class, compiling all the different potential structures and talking through each one. It makes sense for students to record the possibilities you discuss in their notebooks as it gives them a map of possible mentor text structures to work with. These whole-group conversations also help students make connections between texts and extend their understandings in important ways. During the This I Believe study, for example, students noticed that half of the six mentor texts had what we came to call the "and now" paragraph, a paragraph where the writer shares how the belief makes a difference in his or her life now. In addition to noticing the structure of each text, students identified a distinctive feature of the genre that they hadn't noticed before.

As you discuss what students have noticed about structure, you'll need to informally check for understanding. You need to know, "Do these students understand what they are seeing in the mentor texts? Do they understand what *structure* means in writing?" Listen carefully to students' comments and suggestions in both small groups and whole-class discussions, even read their faces to help you check for understanding. If just a few students seem not to understand the concept of structure, bump them up to the top of the list to conference with later in class. If a majority of students seem to be missing the mark, you'll need to regroup, reteach, pull some additional mentor texts, and try again.

MAKE WRITERLY CHOICES

Once students have shared what they have found, they need to start making some choices. Ideally, each text in your cluster has shown students a different possibility for structure. In the This I Believe study, students had six templates for possible structures in their notebooks. In conversations with writing groups and in conferences with a teacher, students consider which structure they like best and which might best fit their idea. From there, they simply make a choice—or choices. In this study we saw that some students chose a single mentor text to use as a planning template, while other students chose a combination—the lead from mentor text #1 with the rest of the structure from mentor text #4, for example.

Once students have selected a structure, it's time to begin drafting. Encouraging students to select a structure before drafting gives them a starting place at a point in the process where they often feel unsure, and it helps them get that first draft on paper, however tentative. Once they are drafting, the structures students started with often change and grow and adapt along with the content of their writing. That's fine! It's a natural part of the recursive nature of process. A structure is a start, and from there, from that baseline, students can begin to dig into craft.

Conversations with Individual Writers

We find that some of our best teaching about structure happens in conferences with individual writers. After the writing lesson and just before students settle in, we take a quick survey of where students are in their current writing projects. This status-of-the-class check is particularly important during the planning stages when writers can falter and fall behind without proper guidance. Students who report they are "beginning to draft" can be left to their own devices for a day or two. Students who have demonstrated a gap in understanding during the whole-class lesson, who request conferences, or who report they are "brainstorming topics" are the students to report to first. Mentor text binder and writer's notebook in hand, we pull up a chair next to these students' desks and see how we can help.

We don't always confer with mentor texts. Sometimes the questions writers have are so specific and so much about the individual writer's words on the page, it makes more sense to keep the conversation between student and teacher. But when the student's need demands a model or some inspiration, we like to bring a mentor text or two into the mix. It's like having a third writer present, an expert writer whose knowledge we draw on as we work through various writing situations. As the teacher, it's so nice to be able to point to something concrete and say, "See how this writer does it?"

Conferring with mentor texts is similar to conferring with readers: It's about putting the right text in the student's hand. Whose writing might inspire Peter? Which writers are going to be able to help Paige move past her initial brainstorm? Which mentor text has brilliant transitions that can help Drew smooth out his writing and make connections from one idea to the next? Who is writing about the same topics Michael is writing about?

Even more than your students, you will need to be well acquainted with the writing and the writers behind the texts to do this well. Conferring with students can be nerve-racking because it is one facet of classroom life you just can't prepare for. While we know the types of questions students typically have, there isn't a lesson plan for each and every individual question we will encounter. The teacher has to be ready. The habits of mind discussed in Chapter 2 will help you greatly—the close, writerly reading of your mentor texts, the list of go-to sources when you need to pull a new mentor text quickly, the digital storehouse of wonderful texts that can serve a variety of needs at a moment's notice. Cultivating these habits enables each of us to be ready for whatever a writing conference throws our way.

CONNECTING WRITERS' PLANNING STRUGGLES TO MENTOR TEXT SOLUTIONS

For many writers, the planning stage is the most daunting part of the writing process—a blank page and nothing to say. Where to begin, what to include, what to put next—these questions trouble writers who don't have a vision for the writing they're about to do.

The ways in which we use mentor texts to coach students through writer's block and blank-page anxiety vary from writer to writer. In the opening vignette, Allison chose to lead Gianna to a specific mentor text because Gianna couldn't articulate what she needed help with. Some students, though, are able to clearly identify their problems. In Figure 6.3, we give brief illustrations of students' common writing quandaries and show how you might skipper them through these setbacks.

The last dilemma arises when students are choosing the genre in which they will write. For example, one student, Ginnie, noted that she wanted to "start drafting little pieces" of her writing but needed to pick a genre first. She wanted to write about her relationship with her sister. Reflecting in her notebook, she wrote, "I like the thought of doing an infographic of siblings, and I think that it would turn out to be very good. I also want to do a poem more than a memoir. I want to find a mentor text that will help me with my poem or my infographic. Then I will begin to draft an outline of special lines that I want to include." In a conference, Allison invited Ginnie to study a multigenre cluster of texts that explored family relationships (see Figure 6.4). She eventually settled on a poem because she felt the form would best suit the emotions she wanted to draw out in the writing.

Of course many of the dilemmas writers run into are unique to the writer and the writing. They do not fit neatly into a chart. Regardless of the writing puzzle, mentor texts offer students powerful models that can help transform their initial ideas into something much more substantial, something that has a life beyond the mind and the notebook jottings and the seed ideas that beg to grow.

"I don't know where to begin."	Gather a few texts in the genre, and have the student read the first few sentences of each piece out loud. Have him describe what each writer is doing. Ask him what he likes and doesn't like about the various beginnings. Invite him to try writing one or two of his own leads based on the models.
"I don't know what to put into my piece."	Choose one or two texts in the same genre with different content—a book review with a heavy focus on author style and another with an emphasis on characterization and plot. Ask the writer to list all the different types of information included in each review. As she plans, ask her to consider what information she might want to include in her own review and what she might want to leave out.
"I don't know what to research."	From memoir to editorial, research has a place in all writing. You might ask a student to highlight all the details in a memoir he thinks the writer couldn't possibly have remembered without talking to others who were involved. Or ask the writer to underline all the stats, facts, and expert testimony present in a piece of commentary. Then have him see where there might be gaps—missing details or places for evidence—in his piece that could be researched and brought into the outline.
"I have an idea, but I don't know what kind of piece to write."	Gather a cluster of mentor texts that address a similar subject in different genres. Have the student skim through the mentor texts and consider the advantages each genre has over the other. For example, what does an infographic allow a writer to do that a memoir doesn't? What are the limitations of editorial? The topic is the same, but how does the purpose shift from genre to genre? What is your purpose and which genre seems most conducive to sharing your message?

Figure 6.3 Common Planning Quandaries and Conferencing Solutions

TIPS FOR CONFERRING AND PLANNING WITH MENTOR TEXTS

Helping students plan is one of our favorite things to do with mentor texts. The energy in the room when a group of writers is about to embark on new writing projects is palpable. The possibilities are ripe. But it can also be difficult to manage a room full of writers who are preparing for takeoff. These tips apply to conferences at every stage of the writing process, not just planning. Writing will always need to be modeled and mentor texts pulled out at a moment's notice. A little bit of organization goes a long way in helping you and your students move forward in their planning and writing.

* *Keep the main thing the main thing.* If a student asks for help with ideas, show him mentor texts that will help him with ideas. Mentor texts have so much to offer, it's easy to get sidetracked and encourage the student to look at form when he needs help with content. The same mentor texts can be returned to again and again throughout the process for different purposes, but it's important to limit the scope of each conference.

"A Lesson Not Learned" by Carol Sherman-Jones (memoir)

"A Lesson Not Learned" by Carol Sherman-Jones. In *I Thought My Father Was God: And Other True Tales from NPR's National Story Project*, edited by Paul Auster.

"My Mother's Death Cured My Anxiety" by Eliza Berman (memoir)

Text 6.8 "My Mother's Death Cured My Anxiety" by Eliza Berman *http://www.slate.com/articles/double_x/doublex/2014/08/how_my_mother_s_death _cured_my_anxiety.html*

"The Science of Raising Happy Kids" by happify.com (infographic)

Text 6.9 "The Science of Raising Happy Kids" by happify.com *http://www.happify .com/hd/the-science-of-raising-happy-kids/*

"My Papa's Waltz" by Theodore Roethke (poem)

Text 6.10 "My Papa's Waltz" by Theodore Roethke *http://www.poetryfoundation .org/poem/172103*

"Parental Involvement Is Overrated" by Keith Robinson Angel L. Harris (editorial)

Text 6.11 "Parental Involvement is Overrated" by Keith Robinson and Angel L. Harris *http://opinionator.blogs.nytimes.com/2014/04/12/parental-involvement-is -overrated/*

"What Remains: A Review of *The Lovely Bones*" by Katherine Bouton (book review)

Text 6.12 "What Remains: A Review of *The Lovely Bones*" by Katherine Bouton *http://www.nytimes.com/2002/07/14/books/what-remains.html*

Figure 6.4 Multigenre Mentor Text Cluster Exploring Family Relationships

A WAY IN

Conferring with students can make us feel anxious. It defies our carefully sculpted lesson plans and calls for improvisation as we respond to the
students' needs in the moment. But you know your students, and you know
what they typically struggle with as they work to get started on a new piece
of writing.

Spend a couple of minutes right now anticipating your students' questions and the hurdles they'll face as they plan for writing. Jot them down, then
add this list to your conferring binder. Next, consider how your collection of
mentor texts might address the student needs you anticipate. Use sticky notes
or flags to mark places in your mentor texts that might be helpful for your
students as they plan.

The more experience you have conferring with mentor texts, the more
internalized this process will become. But for now, having this little support in
place can give you worlds of confidence as you chat with your student writers.

* *Be prepared to demonstrate.* Some students need to see someone else plan or
  write in front of them before they attempt to do the same. Show the student
  how the mentor text inspires your planning and begin to sketch out some
  possibilities in your notebook.
* *Carry a binder of the study's mentor texts with you.* It's a good idea to have a
  few texts you haven't yet introduced that you can use for enrichment with
  students who need additional models. Use tab dividers to keep the binder
  organized by genre, topic, and technique. Sticky notes in various colors can
  be used to mark the mentor texts you think will be particularly helpful to
  students during the planning phases: texts with strong beginnings and clear
  roadmaps, for example.
* *If students are choosing the genre in which they'll write (as they will in a technique study), you should have at least one cluster of mentor texts in your binder
  that explores the same topic across different genres, like the multigenre cluster
  about family relationships in Figure 6.4.* This multigenre cluster doesn't need
  to be on the same topic your student is writing about in order for it to be
  helpful during conferences. Rather, these mentor texts—on any topic—can

be used to help when students are struggling find the right form to fit
their ideas.

* *In all conferences, strive toward student-led conversations, and let students do*
  most of the talking. All the notebook time work you've done with your students has prepared them for reading mentor texts like writers and taking the
  ideas and structures back to their own writing. Use the same questions to
  guide conferences that you use in notebook time: What do you notice? What
  would you like to try?

Writers have plans. They keep lists of the writing they want to do. They use cocktail
napkins and the corners of grocery lists to jot down first lines and characters' names before they disappear into oblivion. They share their ideas with colleagues and family mem-
bers, searching their faces for a flicker of interest. When we teach whole-class lessons and
conference with individual writers about their ideas, we are priming the pump. We are
ensuring that every writer is ready to write because they have a plan in place.

Matthew: One Student's Writing Plan

Finally, we'd like to give you a glimpse of a very typical way whole-class teaching and conferring interact to support students as they're planning. We all know it's rare for students
to "get" all they need to get from one instance of teaching. This is why we carefully weave
our lessons in and out of students' processes as writers, just as Rebekah did with Matthew,
a student in her English 9 class, who was working on his This I Believe essay.

At the beginning of the study, Matthew
knew immediately the belief he wanted to
write about: "On the first day of school, you
should lay low." After the lesson on structure,
he also identified the structure of "The Triumph of Kindness" (option 2 in Figure 6.2) as
a structure he wanted to emulate because it
also told the story of a childhood memory
that yielded a strong belief (Figure 6.5). Matthew was ready to get started, and he drafted
his This I Believe essay (Figure 6.6).

Though not polished or perfected, Matthew's draft adhered pretty closely to the

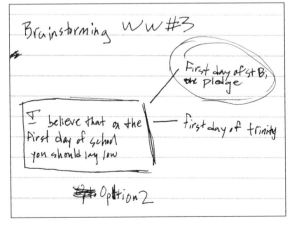

Figure 6.5 Planning from Matthew's Notebook

I believe that on the first day of school, you should lay low. If you have ever transferred schools, you know that the transition is hard because you don't know anyone. In third grade, I had been transferred to Saint Bridget School since I was not getting a very good education at [my former school], which was the heaven I went to previously. I had never heard about this school besides in the tales from my neighbor, who was there at the time. However when I entered the building, it was like I had traveled to another country, everything was different from [my old school].

It was the first day for me at Saint Bridget School, and I was really animated about going into the building for the first time. Also, I would get to see what school life was like through the eyes of my neighbor, who had been going to this school. The pressure was unbearable; I couldn't take it. It was time for the pledge, and I was about to explode.

". . . one nation under God . . ." My life went into slow motion. ". . . indivisible, with liberty and justice for all. Have a great day everyone," said my vice principal, Mrs. Beachley. Once those words flew off of her tongue, Mt. Vesuvius erupted.

"HUUUUUURRRRRRRAAYYYYYY!" I bellowed as loud as I possibly could. As I caught my breath from that shriek, all that happiness fell off my body and landed on the ground with a thud. Everyone stared at me as if I was running around in my underwear. Apparently, you were not supposed to talk after the pledge was done.

My day got even worse. When it came time for handwriting, we were doing cursive. I did not know what alien language they were even writing. During third grade, I was basically taking second grade again as well as doing new third grade things.

Figure 6.6 Matthew's Draft of a This I Believe Essay

structure he identified—introduction with a statement of belief and then a multiparagraph narrative of how that belief came to be. At the time of this draft, he had not yet restated his belief as a final, concluding paragraph, but that could be added pretty easily. The whole-class lesson on structure worked well for Matthew and gave him a starting place so he could get his big ideas on paper.

Matthew's big question during one writing conference, however, had to do with his ending. Even if he restated his belief, he explained, it just didn't feel right. It didn't feel like an ending to him. Rebekah directed him back to his mentor texts. Perhaps there was an ending from one of the others that would fit? Looking at the other mentor texts, Matthew noticed the "and now" paragraphs at the end of several of them and remembered his class had named this kind of ending in their early discussions about structure. Maybe that would work. Flipping back to his initial planning, Rebekah pointed out that, sure enough, his original idea had an "and now" dimension to it—his experience as a new student in a new school once again. Matthew left the conference with a plan for a modified structure, one that would better fit his experiences and intentions as a writer.

Closing Thoughts

Every writing-process chart hanging on a classroom wall lists planning as the first step. But the meaningful, authentic planning that will happen in your classroom can't be contained by a single worksheet or graphic organizer. Mentor texts provide a bigger, better vision for students' planning. Mentor texts help students anticipate the choices they will need to make as writers and give them the latitude to do just that—consider options and make real choices.

Of planning, George R. R. Martin, author of the *Game of Thrones* series, says, "I think there are two types of writers, the architects and the gardeners. The architects plan everything ahead of time, like an architect building a house. They know how many rooms are going to be in the house, what kind of roof they're going to have, where the wires are going to run, what kind of plumbing there's going to be. They have the whole thing designed and blueprinted out before they even nail the first board up. The gardeners dig a hole, drop in a seed, and water it. They kind of know what seed it is, they know if they planted a fantasy seed or mystery seed or whatever. But as the plant comes up and they water it, they don't know how many branches it's going to have, they find out as it grows" (Continetti 2012).

We teach both the architects and the gardeners. In truth, most of our writers are a little bit of both. And mentor texts meet them wherever they are.

CHAPTER SEVEN

Mentors Show Students How to Draft and Revise

As the bell rang and he walked out of class, Q yelled over his shoulder, "Mrs. O'Dell, will you look at my draft sometime?" I promised I would.

Later, I pulled up his analysis of an episode of The Walking Dead and scanned it, knowing that Q would press me for detailed feedback. Most students were finishing and revising their television analysis pieces, but Q had written just one paragraph. It was strong, full of voice, and painstakingly crafted. Though not a strong writer by nature, Q was a perfectionist. He worked at it. He had spent days drafting just the right introduction. And the introduction worked, but I was nervous—what was next? Did he know how to fill this out? How would he finish?

I jotted Q's name at the top of my conference list for the next day.

The next afternoon, after the lesson on punctuating titles of series and episodes, students got back to the business of writing, and I made my way over to Q for a conference.

"Q, I read your introduction. I love it. I especially like the metaphor you're using about wolf packs versus lone wolves. It really opens up your ideas about this episode."

"Really?" he asked, his eyebrows arched hopefully. Knowing me well, his eyes narrowed. "Okay. What else?"

"Well, you've done a fantastic job pumping your introduction full of voice and analysis, but I'm a little bit nervous about what's next. Our study is wrapping up. What are you going to do from here? How are you going to finish this?"

Without a word, Q unzipped his backpack and started flinging papers onto his desk. I leaned in, anxious to get in on Q's secret. The papers were our mentor texts, inscribed with giant pencil circles here and there.

"I like how this one gives a summary of the episode, so I'll do that," Q said, pointing to one of the mentor texts. "And this other one talks about minor characters. I like that idea because I liked Morgan and Duane in the show."

He kept going, showing me what he had marked in each text. He walked me through all of his plans, including the "smart, tight tone" he noticed and was working to achieve in his essay.

Surprised and impressed, I said, "Okay, well, good. You've got it, then." As I walked away, Q stacked his mentor texts on one side of his desk, booted up a laptop, and got back to work.

—Rebekah

Students have chosen an idea and used mentor texts to begin planning the new piece of writing they will compose. This can take a few days as students brainstorm, sketch, read, and tinker. When most students begin reporting they have moved to drafting, we know that the class has moved to a different phase of the study. Planning and brainstorming have turned to writing and revising—a phase that Georgia Heard says is "really ONE process" (Heard 2014). As students write and rewrite, we learn a lot about them. The divers, the patchwork writers, the grand planners, and architects (Creme and Lea 2008)—they all emerge during this period, and we have to figure out how to best support each type of writer. Although Rebekah was feeling anxious about Q's seemingly delayed progress, the fact of the matter was Q had a plan. He had a stack of carefully annotated mentor texts. He had a solid introduction. He had next steps. This was his process, and he owned it. He *was* moving forward.

Like Q, all writers need time to think and write. They need freedom to experiment and write slowly (or quickly!) and revise extensively without our breathing over their shoulders. Likewise, writers benefit from different kinds of support during this phase. Some students thrive on their own, pulling their computers into a small corner of the room, notebooks beside them. Others crave more hands-on support from the teacher or small groups of writers working on similar projects. And everyone gathers together for whole-group lessons that address common needs of the group.

While the organization of the classroom space shifts to accommodate independent workers and small groups, the work with mentor texts shifts, too. They remain central to the writing process, but writers begin to use them in different ways as their needs become more definitive and contextualized in a specific piece of writing. Students study texts on a deeper level—not just for structure or ideas or length but for crafting. They read closely for syntax, transitions, and diction. Q had noted the "smart, tight tone" in one of the reviews, an observation that resulted from several draft readings of a mentor text and careful consideration of word choice.

As students branch off in different directions and begin to show independence, the teacher's work with mentor texts also changes. We bounce back and forth between individual conferences and small groups, between whole-group lessons and the monitoring of independent work. We actually become more dependent on the students, pulling additional mentor texts according to their needs and requests and planning lessons based on what we see emerging in their writing. As students write, mentor texts allow for personalized coaching when students need it most.

John Updike says that "writing and rewriting are a constant search for what it is one is saying" (Temple 2013). In this chapter, we will share with you the different ways in which students interact with mentor texts to support this search. Independent work, one-on-one conferences, various independent and small-group reflection activities, whole-class lessons—all of these things, with the help of mentor texts, allow our students to write freely, build momentum, and gain independence.

Helping Students Find Touchstone Texts

During notebook time and the first days of a new writing study, the teacher repeatedly drives students back to the mentor texts for inspiration and wisdom on how to proceed in a new piece of writing. But as students settle into the work of crafting, they drive *themselves* back to the mentor texts again and again. This is where all the practice designed to encourage independence with mentor texts pays off—both independence of thought and independence of process.

Independent work can be supported in many ways. We introduce students to the concept of touchstone texts to ensure they are reading and writing deeply and not just widely (Isoke Nia, as cited in Ray 1999, 134). A touchstone text is a piece from the mentor text cluster a student has personally chosen to read more closely and learn from. This helps students who are overwhelmed by a cluster of mentors because they can hone in on one text for more focused writerly reading. Those who want more options can do a closer reading of a touchstone while continuing to pull inspiration from the other texts in the cluster. When we ask students to choose a touchstone text, we are not asking them to ignore the others in the cluster; we are simply asking them to identify one or two they particularly admire and go deeper in their reading with these texts.

Students use their touchstone texts to explore an author's craft on a more personal level, spending more time noticing and theorizing and borrowing the techniques that interest them. The time students spend with these texts often leads to inquiry that drives better rewriting. For example, a student writing a book review who has chosen John Green's review of *The Dead and the Gone* and *The Hunger Games* as his touchstone may wonder about the following bookish words and phrases:

*   "these books transcend their premises"
*   "'The Dead and the Gone,' a companion to Pfeffer's acclaimed 'Life as We Knew It'"
*   "some of the plot seems more symbolically resonant than realistic."

Text 7.1 "Scary New World" by John Green *http://www.nytimes.com/2008/11/09 /books/review/Green-t.html?pagewanted=all*

Upon further investigation of the words "premise," "companion," and "symbolic resonance," the student may be inspired to substitute some of the more generic words he's used to describe his book in favor of a more precise literary vernacular that many writers adopt when reviewing books.

Because students will be using their touchstone texts in so many different ways, consider asking them to do some writing about these texts in addition to the writing they are doing for their study. This could be done as an exit ticket before leaving class or as a brief homework assignment. Students' reflections on their touchstones will help you see how they are learning from mentor texts and assess their understandings of the mentorship process. Figure 7.1 shows Ravenel writing about her touchstone, *When I Was Young in the Mountains*, during a study of memoir. Notice how closely she has attended to a variety of crafting elements her mentor, Cynthia Rylant, employed in this beloved picture book.

Sometimes the writer is only beginning to think about craft and hasn't yet had a chance to play with it in her own writing. In Figure 7.2, Alessandra demonstrates her admiration of a touchstone text as she continues to make sense of the genre and considers the elements she may want to use in her own review.

One of the mentor texts I used is *When I Was Young in the Mountains*. Even though this is a very different story than mine, after closely examining it as a writer in class I took away some of the patterns and used them in my writing. For example the repetition of the important phrase (in her story), "When I was young in the mountains." She repeats this at the beginning and end as well as every other paragraph in the middle. I decided to repeat the phrase "I was only six" in the very beginning, the very end, and once in the middle. I also repeated the main couple of sentences that I thought to be some of the most important at the beginning and then at the "climax" of the memoir. These lines were "But I remember the old smell of her room. The sweet taste of the cookies. The rush of zooming around on her wheelchair." Another thing I noticed from this text was how often she used descriptive adjectives such as *black* dust, *hot* corn bread, *white* butter, *sweet* milk, *white* shirt, etc. I tried to do this as much as I could in my own writing. For example, *old* smell, *sweet* cookies, *brown wooden* desk, *warm* neck, etc.

Figure 7.1 Ravenel Writing about the Touchstone *When I Was Young in the Mountains*

I have chosen "Young Love, Complicated by Cancer" by A. O. Scott as my touchstone text for my writing. I admire this writing piece because first of all, it starts out with a quote. I think starting a critical review, memoir, or any written story with a quote is very powerful. And second of all, because the overall voice of this piece is very positive and sympathetic. I selected this writing as my touchstone text because even though it is about the movie, since *The Fault in Our Stars* is also a book, this can be a good touchstone text for someone that is reviewing a book.

The three specific things I have learned about writing reviews from this writer are: 1. In a critical review for a book, it is best not to start out with what you think about the book, but rather start out setting up the emotion of the book and framing small parts of the main characters' lives. You can put personal opinions throughout the review, but definitely start out with an overall description of the story and the characters. 2. This review asks many questions throughout the piece—sometimes answering them, sometimes leaving them be. 3. The two things that this review has a lot of are similes and adjectives. The adjectives seem to be very descriptive and advanced words. The similes are scattered throughout the piece. I will try to use some of these things I mentioned in my critical review of *If I Stay*.

Figure 7.2 Alessandra Writing about the Touchstone "Young Love, Complicated by Cancer"

Students who choose touchstone texts begin to identify more with the writers of these texts rather than just the writing. They develop preferences for certain writers and styles. They become "well-versed" in certain pieces and begin to internalize the craft they have spent time examining. Later in the chapter, we'll show you how students can use their touchstones to form writing groups and collaborate with other writers on their projects.

Checking In as Students Draft and Revise

Teachers offer important support for writing in one-on-one conversations. While students are busy doing the heavy lifting, teachers support the writing process of individual students in two main ways: conferring with students to answer questions, offer support, and troubleshoot their writing, and monitoring student progress through regular checkpoints or process letters.

Conferences

While the approach remains the same as the approach we shared in Chapter 6, conversations with students are very different during the writing phase of a study. They no longer center on finding ideas or a way to get started. These writing conferences are often more about pulling students out of the weeds and helping them use mentor texts to address the stumbling blocks they are encountering. Conferences aren't only for struggling writers, though. Writing conferences help every student—even the student who doesn't think he needs help—raise the level of his writing.

We still encourage students to ask for conferences when they feel they need one, but we monitor students' progress a bit more heavily in this phase as it's the easiest place for students to get lost. We peek over their shoulders and glance at their notebooks or computer screens daily to ensure that progress is being made. If it looks like a student is getting words down, we check in with her periodically, but for the most part, we give her space. However, if it looks like little writing is being committed to paper, or if it's happening very slowly, we make a conference with that student a priority.

As students write and rewrite, we run into some common questions and writing problems. These issues are typically more nebulous than those students encounter as they are starting a piece. Many students ask for a conference at this point and, when we make it to their desk, their first words are, "I just don't know. I need help." The first minutes of these conferences work to simply get at the heart of the problem the student is encountering. There will always be some questions that are so specific to a particular student's paper that using a mentor text doesn't make sense. But many common dilemmas can be answered by redirecting students to mentor texts (see Figure 7.3).

"I don't have anything else to say."	Pull out a mentor text in the same genre as the piece the student is working on. While this mentor text probably won't have the exact same topic as the student, it should have a similar kind of topic. For example, if your student is writing an editorial about the problem of concussions in football, you might find a different mentor editorial about an issue in sports.
	Walk through this text with the student and search for the movement of ideas and topics in the piece. Ask the student to compare these topics to the topics the student has covered in his piece. What has the student not yet covered? Does the student *want* to cover the additional topics offered by the mentor text? Encourage the student to do this with the additional texts in the cluster and then make a decision about whether he is truly finished with the piece (and sometimes, the answer is, he is!).
"I know what I want to say, but I'm not sure how to say it."	Begin by asking the student what he wants to say, and then try to give it a name. Maybe he needs a wrap-up statement at the end of a paragraph. Pull out a mentor text or two, and find similar places in the text for the student to read and consider. This does require an intimate knowledge of the mentor texts in your repertoire. If the student wants to write a wrap-up statement, find and highlight some wrap-up statements in different mentor texts. This is where sentence study in notebook time pays off because students know how to study sentences on their own. All you have to do is point them in the right direction, encourage them to study how the mentor text demonstrates the effect they are trying to achieve, and then adapt it for their own piece.
"I don't know how all of this is fitting together."	The "fitting together" of a piece of writing usually boils down to organization or transitions. If the problem appears to be organization, direct the student to look at the order of the mentor's ideas in her chosen touchstone text. What does the writer need the reader to understand first? Second? Last? Compare this to the student's order of ideas.
	If the problem is a lack of meaningful transitions between ideas, have the student highlight the last sentence and first sentence in each paragraph in the touchstone text. What transitioning language or framework can the student borrow for her own piece?
"I don't think this is working anymore."	This conference starter can indicate many different problems in a piece of writing, but it almost always points to a need for revision, sometimes deep revision, if the movement from beginning to end just isn't working. Use a mentor text with a similar kind of topic to help the student see the development of an idea from start to finish. Where the writing feels stilted or stale, a complete organizational overhaul can do wonders. Have the student cut the piece of writing up into different sections. Then, with a favorite mentor text in hand, invite him to rearrange the parts of the writing to mimic the mentor text's organization. This sense of play can sometimes have dramatic results, breathing new life into the writing. Alternatively, lead your student to a mentor text with a strong sense of theme or purpose. Texts that use effective repetition or an "echo structure" often resonate best with students. Using the mentor text, show the student how repetition can be used to create cohesion across a piece of writing that feels broken.

Figure 7.3 Common Writing Quandaries and Conferencing Solutions

In each of these writing predicaments, only so much can be accomplished in a single conference. Students have to do the legwork on their own. Once you direct a student to a useful mentor text and give him a direction to pursue, leave him to it, move on to help the next student, and circle back around to check on the student's progress.

Julia was one of those "this just isn't working anymore" writers as she crafted a This I Believe essay. She planned an essay about her belief in the power of learning a foreign language. She spent a few days drafting, and, when she wrapped up a draft, she asked for a conference. Although she couldn't articulate what was bothering her, she knew something wasn't working. "I just don't think this is right," she said as she asked for help.

In her draft, Julia told the story of how she learned German by spending time with her friend's German-speaking family. One night, her friend's parents got into a heated argument that involved yelling and name-calling. While Julia couldn't understand every word, she was able to use cognates and context to piece together what was happening. As Julia read her work aloud, Rebekah realized the problem was that Julia wasn't really writing about the power of learning a foreign language at all. That is where she began, but as she wrote, her story became about a moment of family crisis and being the kind of friend who is truly a member of the family. The pieces weren't fitting together because the belief that Julia stated in her introduction and conclusion wasn't actually the belief she was sharing.

It was an idea that needed revising. Rebekah grabbed her laptop and quickly pulled up two essays from the This I Believe website—one with a more academic tone about the power of education, and one about struggles in a relationship. She left Julia to read each. When she returned, she asked, "Which essay sounded more like the story you are telling?" Julia agreed that the relationship essay sounded more like her draft. "So, what's your belief?"

Julia had to spend the rest of class rereading what she had written. She now understood that the belief at the center of her essay involved relationships rather than the importance of learning foreign languages, but it took some time for her to unpack what she was saying through her relationship with her friend's family. By the next day, Julia had identified her new belief: Friends can become as close as family and support you through hard times. The process of writing uncovered a problem in Julia's draft that needed attention, and the process of conferring and using mentor texts helped her find a new purpose for her piece.

Checkpoints

Professional writers are beholden to deadlines, of course, but so are people who write as part of any other profession. Writers of reports, summaries, sales projections, and so forth all work with specific time parameters guiding them, and our students need target dates just the same. But we can't just release students into writing and say, "Good luck! See you in three weeks!" We have to monitor their progress so they feel supported and so they continue moving forward.

Tracking students' progress in a study can happen in different ways. Checkpoints—reflective questions assigned periodically throughout the study—are one tool for accomplishing this. We use checkpoints to encourage students to share anything related to their writing process: setbacks they've run into, thoughts on what they would like us to focus on while reading their drafts, future plans for their writing. Checkpoints can also be used to reinforce work with mentor texts and ensure students are utilizing mentors to enhance their writing instruction. Here is a list of questions you might consider asking as checkpoints along the way.

* What topic did you choose for your piece? Did any of the mentor texts influence your choice?
* What was your process for getting started? Where did you begin and why? How did the mentor texts facilitate this?
* Have you run into any roadblocks? How did you get past them? How did the mentor texts help?
* What material do you already have in your notebook? Please mark the influence of the mentor texts directly on the material.
* What are your plans for continuing to work on your piece over the next few days? How might you use mentor texts to support you in this writing?
* What revision tools have you used? How have the mentor texts inspired revision?
* What should I pay attention to as I read your draft?
* If you had the chance to work with one of your writing mentors, what would you ask him or her to focus on when responding to your draft?

Figure 7.4 shows two of our students responding to one of these checkpoint questions. The students have been asked to explain their choice of touchstone text, why they admire the writing, and then detail three things they have learned about writing reviews from the writer. You'll notice that we allow students to write casually in these checkpoints and choose a format that is most comfortable for them. The students in Figure 7.4 respond in paragraphs, in lists, and in combinations of sentences and bullets. All of these are fine with us. The goal of the checkpoint is simply to ensure students are progressing and continuing to reflect on their intentional choices as writers.

My Touchstone Text: *A Lesson Not Learned* by Carol Sherman-Jones

Why—

1) I like her balance between scene and summary. (Starts with summary then scenes in the middle finishing with summary again.)

2) I like her variation of sentence structure. (Very short and to the point or detailed and longer.)

3) I like how the "so what" or lesson of her writing was mentioned at the very end. (It was very intentional because the slap came out of nowhere just like her final sentences. Also, Sherman-Jones ended with short abrupt sentences just like in the beginning, which gives the piece a sense of closure.)

—Logan

I chose *A Lesson Not Learned* by Carol Sherman-Jones for my touchstone text. I really admire her writing because she uses a lot of (I don't know the specific name for it) but phrases with references to objects or not literal. Example: It hit me like a whip. Or: Whatever made its way into my hands I chewed on, mangled beyond recognition, or sent to a premature death. I want to use some of those for my memoir. I also like how she starts with a summary, then moves on to a few scenes, and ends with musing.

The three things I have learned about writing memoirs from this writer are: 1. You can never be too specific in writing memoirs. 2. To intrigue the reader in the memoir, you really have to dive deep while writing and think of exactly how you felt when it was happening. 3. To make things interesting, you can start with a summary or different memories, add scenes in the middle of the piece, and end with musing.

—Alessandra

Figure 7.4 Sample of Student Responses to a Checkpoint Question

Checkpoints can be assigned at any point during the study, or all at once at the beginning of the study. They can be used as a stopgap to prevent wayward students from veering off the path, or they can be used as a whole-class reflective assignment to keep everyone on a similar time line. Consider giving your students a handout with all the checkpoints and their due dates in advance to allow writers to work at their own pace (see Figure 7.5).

The frequency with which you assign checkpoints will depend on a number of things: the length of your study, the level of support your students need, and the number of students in your class. For studies that span three to four weeks, weekly checkpoints allow students enough time to make progress in their writing while keeping their progress in check. For shorter studies, you may consider assigning two checkpoints per week. The number of students may also factor into your decision. For instance, if you teach a small class and are able to confer with every student every day, you may not need to have them write about their process as frequently since you are privy to it in conferences and can collect that information verbally. You might also consider tailoring checkpoints to individual students: Writers who may benefit from your "checking in" more frequently can be assigned additional checkpoints, whereas writers who are showing more independence may be trusted to check in once in a while.

Checkpoints keep students working steadily throughout a study. They also engage students in important self-reflection, a skill that will strengthen their writing and their understanding of themselves as writers. And while checkpoints do not in any way replace conferences, they can be a useful tool for assessing students' growth at the end of a study.

PROCESS LETTERS

An alternative to checkpoints, process letters invite students to share about their current writing project and their process in the form of a letter. Inspired by Nancie Atwell's literary letters, these epistolary reflections invite students to tell how they are feeling about a piece of writing and why. Students are free to tell us anything they would like about their writing in these letters, but they often share

* what they have noticed about their mentors' writing
* something they have tried in their writing and why it was successful or not
* future plans
* anything about their writing and their process that will help the teacher better support them in future conferences.

Figure 7.6 presents a process letter by Jake, a student who was approaching the final draft of a piece of news satire in the style of *The Onion*.

CHECKPOINT 1: Due Tuesday, 11/4 at the beginning of class

1. Describe the topic you have chosen for your review. Explain in as much detail as you can how and why you have chosen this topic.

2. Tell me about the material you already have in your writer's notebook related to your topic. Then, write about the notebook work you want to do in the coming days to support you in writing your review.

3. How will mentor texts support the work you have planned?

CHECKPOINT 2: Due Monday, 11/10 at the beginning of class

1. Name the review you are using as a touchstone text for your writing. A touchstone text is a text you have personally selected from the cluster that you want to read more closely as a writer and learn from.

2. Explain why you admire this writing and why you selected it as a touchstone text. Then detail three specific things you have learned about writing reviews from this writer.

CHECKPOINT 3: Due NLT Friday, 11/14 at the beginning of class

1. You should have a copy of the most recent draft of your review in your folder. Please title it REVIEW DRAFT.

2. Write a reflection that tells me about drafting and revising your review up to this point. Consider the following questions:

   * How did you get started?
   * Did you revise a lot as you drafted, or did you get it down first and then go back through it? Has another writer given you feedback?
   * Have you read it aloud to yourself?
   * Which mentor texts have you revisited as you have worked on revisions?
   * Have you tried any tools for revision that we've studied?
   * How did your touchstone text(s) help you?
   * What are your plans for continuing work on this review?
   * What would you like me to pay special attention to as I read your draft?

CHECKPOINT 4: Due Friday, 11/21 at the beginning of class

Have a finished copy of your review in your folder. Please title it REVIEW BEST DRAFT.

Figure 7.5 Sample Checkpoint Handout

Dear Ms. Marchetti,

Even though ["Obama Spends Another Night Searching Behind White House Paintings for Safes"] does not contain a similar topic to me, it was one of the funniest in my opinion so I decided it would be smart to use as my touchstone. The first thing that I learned from it was how the beginning gives the location [followed by] an em-dash. Second was how many participle phrases were used at the beginning of sentences to give a good visual description. Lastly how the lede was gripping and funny all while giving the setting of the article.

Text 7.2 "Obama Spends Another Night Searching Behind White House Paintings for Safes" http://www.theonion.com/articles/obama-spends-another -night-searching-behind-white,35850/

The first big change I made in my piece was at the beginning of the article with the who what when where and why. This is done in my first sentence of my story. Second was the use of my first quote in the middle to end of the piece. I inserted the quote to enhance the humor of the story and the character of Donald Sterling. Last was how I changed the way that Donald was dropped off in Compton by the cops and found by the Bloods. I made it make more sense by stating that they were working with them behind Donald Sterling's back.

My proofreading process was the same as always. I read the story multiple times normally to catch grammatical errors and twice backwards.

I don't personally think my favorite thing I learned while writing this genre was anything to do with writing-based stuff but techniques on how to write funny and make jokes in writing because this is something I have never done or known how to do.

Figure 7.6 Jake's Process Letter

While similar to checkpoints, process letters give students the freedom to write about whatever topic is on their minds rather than require that they respond to a teacher-created-and-assigned question. Additionally, these letters reinforce the skill of letter writing and give those students who may not be as comfortable with conferring an opportunity to have a written "conference" on the page. Checkpoints provide more scaffolding while letters provide more autonomy. You may choose to alter checkpoints and process letters or use one type of reflection exclusively. Regardless of the method you choose, students should have an opportunity to reflect on their process and show how the mentor texts have supported them.

Supporting Small-Group Work with Mentor Texts

While whole-class craft lessons support writers by presenting them with options for enhancing their work, writers also benefit from the support they find in more intimate groups of peers. Writers know that community supports the writing process, and students can find community in small mentor text response groups. When students are in the throes of writing, we convene these groups about once a week so students can share their writing and have multiple sounding boards for their ideas. But writing groups can do even more than listen and give general feedback—they can help ensure every student is making the most of mentor texts.

In writing response groups, each student reads his or her piece aloud just as it is. Everyone's writing is unfinished and imperfect at this stage. That's the point. We encourage students to embrace this, and no matter where they are in the process, they share what they have written so far. Then, the group zooms in on how mentor texts have been used and how they can be used as writing continues. To these group meetings, students bring their mentor text cluster as well as their writer's notebooks for borrowing ideas from their friends. We group students in two strategic ways for writing response.

Same-Text Response Groups

Students who are all focusing on the same touchstone text can be grouped together to support one another as they uncover the deepest potential of their chosen mentor text. In these groups, after each student shares his or her work in progress, the student highlights places where the touchstone text has directly inspired his or her work. As they share, other students in the group are able to see the touchstone text through new eyes, which can be particularly helpful in the early stages of crafting as students are still gathering and refining ideas. The group then recommends additional ways the craft of the touchstone text might enhance their peer's work or guide the writing of the rest of the piece. Since every student in the group has chosen the same touchstone text, each student's expert knowledge enables him to push his peers' work to the next level.

Before we ever put students in mentor text response groups, they have had conversations about mentor texts modeled for them again and again. They know how to extract ideas and inspiration from a mentor text and apply it to a piece of original writing. In these groups, the new skill is using the same habits of mind to apply the inspiration of mentors to a peers' writing. Like any feedback circle, students need time to practice having these meaningful conversations; they don't always come naturally. To scaffold this work, we provide groups with the following guiding questions:

* How has each member of the group used the touchstone text in his or her own piece?
* What ideas can you borrow from the ways the touchstone text has inspired your peers? What have your peers tried that might also work for you?
* How might each member of the group use the craft of the touchstone text to enhance what he or she has already written?
* How might each member of the group use the touchstone text to decide what to add or revise as they continue writing?

Varied-Text Response Groups

Another way to group is to place students with different touchstone texts together. In groups centered on a common touchstone text, the goal is depth—how many different ways can we use the touchstone text to inspire writing? In varied touchstone text groups, the goal is breadth—are there elements of many different texts that can inspire a piece of writing? For this reason, we use mixed groups in the latter days of writing while students are finishing and polishing their work. After a student shares his or her writing in these groups, students become advocates for their own touchstone text, sharing how it might benefit peers' writing. We offer these guiding questions to mixed touchstone text response groups:

* What do you see in your touchstone text that might enhance the writing of your peers?
* What ideas are present in your touchstone text that might help your peers revise or add to the writing they have right now?

Whenever you talk to students about a mentor text, no matter how many times you have read the text, you notice craft elements you have never noticed before. This same phenomenon happens when students work in mentor text response groups. New possibilities and deeper layers of potential are unlocked in both the mentor texts and in the students' in-progress writing.

Teaching Whole-Class Lessons in Craft and Revision

Some support is best offered to the class as a whole because it's universally applicable, regardless of what a student is writing. For this kind of support, we use mentor texts in whole-class craft lessons that can benefit any piece of writing.

Craft Lessons in Content, Organization, and Style

Chapter 3 led you through the process of using mentor texts to develop writing lessons, and this is where you will teach the majority of those lessons. As we have mentioned before, these lessons are brief (ten to fifteen minutes) so students have plenty of time during class to get to the main event—the writing. Planning lessons help students get going. Craft lessons in content, organization, and style provide daily, bite-sized guidance for crafting the actual words and sentences that give life to students' ideas, and for revising the initial plans they have made. As in all writing lessons, the teacher's job is to offer students craft options, not craft requirements. We don't want these lessons to dictate the way students write but rather to open their eyes to all the ways great writers communicate their ideas.

Mentor texts in the cluster help determine which craft lessons to teach in a unit of study. Some elements of craft are unique to the writers, and others are more characteristic of the genre. We consider our students' needs, and then we study the mentor texts to identify which craft moves students would benefit from most in the current study. Then, we show students how their mentors make these moves in the mentor texts. In any study, we might teach

* playing with sentence length
* writing concisely
* using effective transitions
* considering word choice
* combining and decombining sentences

* breaking writing rules for effect (e.g., beginning a sentence with a conjunction, using sentence fragments)
* using sound devices in writing
* crafting effective dialogue
* writing with parallel structure
* playing with figurative language
* developing voice
* using effective repetition
* shaping autobiographical significance/so what?

These lessons help students look beneath the surface of the mentor texts and beyond the structure and the ideas. The study of a writer's style asks students to look more deeply at the individual pieces that create the whole.

A WAY IN

To get started with some of these lessons in your classroom, pull out a mentor text—either one you have found in this book or one you have found on your own. Which of the lessons listed here could be taught using just this text? What other lesson possibilities do you see in the text? How many writing lessons could you teach, either to the whole class or in individual writing conferences, from this single mentor text?

Revision Lessons

During the writing stage of a study, writers sometimes discover that their initial plans and intentions aren't quite working or could use tweaking, so we offer brief lessons in revision as students start completing first drafts. And many of our young writers like to stop right there, believing that a one-and-done draft is where their work ends. These lessons are critically important in serving as a continual reminder to students that, as Roald Dahl says, "good writing is essentially rewriting."

In *Teaching Adolescent Writers* (2006), Kelly Gallagher uses the acronym STAR to teach the essential functions of revision: substitute, take out, add, and rearrange. Truly, all revision boils down to these fundamentals. We find that the best way to teach revision lessons is through modeling in our own writing. Projecting a piece of our writing for students to see, we model the process of identifying weaknesses in our own work and then searching for solutions in our mentor texts. For example, we might read through a piece in front of the students and notice aloud that our ideas seem a little flimsy and in need of additional, persuasive support. Then, we would project a paragraph from the middle of Matt Zoller Seitz's analysis of *Seinfeld*'s impact on current television culture (Figure 7.7). After reading Seitz's paragraph aloud, we would go back through it, highlighting ways he supports his idea that *Seinfeld* gave rise to the selfish television characters that followed. We might note that

* Seitz has a very clear topic sentence at the beginning of the paragraph that states the point he will make in this paragraph.
* He supports his argument by referencing characters from other television shows as evidence.
* He persuades the reader by using a list.
* He persuades the reader by using a rhetorical question.

Text 7.3 "How *Seinfeld* Paved the Way for Tony Soprano" by Matt Zoller Seitz
http://www.vulture.com/2014/06/how-seinfeld-paved-the-way-for-tony-soprano.html

Before *Seinfeld*, there were never any sitcoms that let their characters be purely selfish, treating the rest of humankind as a resource or obstacle while standing back and observing their shenanigans with a jaundiced detachment. But David's "no learning" ethos has since become a mantra for the medium . . . and not trouble themselves too much with whether you approve of what the characters say and do. Would Tony Soprano have strangled that snitch in the woods, would *Six Feet Under*'s Nate Fisher have been a sonofabitch right up to his final moments on Earth, would *30 Rock*'s Jenna have treated the entire known universe as a ladder leading to her own career success, if *Seinfeld* hadn't steamrolled an artistic path for them back in the early '90s?

Figure 7.7 An Excerpt from "How Seinfeld Paved the Way for Tony Soprano"

Armed with some new ideas, we'd go back into our document and show students how we add the support our writing needs.

Revision lessons help students see the writerly choices they might make. Students are not required to make a certain number of additions or substitutions. We don't insist they rearrange their writing if they don't need to rearrange their writing. Real writers don't work in this artificial way, and we don't want our students to work within such strictures either. What we *do* want is to give students tools and models for revision and the regular nudges they need to look at their writing in a new light.

Five Mentor Texts, Twenty-Five Different Pieces

In the midst of planning, writing, and rewriting, students become intimately familiar with the mentor texts in the study. Although we do encourage students to add to the mentor text cluster if they choose (more on that in Chapter 9), for the most part, students are using the same handful of texts for inspiration. So, how varied and unique can the students' work be when everyone studies the same group of mentor texts inside and out?

While the class collaborates during daily craft lessons and in mentor text response groups, students largely move forward on their own as they draft and craft, mentor texts on one side of the desk and notebooks on the other. Here, they make the choices writers make: what to put in, what to leave out, how best to communicate their purpose, which pieces of mentor text inspiration to include and how to include them. They write, pause, consult a mentor text for the noticings they have marked, and write some more.

Even though the whole class works from the same mentor text cluster, the writing that results from the study of these texts is entirely unique to the writer. In a study of television and film analysis, our eleventh-grade students studied the same four texts to very different effect in their finished pieces:

"*Doctor Who:* 'Listen'" by Alasdair Wilkins, *A.V. Club*

Text 7.4 "*Doctor Who:* 'Listen'" by Alasdair Wilkins *http://www.avclub.com/tvclub/doctor -who-listen-209034*

continues

"*Sharknado 2*: Winner and Still Chomp" by Linda Holmes, *Monkey See*

Text 7.5 *"Sharknado 2:* Winner and Still Chomp" by Linda Holmes *http://www.npr.org /blogs/monkeysee/2014/07/30/336573454/sharknado-2-winner-and-still-chomp*

"*Into the Storm* Is a Witless, Wild Ride for Disaster-Film Junkies" by Bilge Ebiri, *Vulture*

Text 7.6 *"Into the Storm* Is a Witless, Wild Ride for Disaster-Film Junkies" by Bilge Ebiri *http://www.vulture.com/2014/08/movie-review-into-the-storm.html*

"Why We Absolutely, Definitely Do NOT Need Another *Arrested Development* Season" by Haley Blum, *USA Today*

Text 7.7 "Why We Absolutely, Definitely Do NOT Need Another *Arrested Development* Season" by Haley Blum *http://entertainthis.usatoday.com/2014/08/08 /why-we-dont-need-another-arrested-development-netflix-season/*

Jilly chose to analyze the power of perception in the Will Ferrell flick *Blades of Glory* (2007). The personal tone of her introduction and use of amusing parentheticals (Figure 7.8) were drawn from Linda Holmes' introduction in her review of *Sharknado 2*.

Kellan (Figure 7.9) cites the review of *Dr. Who* for the idea to connect his chosen episode of *Wilfred* to the other episodes in the series as a way of drawing his analysis to a meaningful conclusion.

Remember the "smart, tight tone" Q was trying to emulate in his writing? In addition to "cutting out stuff I didn't need" and focusing on finding just the right word, Q took sentence-level inspiration from Ebiri's review of *Into the Storm*. He noticed that the use of dashes and the occasional sentence fragment for impact gave Ebiri's piece an "in your face" assertive tone he liked and wanted to try in his own writing (Figure 7.10).

The class noted the personal tone and anecdote Jilly adopted for her piece; however, the way she used it was entirely her own. Kellan and Q also made their discoveries independently. Under the influence of mentor texts, students have more possibilities to consider for their own work than ever before. As they study and experiment and try different craft moves, their writing becomes clearer, more assertive, more *their own*.

I can confidently say that I have forced at least 18 people to watch *Blades of Glory* (2007) against their will. It's an unspoken agreement between my friends and me that when they come over to my house that is what we will be watching, whether they want to or not. There are multiple reasons for this: because I am the host (and you're eating my popcorn), because I say so (don't question it), and because (most importantly) *Blades of Glory* is my favorite movie.

Figure 7.8 Excerpt from Jilly's Analysis

"Happiness" truly was what set the stage for future episodes of *Wilfred*. Not just because it was the first episode but because of the way it portrayed Ryan's emotions. Even without dialogue, the music throughout the show gives the viewer a pretty good idea of what is going on and how the characters are feeling, particularly the protagonist. This becomes a regular feature of the series. The use of the music opens the characters up so the viewer can really see what that character is truly like.

Figure 7.9 Conclusion to Kellan's Analysis

There's more to [*The Walking Dead*] than meets the eye. It provides a valuable life lesson; helping one another can lead to genuine camaraderie. In the first episode—and throughout the whole show—working together during a crisis (especially a zombie apocalypse) proves to be more effective than being isolated. Because in the end no one wants to go at it alone.

Figure 7.10 Excerpt from Q's Analysis

Closing Thoughts

There is nothing like the buzz of writers at work. A flurry of mentor texts, the whispered conversations of a writing group, the clicking of keys—the sounds of students who have been well prepared for the demands of writing, through mentor text work and careful planning. The sounds of writers who have found their stride in workshop.

As they get deep into the writing process, students become more comfortable using mentor texts, their knowledge of what's possible expands, and their reliance upon us diminishes. They learn that mentor texts can offer more than just an initial idea or a notion of structure; mentor texts can actually buoy them up and provide ongoing support throughout the writing process. And while they're busy writing, you'll learn to let go a little. While this stepping back may be frightening at first, if your ultimate goal is to help your writers gain independence, you'll set them free. You'll let go of the reins. You'll give them the time and space they need to think and make their own choices and write. And you'll discover that the mentors you've entrusted to them can give them almost everything they need.

CHAPTER EIGHT

Mentors Show Students How to Go Public

A steady stream of Google Docs comments flooded my inbox one evening. Skimming the top email, a comment from Griffin (Figure 8.1) showed that he was looking for a way to provide necessary background information about the Arsenal football club—the subject of his critical review—without cluttering his writing.

Although Griffin actually meant parentheses (not quotations), he had identified a problem. Parentheticals overwhelmed his writing, but many of them provided information that was

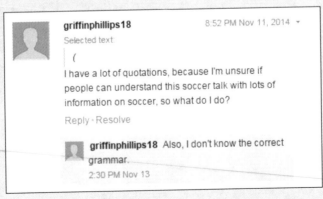

> **griffinphillips18**   8:52 PM Nov 11, 2014 ▾
>
> Selected text:
>
> (
>
> I have a lot of quotations, because I'm unsure if people can understand this soccer talk with lots of information on soccer, so what do I do?
>
> Reply · Resolve
>
> > **griffinphillips18** Also, I don't know the correct grammar.
> > 2:30 PM Nov 13

Figure 8.1 Griffin's Comment

necessary for readers like me who knew little to nothing about soccer and needed some support. I scribbled a note in my plan book to look into how writers get around this problem of providing additional details without encumbering the writing or sacrificing essential background information. Later, I pulled out the mentor texts from our study. I discovered that one solution was to provide pictures or video to illustrate difficult concepts. Another was to link to this information outside of the piece.

The next day, I circled back to Griffin's table. I showed him the mentor texts that used images and hyperlinks to convey information. I gave him a thirty-second tutorial on how to insert photographs and links into his writing in a Google Doc, noting in my plan book that I needed to teach a lesson on proper citation of images soon. As we chatted, he began to search for strategic places in his writing to embed links.

"What do you think?" I queried. "Can hyperlinking solve your problem?" He nodded enthusiastically and got back to his writing.

—Allison

Griffin knew from the get-go he wanted to write a piece about the Arsenal soccer team for readers of the *Bleacher Report*, a sports website covering hundreds of teams and sports around the world. An avid reader of the website, Griffin had a good idea about what visitors to this site look for, and throughout the drafting process, he kept these readers in mind. Thinking about his intended audience helped Griffin make drafting decisions. For example, he knew he would not have to give a detailed biography of Arsene Wenger, long-time manager of Arsenal, because his readers would know a lot about him already.

As Griffin's essay approached final draft form, he began to wonder if the parenthetical explanations he employed throughout—an element that initially seemed like a good idea—were really effective. The more he thought about it, the more he realized not all readers would need this level of detail. In his final piece, he linked to the information instead.

Like Griffin, all writers need to keep their readers in mind. This doesn't come naturally to most students, though, since they have been writing for their teachers their whole lives. They need constant reminders. More important, they need opportunities to share their work with readers outside the classroom.

In this chapter we will show how we use mentor texts to help students ready their work for readers—throughout the writing process and at the finish line, when it comes time to making final, important overall decisions about the writing.

Using Mentor Texts to Polish Student Writing

Most writers do some level of crafting throughout the writing process. They think about how they want their writing to sound, they contemplate word choice, and they mull over punctuation. We certainly teach them lessons focused on craft throughout the process, as you saw in Chapter 7. But these things are secondary to content, and until a writer (particularly a student writer) has settled on all his ideas and organized them, he's not really ready to polish his writing. Polishing involves making sure every sentence is crafted as well as it can be, and it also means checking for errors in grammar and mechanics.

Luckily, crafting better sentences and understanding grammar and mechanics are really two sides of the same coin. The more basic grammatical understandings students have about writing, the better they are able to craft their sentences and also find their mechanical errors. For this reason, as students are near finishing their writing projects, we turn our attention to craft lessons that support an understanding of grammar and usage. For these lessons, students need to study a slew of effective sentences and build a basic understanding of the parts of a sentence.

In *Mechanically Inclined* (2005), Jeff Anderson writes about using powerful literature to teach the rules of language. He believes grammar and mechanics are "inherently linked to craft" (10). Following Anderson's lead, we use mentor texts to help students craft more effective sentences and to teach grammar and mechanics. When we cull examples from the mentor texts students know intimately from weeks of study, they offer relevance and an opportunity for deeper study.

Craft Lessons That Support an Understanding of Grammar and Usage

Craft lessons that support an understanding of grammar and usage encompass a wide range of writing techniques, from selecting the best words to shaping meaning with punctuation to creating emphasis with different sentence patterns. In these lessons, it's important to emphasize techniques over errors and building effective sentences over fixing mistakes.

We decide which of these lessons to teach in one of three ways. We sometimes look at our mentor texts to see if any grammatical concepts are so clear in the writing they would be easy for our students to understand. For example, if one of the mentor texts contains several long, serpentine sentences, we might plan a lesson on crafting effective compound-complex sentences. Sometimes we go back to the original list of noticings students made at the beginning of the study to see if any of those would lend themselves well to teaching a grammatical understanding. And we often use the errors that crop up in our students' writing for inspiration for these lessons. We see what we need to address and then figure out how our mentor texts can help us.

Another great resource for planning craft lessons that support an understanding of grammar and usage is Connors and Lunsford's list of 20 Most Common Errors (cited in Anderson 2005). This list grew out of a study of over 3,000 essays written by college students. It presents a list of the most commonly made errors in order of their frequency—a useful tool for thinking about writing instruction in our own classrooms.

A WAY IN

Connors and Lunsford's list practically begs us to make our own common errors list as well. After all, good grammar instruction—really all good writing instruction—should materialize from our students' writing. So, let's pause here. Take out your notebook. What are the ten most common errors you consistently see in student writing? Be sure to stop at ten. While you might have more, tackle the top ten first.

Craft lessons that support an understanding of grammar and usage will look very similar to the reading like a writer lessons (Chapter 4) and to sentence study during notebook time (Chapter 5). Students study model sentences showing some grammatical concept at work and then create lists of noticings. For example, if you wanted to teach a lesson on participial phrases, you would look for powerful sentences containing these phrases in your mentor texts. Here's an example of three sentences with participial phrases from "Invisible Child—Girl in the Shadows: Dasani's Homeless Life" by Andrea Elliot—a harrowing feature article about homelessness in New York City.

1. "Her small scrub-worn hands are always tying shoelaces or doling out peanut butter sandwiches, taking the ends of the loaf for herself."
2. "Slipping out from her covers, the oldest girl sits at the window."
3. "She then wipes down the family's small refrigerator, stuffed with lukewarm milk, Tropicana grape juice, and containers of leftover Chinese."

Text 8.1 "Invisible Child—Girl in the Shadows: Dasani's Homeless Life" by Andrea Elliot *http://www.nytimes.com/projects/2013/invisible-child/#/?chapt=1*

Your sentence examples will come from texts students already know well, so you can go straight to sharing the sentences you've selected with the class. After you've read each one, ask students what they notice about the craft of the sentences. Welcome all noticings (because you just never know what someone might discover), but after the initial sharing, if no one has commented on what it is you want to talk about, ask them to look more specifically. With the sentences above, for example, you would ask students to think more specifically about the punctuation. Students might notice

* each sentence has at least one comma
* each sentence has a period at the end
* the comma separates each sentence into two parts
* the last sentence has commas in a series.

Once students are noticing in the territory of the sentence you want to explore, you'll need to give them some language for describing what they see. Your direct instruction might sound something like this:

> These are excellent observations. Let's revisit the third point here about the work some of these commas are doing. Look at the first sentence. The comma separates the sentence into two parts. The first part is a complete thought with a subject and a verb. If the writer wanted to, she could have put a period after the word "sandwiches" and ended it there. It can stand alone. The second part of this sentence, "taking the ends of the loaf for herself," can't stand alone. You can hear that it's not a complete thought. What would you think if I came up to you in the hall and said, "taking the ends of the loaf for herself"? You would wonder: WHO is taking the loaf for herself? It's not a complete thought. It can't stand alone. When a writer wants to combine a complete thought and an incomplete thought, she uses a comma.

As you continue to talk about the other examples, focus on what the sentences have in common, in this case a comma separating a complete thought and an incomplete thought. Each of the incomplete thoughts is, of course, also a participial phrase, and you'll want to name and define this for students so they can began adopting the language of grammar to help them talk about writing: *A participial phrase is a group of words that begins with an -ing or -ed verb and adds visual detail to writing.* There is no inherent value in being able to identify a participial phrase in random sentences, but to see the work these phrases can do to add visual detail is priceless for writers in the thick of crafting and polishing their own work. When you use mentor texts to help students understand how language works, you show them what these grammatical tools can do in the hands of master craftsman.

Depending on the level of your students and their understanding of grammatical concepts, you may be able to substitute the phrase "complete thought" for "independent clause" and "incomplete thought" for "phrase." For more information on teaching grammar and mechanics concepts, we highly recommend Jeff Anderson's *Mechanically Inclined*. His book includes over thirty craft lessons, complete with mentor texts, tips for teaching, and student examples.

Teaching About Grammar and Usage Across the Year

We typically teach a few craft lessons focused on grammar and usage in each writing study, and we situate these lessons toward the end of the unit as students are completing drafts and thinking about calling their pieces "finished." This way, students have had time to focus on their ideas and structure before they drill down to the nitty-gritty. We find students give more attention to these lessons after they have had a couple of weeks of dedicated drafting time.

However, some teachers prefer a more frequent or systematic approach to teaching grammar and usage, or they work in a school where daily or weekly grammar instruction is required. Mentor texts can meet you here, too. In *Write Like This* (2011), Kelly Gallagher suggests featuring a new sentence each week with a specific craft or mechanical technique. His students study it over the course of the week and demonstrate their learning in daily quizzes in which they are asked to use the technique in their own writing. This book also offers a yearlong curriculum for teaching grammar and mechanics. You might follow this model and pull weekly sentences from the cluster of texts the class is currently using.

Finding Presentation Ideas in Mentor Texts

Another way writers prepare for readers is to consider a work's presentation—how the writing appears on the page or screen. Think of the articles in the *New York Times* that catch your eye—the front-page images that beckon. Think of the bold headings and subheadings that help you skim week-in-review articles over morning coffee. The title fonts used in *Vanity Fair* that help set the tone for the feature on Jennifer Lawrence. All of these elements help shape the reader's experience of a text and should be taken under consideration by the writer.

Presentation lessons encourage students to think about these elements that attract readers: photography, headers, hyperlinks, and even titles. Title decisions are critically important in order to hook readers. Presentation lessons also encompass the design and layout of a text—how it looks on the page. This is especially important in the writing of digital texts where visual content is everything.

Depending on how much emphasis you want to place on the presentation of the writing, presentation lessons can happen over the course of several days or in one day. For example, in a study of infographics, a highly visual genre, presentation lessons will constitute the majority of instruction. As students create visuals, they must think about how to use lines, color, and font, as well as a variety of design elements, such as space and texture, to promote their message. In contrast, you may need to devote only one lesson to presentation in a more traditional genre like commentary or narrative. A fair amount of teaching toward presentation can happen in one-on-one conferences as specific needs arise and writers have questions that need to be addressed.

Presentation Lessons

In Chapter 5, we wrote about how we use raw data during notebook time to sharpen students' visual literacy skills and inspire future writing pieces. An added benefit of using raw data during notebook time is that students will be well prepared for presentation lessons that ask them to examine the effect of visuals in writing. During a presentation lesson, we guide students through the same kind of thinking as we do during notebook time but the questions we use are a bit more pointed (Figure 8.2).

A single presentation element can have a surprising impact on pulling a student's piece together and reinforcing the writer's purpose. Trey was writing a blog post on zone runs in football. In his post, he wanted to show how zone runs help create running lanes for the running back. In Figure 8.3, Trey explains what the linemen need to do in this run.

Football novices, our heads spin as we read this paragraph. The lineman goes where? The defender covers whom? A picture would have enhanced Trey's overall content and helped tremendously to support readers who needed more scaffolding to understand his meaning.

A study of the mentor text "Better with Age" by Chris B. Brown, a piece about Peyton Manning's historic 2013 season from popular sports and pop culture blog *Grantland*, gave Trey some ideas about how he might incorporate visuals into his writing. Immersed in

* Does the writer use pictures, slideshows, hyperlinks, and other text features to enhance the writing? Can you identify strategic places in your writing for these features?

* Which parts of your writing could be enhanced by a photograph? What about a caption?

* Does the writer use headings or subtitles to organize his writing? Do you see a place for this in your own work?

* Has the writer used color or font in a different or interesting way? Are there opportunities for interesting font or color work in your piece?

* Do graphs, maps, and other visual elements play a role in this writer's work? How might graphics support your content? How about margins? How might they affect the look of your piece?

Figure 8.2 Questions for Presentation Lessons

this mentor text, Trey noticed that Brown incorporates images in a few different ways.

* He uses still frames with captions to illustrate different formations.
* He supplies several GIFs to show Manning's record-breaking touchdown and other important plays.
* He includes a diagram that depicts how Denver ran a certain play.

The linemen against a four-man front will need to zone step either left or right and allow the defender to flow in one direction. Basically, the lineman will let the defender block himself. If the lineman is not covered by the defender, he can double-down and work up to a linebacker. This creates the running lanes needed to get a big gain.

Figure 8.3 Trey's Paragraph on Zone Runs (Draft)

Text 8.2 "Better with Age" by Chris B. Brown *http://grantland.com/features/peyton-manning-denver-broncos-offense/*

Inspired by Brown, Trey decided to add two visuals to his post: an edited still frame of a zone run and a short YouTube video showing zone blocking with double teams. The addition of these graphics created more visual interest in Trey's post as well as strengthened his message through photographic evidence.

Text 8.3 Trey's Blog Post *http://treysfieldnotes.wordpress.com/2014/10/16/zone-run/*

Students can also choose to pull together multiple presentation elements to elevate their writing. After a whole-class lesson about using visuals, Jimmy was inspired to add a visual element to his review of the video game *DayZ*. He borrowed moves from two mentor texts—an *A.V. Club* review of *Titanfall* that incorporated still frames of the video game and a review of M. Wells Steakhouse in *The New Yorker* that included photographs with captions—and was inspired to add captioned still frames of his experience playing *DayZ* to his article.

Text 8.4 "*Titanfall* Supplants Its Ancestors with Speed and Scale" by Ryan Smith *http://www.avclub.com/article/titanfall-supplants-its-ancestors-speed-and-scale-202272*

Text 8.5 "Fred and Barney Would Feel Right at Home" by Pete Wells *http://www .nytimes.com/2014/01/29/dining/restaurant-review-m-wells-steakhouse-in-long-island-city -queens.html*

Text 8.6 Jimmy's *DayZ* Review *https://docs.google.com/document/d/1KgrXBAMpBzi CCYI6y5D49ztbiWgXfG6sFLOScw7qEjE/edit?usp=sharing*

When writers consider the visual layout of a piece, it can impact the way they think about the organization of the writing. Sometimes presentation lessons can even send students back into planning mode. For example, at the end of this study of critical reviews, Jimmy reflected on the presentation lesson, noting that it had influenced more than just the visual elements of his piece; it had actually shaped the way he decided to organize his writing by helping him find a structure for his review. Jimmy writes, "I decided to include pictures and break the paper up into segments. Each segment would highlight an aspect of the game, and the screen shot that followed would usually provide an in-game example of it." Jimmy's reflection is proof that the writing process is recursive and that the best writers are willing to start from scratch for the sake of a better piece of writing. If this happens in your classroom, encourage students to take the necessary steps to make their writing better and furnish yourself with plenty of mentor texts to support their decisions to take alternate routes. In fact, if a student decides to completely rework a piece of writing, you might share this powerful decision with other students and ask the writer to talk about why he ultimately made this decision and how he plans to proceed.

Presentation lessons, and the mentor texts that support them, help students see the big picture of their writing by putting themselves in their readers' shoes. What else do my readers need to know? How can I bring text and visuals together to support the readers' experience? In other words, presentation lessons remind students they are writing not just for themselves but for real readers whose minds and backgrounds and prior knowledge are different from their own.

Exploring Opportunities for Publication

If we're going to be serious about asking our writers to attempt publication—and we should be—we need to create opportunities in class for them to attempt it. We can offer numerous considerations for publication with students. Sharing about submission guidelines, the different types of publications, and query letters will excite and elevate writers as they prepare their work for audiences beyond the classroom.

Resources for Publication

Talking to students about publication opportunities, bringing in print copies of magazines that accept student work, inviting them to browse student-friendly ezines and websites— these overtures can be transformative. Suddenly the writing students have been doing in class takes on a whole new meaning as they begin to visualize people outside the classroom reading their work.

The Writer's Market Guide to Publication presents thousands of publishing opportunities for writers. A simple Google search yields hundreds of options, too. Figure 8.4 shows a compilation of a few of our favorite publication resources, beginning with *Teen Ink*, a national teenage magazine dedicated to publishing student art, writing, and photographs.

Submission Guidelines

Once students begin to think about putting their work out in the world for others to read, they will need to familiarize themselves with the submission guidelines of the publications they plan to submit work to. Submission guidelines are usually printed at the back of a print magazine or linked at the bottom of a website. They often provide a snail mail address or email address to which writers are invited to send their work. Additionally, they give information about formatting, length, and suitable topics. Submission guidelines are also implicitly expressed within the publications themselves—in the genres, topics, and perspectives typically published.

To help students grasp both the explicit and implicit guidelines, consider immersing them in an entire collection of mentor texts—the publications themselves—and asking them to read the work as potential authors, using the following guiding questions to focus their thinking:

* What kinds of topics are common to this publication? What topics
  are missing?
* What genres are explored in this publication? What genres are missing?
* What kinds of attitudes, perspectives, and tones do the published writers
  of this publication take on?

Teen Ink (teenink.com)

A collection curated by the National Writing Project (nwp.org)

A collection curated by New Pages (newpages.com)

Scholastic Writing Contests (http://teacher.scholastic.com)

Writers Digest Competitions (writersdigest.com)

Poets & Writers list of over 800 Literary Magazines (pw.org)

Young Writers Magazine (www.youngwritersmagazine.com)

Figure 8.4 Favorite Publication Resources

* What audience does this publication target?
* Are the writers of this publication established or are some of them emerging writers?
* Do you admire the work in this publication? Would you like to write something like what you are reading here?
* Do you have any extant writing that may fit this magazine's audience?
* Do you notice anything special about the format of the writing?

Students can make a chart in their notebooks tracing the different features of the print and digital publications to which they would like to submit their work. They can add to this running list as they find new places to publish and refer to it as they complete pieces throughout the year.

The final step is to make time for students to prepare their work for these publications. You might consider dedicating one day at the end of each study for publication. You may prefer to let students grow a body of work first and make time for publication at the end of each quarter or semester. On these days, you'll want to make sure your classroom is stocked with the necessary publication tools. Most publications accept submissions by email and regular mail. If your students are submitting work by regular mail, you'll want to stock your classroom with the following materials:

* 8½ × 11" manila envelopes
* resume paper, or nice paper for printing
* school stationery for the cover letter
* writer's market guides
* examples of well-written query letters (more on this below).

You'll most likely have to show your students how to address envelopes and take an in-class field trip to the main office where they can mail their work and receive immediate gratification. If your students are submitting their work through email, show them how to create a proper subject line, and be sure to remind them to check their mail for confirmation that their submission was received (in our experience, many students have a habit of sending emails but not checking back for a response).

We typically teach students about publication and style guidelines after the second or third unit of study when they've written a few different pieces. However, once students understand that publication is a natural end point, it makes sense to study submission guidelines earlier in the process. The desire to publish can become the impetus for future projects rather than an afterthought. The issue of length, for example, is really critical to know before a writer starts. Some publications have strict word limits. The vision a writer has of a 500-word article and a 1000-word article, for example, would be really different. If a student plans on writing for a particular publication, she needs to be familiar with the submission guidelines from the start.

A NOTE ABOUT ACADEMIC STYLE GUIDES

Teaching students how to write in MLA or APA format is an important and necessary part of writing instruction. It's easy to get bogged down in the mechanics of these styles, though, and forget to talk about the why. When students are planning to write for a particular publication, the why will become immediate and clear.

While most English teachers ask their students to write in MLA style, we also ask our students to write editorials and commentary like the articles they read in the *New York Times*. But *New York Times* writers don't use MLA format; they use the *New York Times Manual of Style and Usage*.

Every time we read a *New York Times* book review, students point out that the writers put book titles in quotation marks rather than italicizing them. This is difficult for them. After all, italicizing book titles has been drilled into their heads since the day they wrote their first book report. To clarify the guidelines, consider studying the style guides of different publications when you study the relevant genre. Teaching this kind of flexibility will help students far more in future writing than marrying them to a single style. The more practice they have, the more students should be able to figure out style by looking at the publications themselves—even if they don't have the guidelines!

Additionally, if your students are using images and video in their writing, you will need to talk about copyright. We use mentor texts to teach this aspect of writing, too. You can help your students understand how to cite images by studying how professional writers cite images in their work. For example, after reading the *New York Times* article "Connecticut Teenager with Cancer Loses Court Fight to Refuse Chemotherapy," you might direct students' attention to the picture in the article and the words below it. The picture shows a close-up of a happy teenager with heavy eye makeup wearing a bright pink sweatshirt. Below the picture, the caption reads: Cassandra C. learned she had cancer in September. Below the caption, a citation: Cassandra C./Cassandra C. via Associated Press. This citation raises the following questions: Who took the picture? Who gave the *New York Times* permission to print it? Why is Cassandra's name printed there twice? Who is the Associated Press and how are they involved? Upon further exploration of additional *New*

York Times articles with photography, you and your students can tease out the rules for citing copyrighted material.

Text 8.7 "Connecticut Teenager with Cancer Loses Court Fight to Refuse Chemotherapy" by Elizabeth A. Harris *http://www.nytimes.com/2015/01/10/nyregion /connecticut-teenager-with-cancer-loses-court-fight-to-refuse-chemotherapy.html?_r=0*

Lessons on style guides and citation present opportunities to explain to students why these things matter and to prove to them that formatting and citation are important in the world of writing and reading and not just something we do in school.

The Query Letter: A Genre Study

Another unit of study will present itself while you and your students are preparing for publication: the query letter. Writers send query letters to magazine editors, literary agents, and publishing companies to propose writing ideas. Your students will need to be familiar with the purpose and etiquette behind query letters, making this a perfect opportunity for a brief foray into formal letter writing.

As in all studies, you'll want to gather a few query letters to share with students. A quick Google search yields several possibilities. *Writer's Digest*, for example, offers over sixty examples of successful query letters and a brief explanation from editors as to why they worked. Mediabistro, a website for media professionals, shares query letters that worked in over two dozen different genres with everything from fantasy, to children's books, to historical fiction.

Students can approach a query letter study as they would any other study. While reading through the query letters independently or in groups, they can record their noticings across query letters or study various query letters for specific genres of writing. Figure 8.5 lists some guiding questions to focus their study.

In our experience, query letter studies can really "turn" the students who are initially wary of publication. Even the students who show little to no interest can't help but feel the pull of publication as everyone types up query letters, stuffs envelopes, licks them shut, and mails them off. Figure 8.6 shows an example of a query letter written by a student.

* What information belongs in a query letter?

* How do writers make their query letters stand out?

* How are query letters formatted?

* To whom are query letters directed?

* What is an appropriate tone to adopt in a query letter?

* What is the typical length of a query letter?

* How do query letters for specific genres of writing work? Are there clear differences? Are there things you should do in a query for a work of fantasy, say, that are different from memoir?

* What kinds of prewriting work do writers of query letters do? In other words, do they need to research the publication before writing the query?

Figure 8.5 Questions to Focus a Study of Query Letters

May 7, 2014

Dear Ms. Josephine Mandarano:

I'm contacting you in hopes that you will consider my 2,530-word short story, *Define Yourself*, for your magazine, *Lip*. The thought-provoking articles and stories that encompass your magazine are truly uplifting. Being that my target audience is young adults too, I was inspired by many of the articles in *Lip*.

The nameless narrator paints the story of her first romance with an aspiring New Yorker whose raspy voice entices her. Although all the signs point to heartbreak, she eagerly pursues him, unable to escape his enchanting aura. At first, she experiences a real life fairytale filled with pure bliss and childlike wonder. Things turn for the scandalous when the New Yorker's true colors shine through, allowing the narrator to free herself from their toxic relationship. Through her experience she learns the most important lesson every young woman should be taught: independence.

continues

The theme of this story is freeing oneself from the self-destructing relationship standards set by society. Through the narrator's experience the reader learns that women should not define themselves or their self worth on the opinion of their significant other.

A copy of the story is attached to this email, per your submission guidelines. Thank you for your time and consideration.

Sincerely,

Catie P.

Figure 8.6 Catie's Query Letter

Author Recordings: An Alternative to Print or Digital Publication

Some students may prefer to publish their work through a different medium: audio and video recordings. With today's technology, this has never been easier: Students can record, promote, and share originally created audio and video within seconds. From there, recordings can be posted on student blogs, websites, and Twitter accounts. Figure 8.7 shows a list of audio and video platforms students can use for free.

Audio	Video
Audacity—Audacity has a wonderful built-in editor that gives users the ability to mix tracks, adjust the volume, create fades, and more.	**YouTube**—Students can use the free YouTube Capture app to record video on their phones. Then they can upload it to YouTube to share.
Vocaroo—Vocaroo is a hassle-free service that lets users create audio without installing software or making an account.	**Vimeo**—A free Vimeo account grants users basic editing privileges and plenty of space to store and share videos.
SoundCloud—What sets SoundCloud apart is the option to comment on an audio track as it plays. Just imagine the possibilities!	**Flickr**—Unbeknownst to most people, Flickr supports video-sharing as well as image-sharing. A free account grants users two video uploads per month, up to 90 seconds each.
Audioboo—Students can create audio right from their phones using the free Audioboo app. Alternately, they can record directly on the website.	

Figure 8.7 Audio and Video Platforms

There are mentor texts for this kind of work, too—audio and video recordings of authors presenting their work. For example, The Academy of American Poets has a YouTube channel dedicated to videos of poets reading and talking about their work. The Library of Congress is another wonderful resource for finding audio and video recordings. Their "Poet and the Poem" series provides live interviews at the Library of Congress with distinguished writers. Their website also offers the best compilation of author audio recordings we can find on the Internet. Other sources for recordings include the BBC Poetry Out Loud website and the HarperCollins collections of recordings from major writers and poets.

Additionally, podcasts of authors reading excerpts from new books and discussing their work make for excellent audio mentor texts. Check out NPR's *This American Life* or *The Reading Life, Serial* (a podcast from the creators of *This American Life), The Guardian Books Podcast,* Sherman Alexie's podcast *A Tiny Sense of Accomplishment* (he reads excerpts of his works in progress!), and the BBC's *Open Book.*

As students listen to or watch a recording, give them a copy of the poem or piece being read, and present the following guiding questions to support their listening:

* How does the writer make the piece captivating by reading it out loud? How might you make your reading captivating?
* Does the writer place emphasis on certain words? Why do you think he or she does that? Which words might you choose to emphasize in your piece?
* Does the piece sound different to you when read aloud by the writer? How might a reading of your piece change the meaning for someone else?

Conferring to Prepare Student Writing for Readers

We continue to confer with students as they prepare their work for readers. At this point, students have a tendency to revert to the least focused and least helpful conference starters. Most often, they want to know, "Is this right?" "Do I have any mistakes?" and "Am I done?" Thus, conferences at this stage are more teacher-directed. The trick here is to give students the kind of assistance that will still ultimately promote their independence. For example, we don't want to correct their commas for them; we want to give them the tools to figure out how to fix their commas themselves. It's important to bear in mind that students can fix only the things they know need to be fixed. A student isn't being sloppy or careless if she doesn't know something needs fixing. Mistakes show us what information students still need to be able to craft more effective sentences independently. Figure 8.8 highlights some common issues teachers see as students put the finishing touches on writing and shows how mentor texts might help address them.

Teacher notices . . .	In the conference . . .
A student makes the same grammatical or mechanical error over and over again.	First, to discern whether the student just missed something entirely or truly doesn't know, point to a section of text and have her read it to you and then talk to you about how it's written. If appropriate, direct the writer to check her draft against her independent proofreading checksheet (Atwell 2002), independent correction sheet (Gallagher 2006), or a list of errors she's made in previous pieces. Alternatively, introduce her to express-lane edits (Anderson 2005), a fun activity that helps students proofread their work. Where does she see errors in her current draft? How might she correct them? What mentor sentences might she draw from for support? Keep in mind that, while a paper may be riddled with errors, if the student is making the same error over and over again, you need to teach only one thing to make a huge difference in the writing. We spend a lot of time reteaching in conferences; sometimes it takes a while for students to get the hang of something we've taught.
A student recognizes an error but doesn't know how to fix it.	Hand the student an applicable broadsheet (Figure 8.9), a small laminated poster that shows effective writing (Heard 2014). Ask him to study the sentences and consider: What kinds of punctuation do you see the writer using? What punctuation do you have in your writing? The student can then use the samples on the broadsheet to build stronger sentences.
A student has trouble fully explaining necessary context or complicated ideas.	Share mentor texts that use hyperlinks to deftly share background and other context a reader might need in order to access the writer's piece. Ask the student to consider what she might link to that would open up her ideas for readers who need a bit more. Sometimes a complicated idea can best be explained through an image, video, or graphic. Share some examples of these with the student. Is there an image or video that might demonstrate the idea she is trying to share? Other complicated ideas are helped when broken down into different sections. Suggest a few mentor texts that have separated their ideas into smaller chunks with subheadings.
A student is finished and needs a place to go next with the writing.	When a student is really, truly finished and needs something meaningful to do, send him to the publications! Suggest three places for publication you think might fit the student's work. Ask the student to study the submission guidelines and choose one place to submit his work. The student can also use the running publications chart from his notebook to figure out where to submit. Have the student make a tangible goal: "I will submit my piece to at least one place by the end of the week."

Figure 8.8 Common Conferences as Writers Ready Their Work for Publication

A phrase is a small group of words. Writers use participial and absolute phrases to add visual detail to their writing.

A participle phrase begins with an -ing or -ed verb. Sentences with participial phrases (boldfaced):

Now I see cows corralled in their own muck, **stopped by fences just beyond lush green meadows, assailed by armies of flies**.

— "A City Girl Feeds Country Cows," Sandra Becker, 2013

Listening to bumps in the night and crackles in the woods, spotting vague shadows amid trees or at the end of dark corridors, we're reminded that nothing is scarier than nothing.

— "Zombies in the Time of Ebola: Why We Need Horror Movies Now More Than Ever," David Edelstein, 2014

French onion soup is more solid than liquid, **stuffed with poached pork belly and a marrow bone** (tiny spoon provided) that takes the natural beefiness of onion broth to its logical conclusion.

— "Fred and Barney Would Feel Right at Home," Pete Wells, 2014

An absolute phrase begins with a noun and an -ing or -ed verb combination. Sentences with absolute phrases (boldfaced):

So she tells me, **the words dribbling out with the cranberry muffin, commas dunked in her coffee**.

—Laurie Halse Anderson, *Wintergirls*, 2009

The smaller children lie tangled beside her, **their chests rising and falling under winter coats and wool blankets**.

—"Invisible Child, Girl in the Shadows: Dasani's Homeless Life," Andrea Elliot, 2013

Figure 8.9 Conference Broadsheet for Phrases That Add Visual Detail

Closing Thoughts

As students move into the final phases of writing and revision, it's tempting to brush over the presentation and publication lessons. After all, students have succeeded in getting words down and saying something meaningful. But in our experience, it's these very lessons that elevate not just the writing but also our writers. It's these lessons that show our students their work matters—not just to us, not just to their peers or their parents, but to readers.

It's not enough to have students share their work within the walls of our classrooms. If we are going to put true meaning behind the term *writer*, we need to make it real. We need to help our students ready their work for readers and then help them push it out into the world.

CHAPTER NINE

Mentors Show Students How to Be Independent

T he possibility of losing the rings isn't what has been keeping him up at night. It's the toast. The best man's toast is important. All eyes and ears will be on him, and what he delivers needs to be better than good. It needs to be great.

Justin racks his brain as he sits down to pen his speech. What does a best man say anyway? He wants it to be memorable but appropriate, personal but relatable for all of the wedding guests. But how long should it be? What will the guests expect him to include? Where should he even begin?

And then he remembers that old trick from English class—find a mentor text.

Grabbing his computer, he pulls up YouTube and searches "Best Man Toast." Thousands of videos appear. He watches one, then the next. After a handful of videos, he grabs a piece of paper and begins to list the following common denominators he's noticing among the toasts:

- the best man introduces himself
- background on the relationship between the best man and the groom
- usually funny—jokes? Embarrassing stories?
- the bride's influence on the groom
- ends with a wish for happiness and the actual toast.

Okay, *he thinks,* those are the basics of the best man's toasts. I need more specifics so I can actually write this thing. *He goes back and rewatches the toasts he likes best and adds the following to his list:*

- *casual but appropriate language—no cursing, no inappropriate jokes*
- *try to avoid cliches*
- *I like, "Here's to a lifetime of love and joy" at the end. Use this!*

Justin takes a deep breath. He can do this. Opening a blank document, his list of noticings by his side, he begins to write.

The vignette above is fiction. At least, we don't know for a fact this has happened to one of our former students yet. But this is our goal: to teach students how to use mentor texts and develop the independence they will need to continue finding and using mentor texts for the rest of their writing lives. You see, students will leave our classes. They will lose their writer's notebooks. But they will always need to write—in the next English class, in college, at work, in life. In their education, they will need to craft excellent papers, and in their careers they will need to craft well-written emails and business plans and reports and grant proposals and letters of recommendation. But, in their everyday lives, they will also need to write—thank-you notes, eulogies, toasts. When students leave our classes, they will be writers, and in their futures, regardless of their profession, they will remain writers.

Mentor texts will always be present. Over the course of a school year, we introduce students to mentor texts and teach them how to use these texts to support their writing. We hope that by the time they leave us, they wouldn't dream of writing something without consulting one of their mentors. We want their relationship with mentor texts to be a lasting one. Through our teaching, we want students not only to learn about writing, we also want them to learn how to create a writing life, a life supported by mentors and mentor texts long after we have finished guiding their writing.

We begin guiding students toward the independent discovery and use of mentor texts from the very first days of school. As the year progresses, we remove scaffolds, ask more of their interactions with mentor texts, and gradually shift the responsibility of finding mentors and texts onto students' shoulders. This chapter shares a vision for how we move our students toward a future where mentor texts have made a lasting impact, and both our writers and their writing are forever changed.

While we will share some projects that will encourage independence in your students' work with mentor texts, this transformation isn't something that happens because of a single project or activity. There isn't typically a moment of epiphany when a student says, "I'm going to do this mentor text thing forever" (at least not in our experience). The momentum that moves writers forward into their own independent writing lives happens over the course of the school year. It happens because of the constant flood of inspiration and learning that flow from a writing life immersed in mentors and mentor texts.

Inviting Students to Find Their Own Mentor Texts

Mentor texts model excellent writing, and teachers who infuse their instruction with them model the act of finding excellent mentor texts. This is where independence begins. Once students have studied the texts we provide in our initial mentor text unit of study (described in Chapter 4), we make it possible for them to find mentor texts on their own. For us, this is usually around the second month of school.

The invitation for students to contribute their own mentor texts is an open one, but it's not something we spend a lot of time focusing on right away. Many times this happens organically anyway. As students become increasingly familiar with using mentor texts, they bring us texts they have found. We gently encourage all students to find their own mentor texts, though, throwing out reminders: "You can bring your own mentor text if you wish" or "Go back and look at the mentor text cluster and any mentor texts you've collected on your own." We throw the invitation into our routine classroom conversations, keeping the possibility at the forefront of our students' minds. Some students are ready to jump in right away. These students love the hunt as much as we do and immediately think of sources and authors they want to search for this purpose. Other students aren't ready to try until they are required to, and that's fine, too.

As you work to support students' independence with mentors and mentor texts, you will want to offer up frequent, brief, low-stakes invitations for students to begin searching on their own. Use the invitations below as they fit into your writing studies.

* Find a mentor text that has a lead or introduction that grabs you.
* Find a mentor text that has a particularly strong or interesting conclusion.
* Find a mentor sentence—one you think is beautiful or strange or just awesome. Look for one that has a structure or other elements you might be able to replicate in your own writing.
* Find a mentor text that has a surprising use of figurative language.

* Find a mentor text that contains the kind of description that makes you want to keep reading (rather than skimming over it).

* Follow a favorite writer on Twitter. Bring the class three things you learn about that writer from his or her recent tweets. This can be a writer of any kind—fiction, nonfiction, poetry, a writer you have liked for a long time, a writer you discovered through one of our mentor texts, a writer you have heard about but don't know well.

* Find a fun fact about _____ (a mentor from your current writing study) to share with the class.

* Try to find an interview with a writing mentor of your choosing. Read it and report to us what you learn about that writer's process. To find an interview with this mentor, try his or her official website, or do an Internet search of the author's name.

The students who start finding their own mentor texts right away are usually our most savvy readers and writers, so the chance they will bring in something good is pretty high. These students typically read between the lines, see the mentor texts we have offered the class, and find writing of a similar quality on their own. When a student contributes a mentor text for the class to study or for his touchstone text, we make a big deal of it. We shout it out to the class in celebration (and as a reminder to other students). If it's a particularly good mentor text, we project it and read it or copy it for students to add to their current cluster of texts. When a student contributes a new mentor text from an unfamiliar source, we might spend a couple of minutes searching that source as a class to learn what it has to offer for our future mentor text needs.

On occasion, we use the new texts offered by students in the teaching of our writing lessons. We certainly add that text to our working binder of texts to use in writing conferences. When our students discover a great source for mentor texts, we add it to our regular feeds. This gives us great insight into students' interests and reading habits. When students discover great mentor texts on their own, our instruction is also enriched. Our repertoire of mentor texts grows with every class of students we teach because our students add to it. This gives us a head start on texts students will find engaging next year; after all, the new texts we add have been vetted by other students.

If students bring in a mentor text early on that is lacking in quality, that's okay. Let's be honest—our first mentor texts weren't always spectacular either. Over time, as students are exposed to increasing numbers and variety of texts, their ability to discern what's great and what's not will grow. If the text the student brings falls into the not-spectacular category, we thank them for their contribution, congratulate them on their find, and validate their addition by sharing it with the class. We don't teach from it. We don't give substantial class time to it. And we don't stress about it. There is *some* admirable craft element to be found in nearly any piece of writing. If students don't see anything mentor-worthy about a particular text, they won't use it as inspiration for their own work anyway. Nothing is lost.

Sometimes, students find themselves in need of mentor texts beyond what the teacher-selected cluster offers. This is a prime time for them to embark on a mentor text hunt of their own! When students want to write in a genre that we do not teach, haven't taught yet, or don't know much about, we send them to find their own mentor texts. In a study of analytical writing, Griffin wanted to write sports analysis. While we pull inspiration from sportswriters, we don't explicitly teach sports analysis. With a little guidance about which websites tend to have excellent sports writing, we sent Griffin to build his own mentor text cluster before trying his hand at sports analysis (Figure 9.1). Kippy wanted to write a fashion analysis of the work of Coco Chanel. However, we had no knowledge of the ways writers write about fashion—the jargon they use, how they use imagery to paint pictures of garments, how they use photographs to support their claims. In fact, beyond the writing done by fashion bloggers, we didn't even know if this was really a genre. We asked Kippy to solve this problem by finding mentor texts, figuring out what fashion writing really is, and teaching us about it through her writing (Figure 9.2).

As we move into the second or third study of the year, the open invitation to find and share a mentor text of one's own becomes an occasional assignment as we seek to build every student's confidence and independence. When we first require students to find their own mentor texts, though, we ask them to bring little pieces of larger texts. You might ask them to bring an excellent introduction or a persuasive conclusion. Depending on your writing study, you might ask them to find a killer sentence for sentence study or a lovely piece of imagery or a surprising claim. These baby steps are helpful for students because it doesn't require them to find mentor texts that

Wenger must change. His stubbornness in his tactics and buying/selling the team hurts the fans, the team, and himself. Arsenal has 27 players, but only seven are defenders, and there are four possible defensive positions to cover. Two defenders are injured right now, causing major defensive problems. In the last two games, Arsenal has had a 3-0 lead in the UEFA Champions League against Anderlecht, and a 1-0 lead in the English Premier League against Swansea City. In both games they blew their lead, and Arsenal has lost more points than any other team from winning positions this year. There are rumors that the coaching staff doesn't back Wenger and that some players want to leave Arsenal.

Figure 9.1 Excerpt of Griffin's Sports Analysis

are fantastic from top to bottom. Students only have to focus on finding one great tidbit at a time. This also pushes students to think analytically about mentor texts as they identify the parts and pieces that comprise them.

Students use these mentor texts on their own as touchstones and in addition to texts from the whole-class cluster in their smaller varied text response groups we discussed in Chapter 7 (Figure 9.3). In these small group settings, each student is empowered by her expertise with a text no one else has studied.

We proceed this way throughout the year, periodically asking students to contribute their own mentor texts here and there, celebrating when the pieces come together and a student attempts on his own to connect his writing to the writing of others. Later in this chapter, we will share some ideas for larger writing projects that ask students to take the reigns with mentor texts.

The real start of her fashion empire was she started cutting out the corsets in her dresses for her and her sister to wear. Coco's revolutionary thought of the way people dress was the best of designs, inspired by the comfort men had and the class and style women needed. Her wool jersey traveling suit consisted of a cardigan jacket, and pleated skirt, paired with a low-belted pullover top. This ensemble, worn with low-heeled shoes, became the casual look in expensive women's wear.

She lived with Etienne Balsan at the time she started to think of fashion. She would take his expensive, nice quality clothes and make herself modest, free flowing, "masculine" dresses and pantsuits while other high-class women would wear tight corsets, feathers, beads, and large hats.

Figure 9.2 Excerpt of Kippy's Fashion Analysis

When you bring your own mentor text into your response group, your classmates will not be familiar with the text you have found. Think about the four Cs: context, content, craft, and crowd. Use these prompts to support you as you share your mentor text treasure, and use it to enhance writing in our class.

✳ Share the *context* of your mentor text. Who wrote it? Where did it come from? How did you find it? What made you read it?

✳ Share the *content* of your mentor text. In three to four sentences, share what your mentor text is about for those in your group who have not read it.

✳ Share the *craft* of your mentor text. You probably noticed a lot of interesting craft elements in your mentor text. Share just a few of your favorite examples with your group.

✳ Share the *crowd* for your mentor text. Who would benefit most from studying this mentor text more closely? What kind of writer could really use this mentor text? Recommend an audience for your text of choice.

Figure 9.3 Using Your Own Mentor Text in Your Mentor Text Response Group

A WAY IN

Return to the vignette that opens this chapter for a minute. This vignette represents a hope for a specific student, Justin—a student who doesn't always love writing and doesn't always see its relevance to his life. This is what we hope for him.

Think of a student in your class and the dreams you have for his or her writing life. What might her writing future look like with mentor texts to guide her? *This* is what will carry you forward into the work, these hopes and dreams for your student's future.

Craft your own in-the-future vignette.

Bringing Authors to Life as Mentors for Students

When the class studies a mentor text, we talk about the author behind the words (the mentor) as we talk about the choices writers make and their effect on the work. It's important for our student writers to understand there are writers just like them behind the mentor texts they are studying. We humanize these writers as a way of deepening students' connection to the world of words. It is powerful when students can identify a favorite mentor text and use it to inspire their work. But it is even more powerful for our students when they can connect with a human, a mentor, a fellow writer. In *Study Driven* (2006), Katie Wood Ray argues that

> In genre studies, particularly, it's a good idea to find out as much as you can about the
> people behind the texts you're reading and the kind of work they do to support their writing.
> If possible, you may find interviews with writers and either include them in the stack of texts
> for students to read, or in whole-class gatherings, you might highlight what you think are
> the important points from the interviews. Also, ask students to pay attention to any author's
> notes or information on book jackets that might provide insight into the writers and the
> work they do. (128)

These professional writing mentors aren't just writing instruction gravy—nice to have but not necessary. They are important. Professional writers have mentors from myriad genres that inspire and speak to their own writing process. And students need to hear this reiterated again and again. Mentors and mentor texts aren't a crutch for lesser writers; *all* writers have mentors. For this reason, we share the mentors of our mentors with students.

Essayist Joan Didion, a favorite in Rebekah's IB English courses, has famously said that reading and studying Hemingway's craft taught her "how sentences worked." Gabriel García Márquez credits James Joyce and Virginia Woolf—two writers whose work seems vastly different from his own—for teaching him the trick of writing interior monologue. Since students won't always have a teacher who can help guide their way to inspiration, they too need to have an army of mentors available when they need what film critic A. O. Scott calls a "jolt of inspiration" in the *New York Times* feature "Questions for A. O. Scott."

> *There are several critics whose work I return to when I feel like my own writing needs a jolt of inspiration. I admire Paul Kael's passion and cantankerousness, Renata Adler's elegance and impatience, Manny Farber's cranky intellectualism and James Agee's humanism. All of them have influenced the way I think about movies (as have many others, including critics like Jonathan Rosenbaum and J. Hoberman who are still very much active). But the critics to whom I feel the strongest connection—from whom I've learned the most about criticism as a mode of writing and intellectual discipline—didn't write much about movies at all. Randall Jarrell's poetry reviews, Mary McCarthy's essays on theater and the novel and Clive James's pieces on literature and television provide me with durable models of intelligence, insight, and wit. My greatest ambition as a critic is to be able, someday, to write as well as they did (and, in Mr. James's case, still do).*

If we ensure that students have exposure to the mentors behind the mentor texts and use them as "distant teachers" (John-Steiner 1997), the mentors' writing and advice will carry students throughout their writing lives.

Helping Students Identify Their Mentors

How do we help students identify these distant teachers? One simple way to begin establishing connections between your students and the writers who have crafted the mentor texts is by sharing quotes from writers about their process and their advice for other writers. This pushes students past looking only at models for writing and gives them models for living a life as a writer.

In an interview with Semi Chelas for *The Paris Review*, Matthew Weiner, creator and writer of *Mad Men*, reflects on how helpful it can be for young writers to hear about the writing processes of others. He talks about reading the interviews with writers in *The Paris Review* as a teenager: "There were people talking about writing like it was a job, first of all. And then saying 'I don't know' a lot. It's helpful, when you're a kid, to hear someone saying 'I don't know'. Also, they were asking questions that I would've asked, only I'd have been embarrassed to ask them. Like, 'What time of day do you write?'" (2014). As Weiner suggests, students need to have the curtain pulled back and the mystery of writing demystified by the experts. To a certain extent, we want to pull professional writers off their pedestals and have them instead become our students' colleagues, offering helpful suggestions and options for the process of writing.

You might introduce students to writing mentors early on by sharing bits of interviews from the writers of the mentor texts the class is studying. In a study of critical reviews, Allison's students studied a restaurant review by *New York Times* critic Pete Wells. After students completed a first draft reading of the mentor text, the class viewed two brief video interviews linked to the *Times* website that show Wells talking about how critics sneak into restaurants unnoticed and rate the dishes they are served. This brief encounter with the person of Pete Wells helped students connect with the man behind the review.

Text 9.1 "At the Restaurant Critics' Table" *http://www.nytimes.com/interactive/2013 /09/03/dining/2013-dining-critics-videos.html*

We have some favorite sources for interviews with writers (see Figure 9.4). Your students will not be familiar with all of these writers. Some are very classic, and others are just very adult. This presents an opportunity in itself, though, to introduce students to new writers. Consider combining a brief author introduction or book talk with quotes from that writer to help students at specific points in the writing process.

Even better, seek out opportunities for author visits. There is almost nothing as powerful for students as having a real conversation with a fellow writer. It's wonderful

The Paris Review

Poets & Writers

"How I Write" in *The Daily Beast*

"Writers on Writing" in the *New York Times*

Individual author's websites

Figure 9.4 Sources for Author Quotes and Interviews

when these can happen in person, but so many writers are available to talk to your students via Skype. Author Kate Messner even has a wonderful list of authors who will Skype for free! Students can also connect with writers via Twitter, and many writers will tweet them back. Our students literally screamed with excitement in the lunchroom and raced to check Twitter when Ishmael Beah responded to their tweets about *A Long Way Gone*. The list can be found at http://www.katemessner.com /authors-who-skype-with-classes-book-clubs-for-free/.

Just as we eventually share responsibility for finding mentor texts with our students, over time we also begin to share responsibility for learning about writing mentors so students can learn to do this on their own. Periodically, ask students to find out a little something about a mentor whose work appears in your current mentor text cluster and share it with the class the next day. When students bring in their own mentor text, ask them to share what they know about that particular writer. While not every writer will have an in-depth interview in *The Paris Review*, students can find out a lot about writers' processes and influences by visiting their websites, following them on Twitter, and even performing simple Internet searches. Over time, this process reinforces to students that writers follow the same writing habits you are trying to encourage in them.

At other times, you might ask students to go in search of another mentor text from a mentor you are already studying as a class. Sometimes we become so immersed in a mentor text that it's easy to forget that the text is just one island in the vast sea of a writer's work. Encouraging students to examine the larger body of an author's work sets them up for finding favorite writers they will return to again and again in your class.

Supporting Work with Mentors Across the Year

We steadily and intentionally work from the first day of school until the last in the hopes that our students will take the mentor text skills they have learned in our class and transfer them to the rest of their lives. While there isn't a single project or activity that ensures this will happen with absolute certainty, the experiences and projects below are ones we have found promote the kind of independence we want to see in every student by the time they leave our class.

Figure 9.5 shows how the experiences shared in this chapter might fit in throughout the school year. Your time line may look different as your students may be ready for a challenge sooner or may need more support, so consider this a guide as you plan to develop your students' mentor text independence.

Months 1–2	✳ Teacher introduces students to her favorite sources for mentor texts, walks students through these sites, and shows them the different types of writing that can be found there.
	✳ Teacher makes special mention of the authors of each mentor text, giving a couple of interesting facts or background details to humanize them or even sharing brief interviews with the writers.
	✳ Students set up a place for mentor text storage (look back at Chapter 2 for suggestions). Even though they will not be ready to fill it yet, they will want a system ready to go whenever they are.
	✳ Students begin culling a list of personal go-to sources for mentor texts.
	✳ Teacher shares quotes from writers about their process and advice for writing.
Months 3–4	✳ Students find smaller pieces of mentor texts to share with the class: an introduction, a mentor sentence, an example of figurative language, and so on.
	✳ Students find engaging supplementary information about authors of mentor texts to share with the class.
Months 5–7	✳ Students find mentor texts to add to the whole-class mentor text cluster, to use as personal touchstone texts, and to share with peers in response groups.
	✳ Students create collections of mentor texts and annotate them for craft and purpose.
	✳ Students respond to mentor authors using similar craft elements and genre.
Months 8–10	✳ Students develop their own mentor text cluster for use in a multigenre writing project.
	✳ Students complete a mentor author study.

Figure 9.5 A Time Line for Building Student Independence with Mentors and Mentor Texts

Annotated Mentor Text Collection

We constantly remind our students that writers have plans. Part of that planning is finding and collecting mentor texts and also considering how they might be used in writing down the road.

To demonstrate their ability to find and collect mentor texts that will be meaningful to their writing, students create annotated mentor text collections. Using a digital platform for mentor text storage, students share the mentor texts they have found and note some of the craft moves they want to investigate more fully in a future piece of writing. Students can create annotated collections of mentor texts for a variety of purposes: as a cluster for a genre or technique study or even as a cumulative, end-of-year project (we like this activity best as a useful summative assessment to see if students are truly connecting with mentor texts). When students set out to create a mentor text collection, you can keep this invitation wide open—"Find any mentor text that strikes your fancy"—or you can require the mentor texts to center around a specific genre, technique, writer, theme, or topic.

Through this activity, we are seeking to develop a habit in our students. Just like their teachers, once students begin collecting mentor texts, they can continue to collect and store mentor texts they find and want to use later. Our hope is that this collection will grow not just through a single school year but throughout a lifetime of writing.

Responding to Mentors

Having students respond creatively to writing mentors allows them to simultaneously connect with the writer and the writing. Shorter than a full writing study, these activities give students quick contact with a mentor and an opportunity to try their craft on for size. In fact, a few of these opportunities to respond to mentor authors would provide a nice prelude to the more intensive mentor author study described below, helping students zoom in on an author they would like to study in more depth.

Conversation Pieces: Poems That Talk to Other Poems (Brown and Schechter 2007) is a collection of poetic responses to other poems. These response poems are linked in topic, theme, or style to the original poems. In the foreword to this text, Billy Collins posits that "to write a poem is to become part of a Great Conversation," and, as they write, poets write not only for a larger audience but also to communicate with an "inner circle of fellow practitioners."

Let's make our students part of that inner circle! After studying several mentor text pairs from this book, have students select their own mentor text and craft a response to the author. Students will often choose to respond in the same genre as the author's original piece, but we allow our students to respond in any genre as long as their craft and content are inspired by the mentor's craft. Figure 9.6 shows one student's response writing to the poem "Making a Fist" by Naomi Shihab Nye.

Text 9.2 "Making a Fist" by Naomi Shihab Nye *http://www.poetryfoundation.org/poem/241028*

Hands of Mortality

I have seen death and how he works. At first, when I gazed upon his grim visage, I was surprised to see the absence of long black or purple cloaks and long sharp scythes. There must have been bones within his body, but he was not a skeleton as I had expected. His bones were clothed by pale white skin, with blue veins visible underneath the surface, spiderwebbed up and down his arms. And what arms they were. Each one was twice the length of mine, and my wingspan is by no means laughable. But more than that, the number of them shocked me. There were millions, piled upon each other, looking like a curled up centipede. Only this particular beast had no body to speak of; no antennae either. The only visible part of death was his arms.

Once I had gazed upon the macabre spectacle for many a frightened hour, I was shown how he carries out his venomous purpose. He followed a man every second of his life. The arms did not grasp him until he was old, wrinkles on his visage. I watched them slowly apply pressure on the top of his back. Over the span of decades, they slowly pushed harder and harder. At the end, he was hunched over. He had once stood so tall. I witnessed the arms come together to break bones as he got older. I wanted to tell him that the medicine he was taking to strengthen the skeleton living inside him would do nothing. He was in pain at the end. I witnessed them apply sharp metal instruments to his body, making him feel annoyed but not in agony. He was jaded and tired of it all at the end. Then, when the man was old, and molested by the arms and the hands of death that he was blind to, all the hands seized him suddenly at once, while he was asleep. They held him like a vice. He could not move an inch. Every fiber of his being was still. Each one of his fingers were held down. He could not even make a fist.

Figure 9.6 Max's Response Writing to Naomi Shihab Nye

Another way to help students engage with writers is to have them think about the mentors that first made a difference. You might share with them the anthology *First Loves* (Ciuraru 2001), a provocative collection of short essays written by poets about the "essential poems that captivated and inspired them." This book offers over seventy mentor text pairs—the original poem that made each writer fall in love with words and a written reflection of that experience. For example, Sherman Alexie cites his encounter with Theodore Roethke's "My Papa's Waltz" as an indelible moment: "I loved it because it was the first poem that I truly understood. . . . I saw my father in that poem" (33).

These reflective tributes present another possible genre study—gratitude essays—that invite students to pay tribute to the writers who have impacted their work. While *First Loves* focuses on poets and poems, students needn't be limited to one genre in your classroom; they could be encouraged to write about mentors in all genres.

Multigenre Writing Projects

Multigenre writing asks students to write on a single topic in multiple genres. The art of multigenre writing is for every piece to be able to stand alone as a piece of art and also contribute to and enhance the meaning of every other piece in the collection. A great multigenre project should be a collection of little gems and also something more than the sum of its parts. Tom Romano offers wonderful in-depth explorations of all the ins and outs of multigenre writing in *Blending Genre, Altering Style* (2000) and *Fearless Writing* (2013).

Multigenre writing projects stem from many different sources of inspiration. Students can pursue a topic of interest, perhaps one they have identified in their heart maps or writing territories or something they have briefly touched upon in a previous piece of writing during the course. Multigenre projects are often used as dynamic alternatives to traditional research papers. Beginning with a research question and fueled by research, students demonstrate their new understanding with this type of writing. A piece of literature—a whole-class read or a selection from independent reading—can also spur multigenre writing as students explore a character or a theme from the text through different modes of writing.

Most importantly for our purposes, a multigenre writing project provides the perfect ground for demonstrating confidence with mentor texts. Since students can write on any topic and choose any combination of genres in which to write, students are required to develop their own unique mentor text cluster for this study. Students take the lead as they search for pieces that will inspire both their topic and their genres. If students plan to write poems in their multigenre projects, they find mentor poems to inspire and guide them. If they plan to write a news report, they find mentor news reports. They study these mentor texts on their own for inspiration and craft lessons, and they infuse their multigenre projects with the marks of their mentors.

In a multigenre writing project, Nick pulled together *Things Fall Apart*, *Antigone*, and *The Giver* to explore how characters defy their society. The Beastie Boys' "Body

Movin'" and Eminem's "Lose Yourself" inspired him to craft a rap from Okonkwo's perspective (Figure 9.7).

Text 9.3 The Beastie Boys' "Body Movin'" *http://www.azlyrics.com/lyrics/beastieboys/bodymovin.html*

Text 9.4 Eminem's "Lose Yourself" *http://www.metrolyrics.com/lose-yourself-lyrics-eminem.html*

Nick's topic of defiance coupled with his own love of rap music drove him to choose rap as a genre that would aptly express Okonkwo's feelings. Nick used "Body Movin'" as a mentor text for the structure and rhythms of his verse. "Lose Yourself" provided inspiration for the driving, angry tone of the rap and the explosive imagery.

They say I'm like a match next to gasoline cause I'm ready to explode
Everytime I see the white man in the market I want to pull out my rifle
    and unload,
People don't understand that what they're doing is wack
They treat us all like savages just because we're black,
I want my people to rise up and declare war
No one's listening I don't know what to do anymore,
The white men are taking my people and making them pray,
their strange religion until one day,
I let my temper rise up inside me
I cut down the white's messenger like an axe would a tree.
They think of me differently I used to be something great
Now when my people look at me their eyes are full of hate,
What have I done I've made a huge mistake.
I acted for what I believe in, and now I'm thinking about packing up
    and leavin'
Or just "checking out" completely . . . I think those men have finally beat me.

Figure 9.7 Nick's Rap About Okonkwo

As students work on their independent projects, the teacher shares a cluster of mentor texts with them—multigenre writing alive in the wild. We've listed a few suggestions to get you started (Figure 9.8).

Along with a final multigenre product, students share their mentor text clusters. Additionally, they annotate their final projects to show the threads of inspiration and craft that run between the mentor texts they have studied and the writing they have created.

Moby Dick by Herman Melville	The classic tale of Captain Ahab's quest for the great white whale. While not typically thought of as a work of multigenre writing, this novel contains traditional narrative with etymology, charts, quotes, and even a short play.
Monster by Walter Dean Myers	This young adult novel combines journaling and screenplays to tell the story of a young man's murder trial and experiences in jail.
Yes Please by Amy Poehler	This hilarious memoir combines narrative with captioned art and images, screenplays, and poems. Additionally, Poehler's memoir uses interesting bursts of color and design to tell its story.
Important Artifacts and Personal Property from the Collection of Lenore Doolan and Harold Morris, Including Books, Street Fashion, and Jewelry by Leanne Shapton	This fictional auction catalog uses images, captions, and auction listings to tell the story of a failed relationship.
The Collected Works of Billy the Kid by Michael Ondaatje	Inspired by history and fleshed out with fiction, this multigenre masterwork combines prose, poetry, interviews, photographs, and songs. As a bonus, Ondaatje's afterword describes his writing process as he tried multigenre writing for the first time.
Coal Mountain Elementary by Mark Nowak	Poet Mark Nowak weaves together photographs, educational curriculum, newspaper reports, and firsthand testimony to chronicle humans' relationship with coal in both the United States and China.
Op-docs on the *New York Times*	Op-docs combine opinion writing with documentary filmmaking. These short films use interviews, images, and captioning to bring attention to an important contemporary issue.
McSweeney's Quarterly	You never know what you will find in *McSweeney's*. A great mentor text for humor writing, *McSweeney's* includes open letters, poems, lists, narratives, faux Twitter feeds, proverbs, fictional histories, and instructions, just to name a few!

Figure 9.8 Multigenre Mentor Texts

Multigenre writing synthesizes all the work students have been doing in class—finding inspiring mentor texts, closely studying the craft of these texts, using the genres and techniques to support their purposes as writers, and creating compelling original writing.

Mentor Author Studies

In a mentor author study, students choose a single mentor, create a mentor text cluster of his or her work, and use that cluster to inspire a piece of their own writing. Typically, students will situate their original piece of writing within their mentor's primary genre, but they certainly don't have to do this. Any good writing can and should inspire good writing. While each student uses a unique set of mentor texts, the whole class still receives instruction during writing lessons to support students as they analyze the craft of a single writer over multiple pieces of writing. For example, a student interested in studying John Green's writing might pull excerpts from *The Fault in Our Stars*, *An Abundance of Katherines*, *Looking for Alaska*, one of his *New York Times* book reviews, and one of his VlogBrothers Crash Courses on YouTube.

Using this John Green mentor text cluster, students would seek inspiration and craft moves for an original piece of writing. They follow the same process they have practiced over and over again during class studies of mentor texts: Read the mentor texts as a reader, read the mentor texts as a writer, collect noticings about the craft of the mentor texts, and use that craft to inspire their own writing. As a final product, students turn in their mentor text cluster along with their original piece of writing, annotated to reflect the craft moves they borrowed from their mentor.

In this kind of mentor-focused study, not only are students inspired by the writer's craft in each piece, but they are able to see the unique stylistic fingerprints of their mentor. What craft moves does the mentor make again and again? What topics and themes does the mentor circle around? What are this writer's obsessions? Reflecting on a chosen mentor's style begins to clearly distinguish that writer from other writers in the student's mind.

What's more is this reflective practice helps students begin reflecting on their own writing style in the same way. What are their work habits? Their writing processes? Who are the mentors they return to again and again? What are their writing strengths? What are their obsessions? Their favorite punctuation marks? Their go-to sentence structures? Their most-explored topics?

A mentor author study shows the impact a single writing mentor can make on a student writer. In an author study of Sandra Cisneros, Isabella reflects:

The vignettes that have impacted me most are "Hair" and "Four Skinny Trees." I actually got the idea for my vignette "Seasons" from "Four Skinny Trees." I take a lot of my structure from her—like her, I don't want to write poems. I want to take poems and make them bigger. I've noticed that I use Cisneros a lot when I want to write about emotion or setting. And I'm inspired by the poetic way she dances around a topic. These are elements I will take with me in all of my writing.

Through this process, students become even more deeply connected to a writer they admire and will leave with a go-to mentor they can return to time after time.

Closing Thoughts

Imagine students leaving your class not only knowing how to use mentor texts in their own writing but being able to find mentor texts on their own. Imagine students leaving your class with a handful of favorite writing mentors whose work will inspire and inform their writing next year, and the next, and as they continue to write for lots of different occasions and purposes. Imagine students leaving your class with the tools to write successfully and the passion to be writers. Mentor texts and the mentors behind them can give your students all of this and more. Finding writing mentors and using mentor texts isn't only academic. It's life. The ability to find good writing and identify what makes it effective will carry students through their education and into the world of work.

Afterword

THE COURAGE TO WRITE

She was right on time. Two minutes to ten, and she was leaning her bike against the brick facade of my classroom, slinging a backpack heavy with books over her shoulders. In seconds, she appeared at my door, her forehead sweaty from the two-mile bike ride to school.

It was mid-June. The academic building was deserted, except for a few administrators, the librarian, and the custodial staff. The school had agreed to let us meet in my room over the summer to work. Isabella was writing a memoir about her childhood with May-May, the beloved nanny who had watched over her and her brother and sister for nine years and had suddenly disappeared from their lives. She hoped the publication of her book would help her find MayMay or, rather, that it would lead MayMay to her.

"I think I have a lead," she said, unpacking her bag, one book at a time. "An old neighbor of MayMay put me in touch with her sister Bernice. She might know something." She began to recount the details of her week—the long bike rides through MayMay's old neighborhood, the new vignettes she'd written, how hard it was to find time to write, even in the summer.

We filled our time with talking, writing, talking, writing some more. We turned to dog-eared pages in David Sedaris' *Dress Your Family in Corduroy and Denim* and the chapter on finding form in Judith Barrington's *Writing the Memoir*. We studied Sandra Cisneros' vignettes in *The House on Mango Street*, completely awed by her ability to evoke nostalgia and grief and hope all at once. The air was thick with the voices of many writers and their mentors and their mentors' mentors.

I asked Isabella to read something to me. Thumbing through her marbled composition notebook, she searched for a place, and began.

Dirty Laundry

I don't know what it was about the laundromat that felt so safe. The smell was musky, and the floors were dirty with grime. The windows were painted with the handprints of those before me. We said she could wash her clothes with ours and not waste the money. But she dragged us there anyway. We sat and waited, watching the clothes go around and around. It wasn't all bad, though. It was exciting going to the laundromat. I crawled, hands and knees, searching for the treasured coins. I would find pockets full of the cherished objects. The coins were like little movies telling me their story. Sometimes they would be green and moldy, a long boring life. Then they would be dented and scratched, a long fight to get here.

We sat in those old, stained-with-age chairs and watched the clothes go around and around. I would stand and move to the next machine, peering in, and from the clothes, I tried to piece their story together. But I never could really quench my curiosity with a pretend story I thought of. I always wanted to know more, more about MayMay, more about the clothes and more about her world.

MayMay's world was so small and yet so big at the same time—her street, the laundromat, the run-down Kroger, our house, just one big cycle we repeated on a weekly basis. It was boring, but it felt safe, almost like a routine with some religious importance. I never complained because it felt like a secret world I entered, and MayMay was the only way into it. I was almost addicted to the raw reality that MayMay dragged us into and then we ran to catch up with.

She closed her journal and motioned to the Sedaris book. "The first time I read 'Santaland Diaries,' I thought to myself, *I want to be a writer*. He put everything on the table. There was no censorship. I tried to put that rawness in here." She looked up at me, her eyes hopeful.

I could hear the influence of her mentors—Cisneros' poetry. Sedaris' rawness. At the same time, I could hear Isabella. Her memories, her story, had come alive under their tutelage. Their books had given her structure and style. They had given her a vision. They had taught her how to write a conclusion that resonates and how to give her readers goosebumps.

And they had given her something else, too. Courage. The courage to write about something that is deeply personal and a little scary and maybe even taboo. The courage to ask questions, to relive the past, to write the hard stuff. The courage to write a book—and the hope that it will lead you home.

This is why we write with mentors.

Appendix

CHAPTER 1

Text 1.1: "Young Love, Complicated by Cancer" by A. O. Scott *http://www.nytimes.com/2014/06/06/movies/the-fault-in-our-stars-sets-out-to-make-you-cry.html?_r=0*

Text 1.2: "*Titanfall* Supplants Its Ancestors with Speed and Scale" by Ryan Smith *http://www.avclub.com/article/titanfall-supplants-its-ancestors-speed-and-scale-202272]*

Text 1.3: "A Farewell to Twang" by Jon Caramanica *http://www.nytimes.com/2014/10/26/arts/music/taylor-swift-1989-new-album-review.html*

Text 1.4: "Fred and Barney Would Feel Right at Home" by Pete Wells *http://www.nytimes.com/2014/01/29/dining/restaurant-review-m-wells-steakhouse-in-long-island-city-queens.html*

Text 1.5: "Scary New World" by John Green *http://www.nytimes.com/2008/11/09/books/review/Green-t.html?pagewanted=all*

Text 1.6: "Two Against the World" by John Green *http://www.nytimes.com/2013/03/10/books/review/eleanor-park-by-rainbow-rowell.html*

Text 1.7: "Pharrell Williams: Just Exhilaratingly Happy" by Ken Tucker *http://www.npr.org/2014/03/06/286864627/pharrell-williams-new-album-is-as-happy-as-its-hit-single*

Text 1.8: "*Modern Family*: 'A Hard Jay's Night'" by Joshua Alston
http://www.avclub.com/tvclub/modern-family-hard-jays-night-203009

CHAPTER 2

Text 2.1: "Vernal Sentiment" by Theodore Roethke
http://writersalmanac.publicradio.org/index.php?date=2014/06/16

Text 2.2: "On the Eve of Its Finale, It's Time to Compare *How I Met Your Mother* to Itself" by Donna Bowman *http://www.avclub.com/article/eve-its -finale-its-time-compare-how-i-met-your-mot-202733*

Text 2.3: "The Ghost Writer: Lucie Brock-Broido's 'Stay, Illusion'" by Dan Chiasson *http://www.newyorker.com/magazine/2013/10/28/the-ghost -writer-3*

Text 2.4: "*Carrie*" by A. A. Dowd
http://www.avclub.com/review/carrie-104381

Text 2.5: "The New Stephen Curry: How the Warriors' Super-Shooter Has Transformed His Game in the Playoffs" by Zach Lowe
http://grantland.com/the-triangle/the-new-stephen-curry-how-the-warriors-super -shooter-has-transformed-his-game-in-the-playoffs/

Text 2.6: "Bullying: Why Zero-Tolerance Policies Don't Work" by Andrew Zack *http://www.huffingtonpost.com/andrew-zack/bullying-zero -tolerance_b_815231.html*

Text 2.7: "Social Media Can Be Deadly" by Leonard Pitts
http://www.miamiherald.com/opinion/opn-columns-blogs/leonard-pitts-jr/article1956196.html

Text 2.8: "It's Not Just the Guns, It's the Person" by Mitch Albom
http://mitchalbom.com/d/journalism/7800/its-not-just-guns-its-person

Text 2.9: "Better with Age" by Chris. B. Brown
http://grantland.com/features/peyton-manning-denver-broncos-offense/

Text 2.10: "Repetition" by Phil Kaye
http://youtu.be/EILQTDBqhPA

Text 2.11: "Save Us from the SAT" by Jennifer Finney Boylan
http://www.nytimes.com/2014/03/07/opinion/save-us-from-the-sat.html

CHAPTER 3

Text 3.1: "How Teens Read: The Kids are Alright" by Delano Scott and Daniel Vecchitto *hhttp://www.slideshare.net/PenguinRandomHouse/how-teens-read*

Text 3.2: "With Poetic Intensity, Kevin Powers Tackles the Terror of War" by Abigail Deutsch *http://www.npr.org/2014/04/02/295828579/with-poetic-intensity-kevin-powers-tackles-the-terror-of-war*

Text 3.3: *"Modern Family:* 'A Hard Jay's Night'" by Joshua Alston
http://www.avclub.com/tvclub/modern-family-hard-jays-night-203009

Text 3.4: *"Titanfall* Supplants Its Ancestors with Speed and Scale"
by Ryan Smith *http://www.avclub.com/article/titanfall-supplants-its-ancestors
-speed-and-scale-202272*

Text 3.5: "Fred and Barney Would Feel Right at Home" by Pete Wells
*http://www.nytimes.com/2014/01/29/dining/restaurant-review-m-wells
-steakhouse-in-long-island-city-queens.html*

Text 3.6: "Pharrell Williams: Just Exhilaratingly Happy" by Ken Tucker
*http://www.npr.org/2014/03/06/286864627/pharrell-williams-new-album-is-as
-happy-as-its-hit-single*

Text 3.7: Sam Tanenhaus Interview
*http://www.thedailybeast.com/articles/2012/08/08/inside-the-nyt-book-review
-how-i-write-interviews-sam-tanenhaus.html*

CHAPTER 4

Text 4.1: "New York City in 17 Syllables" *http://www.nytimes.com
/interactive/2014/04/27/nyregion/new-york-city-in-haiku.html?_r=0*

Text 4.2: "Child's Play" by Reeves Wiedeman
http://www.newyorker.com/magazine/2014/06/02/childs-play-6

CHAPTER 5

Text 5.1: Facebook Fandom Map 2014 *http://www.cbssports.com/nfl/eye -on-football/24697058/facebook-releases-nfl-fan-map-of-us-jets-have-no-fans*

Text 5.2: "Life in the 30's" by Anna Quindlen *http://www.nytimes.com/1987/09/09/garden/life-in-the-30-s.html*

Text 5.3: "Solitudes" by Margaret Gibson *http://writersalmanac.publicradio.org/index.php?date=2014/09/11*

Text 5.4: "How Much Snow It Typically Takes to Cancel School in the U.S." by Eleanor Barkhorn *http://www.theatlantic.com/education/archive /2014/01/map-how-much-snow-it-typically-takes-to-cancel-school-in-the -us/283470/*

Text 5.5: "Rise and Shine: What Kids Around the World Eat for Breakfast" by Hannah Whitaker and Malia Wollen *http://www.nytimes.com/interactive /2014/10/08/magazine/eaters-all-over.html*

Text 5.6: "Back Road" by Bruce Guernsey *http://www.poetryfoundation.org/poetrymagazine/poem/23632*

Text 5.7: "Ross: Children of the Ghetto" by George Szirtes *http://www.poetryfoundation.org/poetrymagazine/poem/181102*

Text 5.8: "The snow's/feet slip" by Marty Walsh
http://www.americanlifeinpoetry.org/columns/503.html

Text 5.9: "Where Children Sleep" by Jane Mollison
http://jamesmollison.com/books/where-children-sleep/

Text 5.10: "My Mother's Death Cured My Anxiety" by Eliza Berman
http://www.slate.com/articles/double_x/doublex/2014/08/how_my_mother_s_death_cured_my_anxiety.html

Text 5.11: University of Alabama Sports Revenue *http://www.businessinsider.com/university-alabama-athletics-revenue-scholarships-2014-10*

CHAPTER 6

Text 6.1: "How Much Does It Cost to Be Batman in Real Life?" by Sarah Ang *http://mashable.com/2013/07/16/batman-price-infographic/*

Text 6.2: "Find a Good Frog" by Delia Motavalli
http://thisibelieve.org/essay/101469/

Text 6.3: "The Triumph of Kindness" by Josh Stein
http://thisibelieve.org/essay/83477/

Text 6.4: "Accomplishing Big Things in Small Pieces" by William Wissemann
http://thisibelieve.org/essay/39318/

 Text 6.5: "The Beatles Live On" by Macklin Levine
http://thisibelieve.org/essay/469311/

 Text 6.6: "Finding the Flexibility to Survive" by Brighton Earley
http://thisibelieve.org/essay/31840/

 Text 6.7: "Inner Strength from Desperate Times" by Jake Hovenden
http://thisibelieve.org/essay/269411/

 Text 6.8: "My Mother's Death Cured My Anxiety" by Eliza Berman
http://www.slate.com/articles/double_x/doublex/2014/08/how_my_mother_s_death_cured_my_anxiety.html

 Text 6.9: "The Science of Raising Happy Kids" by happify.com
http://www.happify.com/hd/the-science-of-raising-happy-kids/

 Text 6.10: "My Papa's Waltz" by Theodore Roethke
http://www.poetryfoundation.org/poem/172103

Text 6.11: "Parental Involvement Is Overrated" by Keith Robinson and Angel L. Harris *http://opinionator.blogs.nytimes.com/2014/04/12 /parental-involvement-is-overrated/*

Text 6.12: "What Remains: A Review of *The Lovely Bones*" by Katherine Bouton *http://www.nytimes.com/2002/07/14/books/what-remains.html*

CHAPTER 7

Text 7.1: "Scary New World" by John Green *http://www.nytimes.com/2008/11/09/books/review/Green-t.html?pagewanted=all*

Text 7.2: "Obama Spends Another Night Searching Behind White House Paintings for Safes" *http://www.theonion.com/articles/obama-spends -another-night-searching-behind-white,35850/*

Text 7.3: "How *Seinfeld* Paved the Way for Tony Soprano" by Matt Zoller Seitz *http://www.vulture.com/2014/06/how-seinfeld-paved-the-way -for-tony-soprano.html*

Text 7.4: "*Doctor Who*: 'Listen'" by Alasdair Wilkins *http://www.avclub.com/tvclub/doctor-who-listen-209034*

Text 7.5: "*Sharknado 2*: Winner and Still Chomp" by Linda Holmes *http://www.npr.org/blogs/monkeysee/2014/07/30/336573454/sharknado -2-winner-and-still-chomp*

Text 7.6: "*Into the Storm* Is a Witless, Wild Ride for Disaster-Film Junkies" by Bilge Ebiri

http://www.vulture.com/2014/08/movie-review-into-the-storm.html

Text 7.7: "Why We Absolutely, Definitely Do NOT Need Another *Arrested Development* Season" by Haley Blum *http://entertainthis.usatoday.com /2014/08/08/why-we-dont-need-another-arrested-development-netflix-season/*

CHAPTER 8

Text 8.1: "Invisible Child—Girl in the Shadows: Dasani's Homeless Life" by Andrea Elliot

http://www.nytimes.com/projects/2013/invisible-child/#/?chapt=1

Text 8.2: "Better with Age" by Chris B. Brown

http://grantland.com/features/peyton-manning-denver-broncos-offense/

Text 8.3: Trey's Blog Post

http://treysfieldnotes.wordpress.com/2014/10/16/zone-run/

Text 8.4: "*Titanfall* Supplants Its Ancestors with Speed and Scale" by Ryan Smith *http://www.avclub.com/article/titanfall-supplants-its-ancestors -speed-and-scale-202272*

Text 8.5: "Fred and Barney Would Feel Right at Home" by Pete Wells *http://www.nytimes.com/2014/01/29/dining/restaurant-review-m-wells -steakhouse-in-long-island-city-queens.html*

Text 8.6: Jimmy's *DayZ* Review *https://docs.google.com/document/d /1KgrXBAMpBziCCYI6y5D49ztbiWgXfG6sFLOScw7qEjE/edit?usp=sharing*

Text 8.7: "Connecticut Teenager with Cancer Loses Court Fight to Refuse Chemotherapy" by Elizabeth A. Harris *http://www.nytimes.com/2015/01/10/nyregion/connecticut-teenager-with -cancer-loses-court-fight-to-refuse-chemotherapy.html?_r=0*

CHAPTER 9

Text 9.1: "At the Restaurant Critics' Table" *http://www.nytimes.com /interactive/2013/09/03/dining/2013-dining-critics-videos.html*

Text 9.2: "Making a Fist" by Naomi Shihab Nye *http://www.poetryfoundation.org/poem/241028*

Text 9.3: The Beastie Boys' "Body Movin'" *http://www.azlyrics.com/lyrics/beastieboys/bodymovin.html*

Text 9.4: Eminem's "Lose Yourself" *http://www.metrolyrics.com/lose-yourself-lyrics-eminem.html*

Works Cited and Consulted

Albom, Mitch. 2012. "It's Not Just Guns, It's the Person." *Detroit Free Press*. 22 July. Retrieved 1/10/2015 from http://mitchalbom.com/d/journalism/7800/its-not-just -guns-its-person.

Alston, Joshua. 2014. "*Modern Family*: 'A Hard Jay's Night.'" *A.V. Club*. 2 April. Retrieved 1/10/2015 from http://www.avclub.com/tvclub/modern-family-hard-jays-night -203009.

Anderson, Jeff. 2005. *Mechanically Inclined*. Portland: Stenhouse.

Anderson, Laurie Halse. 2009. *Wintergirls*. New York: Speak.

Ang, Sarah. 2013. "How Much Does It Cost to Be Batman in Real Life?" *Mashable*. 16 July. Retrieved 1/10/2015 from http://mashable.com/2013/07/16/batman-price -infographic/.

"At the Critics' Table." 2013. *New York Times*. 3 September. Retrieved 1/10/2015 from http://www.nytimes.com/interactive/2013/09/03/dining/2013-dining-critics -videos.html.

Atwell, Nancie. 1998. *In the Middle*, 2nd Edition. Portsmouth, NH: Heinemann.

———. 2002. *Lessons That Change Writers*. Portsmouth, NH: Heinemann.

———. 2014. *In The Middle*, 3rd Edition. Portsmouth, NH: Heinemann.

Barrington, Judith. 2002. *Writing the Memoir: From Truth to Art*. Portland: The Eighth Mountain Press.

Becker, Sandra. 2013. "A City Girl Feeds Country Cows." *Imperfect Matter*. Retrieved 1/11/2015 from http://writersalmanac.publicradio.org/index.php?date=2014/09/27.

Berman, Eliza. 2014. "My Mother's Desk Cured My Anxiety." *Slate*. 25 August. Retrieved 1/10/2015 from http://www.slate.com/articles/double_x/doublex/2014/08 /how_my_mother_s_death_cured_my_anxiety.html.

Blum, Haley. 2014. "Why We Absolutely Definitely Do Not Need Another *Arrested Development* Season." *USA Today*. 8 August. Retrieved 1/10/2015 from http:// entertainthis.usatoday.com/2014/08/08/why-we-dont-need-another-arrested -development-netflix-season/.

Bouton, Katherine. 2002. "What Remains." *New York Times*. 14 July. Retrieved 1/10/2015 from http://www.nytimes.com/2002/07/14/books/what-remains.html.

Bowman, Donna. 2014. "On the Eve of Its Finale, It's Time to Compare *How I Met Your Mother* to Itself." *A.V. Club*. 31 March. Retrieved 1/10/2015 from http://www.avclub .com/article/eve-its-finale-its-time-compare-how-i-met-your-mot-202733.

Bowman, Robin, and Robert Coles. 2007. *It's Complicated: The American Teenager*. Brooklyn: Umbrage.

Boylan, Jennifer Finney. 2014. "Save Us from the SAT." *New York Times*. 6 March. Retrieved 1/10/2015 from http://www.nytimes.com/2014/03/07/opinion/save-us-from-the -sat.html.

Breech, John. 2014. "Facebook Releases NFL Fan Map of U.S.; Jets Have No Fans." *CBS Sports*. 14 September. Retrieved 1/10/2015 from http://www.cbssports.com/nfl/eye -on-football/24697058/facebook-releases-nfl-fan-map-of-us-jets-have-no-fans.

Britton, James. 1970. *Language and Learning*. Portsmouth, NH: Heinemann.

Brown, Chris B. 2014. "Better with Age." *Grantland*. 30 January. Retrieved 1/10/2015 from http://grantland.com/features/peyton-manning-denver-broncos-offense/.

Brown, Kurt, and Harold Schechter. 2007. *Conversation Pieces: Poems That Talk to Other Poems*. New York: Knopf.

Caramanica, Joe. 2014. "A Farewell to Twang." *New York Times*. 23 October. Retrieved 1/10/2015 from http://www.nytimes.com/2014/10/26/arts/music/taylor-swift-1989 -new-album-review.html.

Charney, Noah. 2012. "Inside the *NYT Book Review*: 'How I Write' Interviews Sam Tanenhaus." *The Daily Beast*, 8 August. Retrieved 12/19/2014 from http://www .thedailybeast.com/articles/2012/08/08/inside-the-nyt-book-review-how-i-write -interviews-sam-tanenhaus.html.

Chelas, Semi. 2014. "Interviews: Matthew Weiner, The Art of Screenwriting, No. 4." *The Paris Review*. Spring. Retrieved 12/30/2014 from http://www.theparisreview.org /interviews/6293/the-art-of-screenwriting-no-4-matthew-weiner.

Chiasson, Dan. 2013. "The Ghost Writer: Lucie Brock-Broido's 'Stay, Illusion.'" *The New Yorker*. 28 October. Retrieved 1/10/2015 from http://www.newyorker.com /magazine/2013/10/28/the-ghost-writer-3.

Cisneros, Sandra. 1991. *The House on Mango Street*. New York: Vintage.

Ciuraru, Carmela. 2001. *First Loves: Poets Introduce the Essential Poems That Captivated and Inspired Them*. New York: Scribner.

Conroy, Frank. 1977. *Stop Time*. New York: Penguin.

Continetti, Matthew. 2012. "Dungeons and Dragons." *The Claremont Institute*. 24 May. Retrieved 1/10/2015 from http://www.claremont.org/article/dungeons-and-dragons /#.VLFtDEvZr8E.

Creme, Phyllis, and Mary Lea. 2008. *Writing at University*. New York: Open University Press.

Deutsch, Abigail. 2014. "With Poetic Intensity, Kevin Power Tackles the Terror of War." NPR. 2 April. Retrieved 1/10/2015 from http://www.npr.org/2014/04/02/295828579 /with-poetic-intensity-kevin-powers-tackles-the-terror-of-war.

Dowd, A. A. 2013. "Review: *Carrie*." *A.V. Club*. 13 October. Retrieved 1/10/2015 from http://www.avclub.com/review/carrie-104381.

Earley, Brighton. 2008. "Finding the Flexibility to Survive." *This I Believe*. 2 June. Retrieved 1/10/2015 from http://thisibelieve.org/essay/31840/.

Ebiri, Bilge. 2014. "*Into the Storm* is a Witless, Wild Ride for Disaster-Film Junkies." *Vulture*. 7 August. Retrieved 1/10/2015 from http://www.vulture.com/2014/08/movie -review-into-the-storm.html.

Edelstein, David. 2014. "Zombies in the Time of Ebola: Why We Need Horror Movies Now More Than Ever." *Vulture*. 21 October. Retrieved 1/11/2015 from http://www .vulture.com/2014/10/horror-movies-in-the-time-of-ebola.html.

Elliott, Andrea. 2013. "Invisible Child, Girl in the Shadows: Dasani's Homeless Life." *New York Times*. 9 December. Retrieved 1/11/2015 from http://www.nytimes.com /projects/2013/invisible-child/#/?chapt=1.

"Famous Author Writing Influences: 20 Famous Writers on What Inspired Their Work." *Huffington Post*. 3 July 2013. Retrieved 1/3/2015 from http://www.huffingtonpost .com/2013/07/03/author-writing-influences_n_3540905.html.

Feuer, Alan. 2014. "New York City in 17 Syllables." *New York Times*. 25 April. Retrieved 12/23/2014 from http://www.nytimes.com/interactive/2014/04/27/nyregion/new -york-city-in-haiku.html.

Fletcher, Ralph. 1992. *What a Writer Needs*. Portsmouth, NH: Heinemann.

Gallagher, Kelly. 2004. *Deeper Reading*. Portland: Stenhouse.

———. 2006. *Teaching Adolescent Writers*. Portland: Stenhouse.

———. 2011. *Write Like This*. Portland: Stenhouse.

Goldberg, Natalie. 2005. *Writing Down the Bones: Freeing the Writer Within*. Boston: Shambhala.

Graves, Donald. 1994. "Conditions for Effective Writing." In *Children Want to Write*, edited by Thomas Newkirk and Penny Kittle, 58–67. Portsmouth, NH: Heinemann.

Graves, Donald, and Penny Kittle. 2005. *Inside Writing: How to Teach the Details of Craft*. Portsmouth, NH: Heinemann.

Green, John. 2008. "Scary New World." *New York Times*. 7 November. Retrieved 1/10/2015 from http://www.nytimes.com/2008/11/09/books/review/Green-t.html?pagewanted=all&_r=0.

———. 2013. "Two Against the World." *New York Times*. 8 March. Retrieved 1/10/2015 from http://www.nytimes.com/2013/03/10/books/review/eleanor-park-by-rainbow-rowell.html.

Hancock, James Gulliver. 2014. *Artists, Writers, Thinkers, and Dreamers: Portraits of 50 Famous Folks & All their Weird Stuff*. San Francisco: Chronicle Books.

Harris, Elizabeth A. 2015. "Connecticut Teenager with Cancer Loses Court Fight to Refuse Chemotherapy." *New York Times*. 10 January. Retrieved 1/11/2015 from http://www.nytimes.com/2015/01/10/nyregion/connecticut-teenager-with-cancer-loses-court-fight-to-refuse-chemotherapy.html?_r=0.

Heard, Georgia. 1998. *Awakening the Heart: Exploring Poetry in Elementary and Middle School*. Portsmouth: Heinemann.

———. 2014. "Writing Poetry: Giving Students the Vision and Tools to Reach for Wider Possibilities as Writers." Central Virginia Writing Project. Charlottesville, Virginia, 13 November.

Holmes, Linda. 2014. "*Sharknado 2*: Winner and Still Chomp." *Monkey See*. 30 July. Retrieved 1/10/2015 from http://www.npr.org/blogs/monkeysee/2014/07/30/336573454/sharknado-2-winner-and-still-chomp.

Hovendon, Jake. 2007. "Inner Strength from Desperate Times." *This I Believe*. 13 May. Retrieved 1/10/2015 from http://thisibelieve.org/essay/26941/.

John-Steiner, Vera. 1997. *Conversations of the Mind: Explorations of Thinking*. New York: Oxford University Press.

Kaye, Phil. 2011. "Repetition." Retrieved 1/10/2015 from http://youtu.be/EILQTDBqhPA.

Kittle, Penny. 2008. *Write Beside Them*. Portsmouth, NH: Heinemann.

———. 2013. "Fearless Writing, Fearless Teaching." Central Virginia Writing Project. Charlottesville, Virginia, 6 December.

Levine, Maclin. 2009. "The Beatles Live On." *This I Believe*. 15 March. Retrieved 1/10/2015 from http://thisibelieve.org/essay/46931/.

Lowe, Zach. 2013. "The New Stephen Curry: How the Warriors' Super-Shooter Has Transformed His Game in the Playoffs." *Grantland*. 10 May. Retrieved 1/10/2015 from http://grantland.com/the-triangle/the-new-stephen-curry-how-the-warriors-super-shooter-has-transformed-his-game-in-the-playoffs/.

Martindell, Cameron. 2014. "Hiking Below the Rim of the Grand Canyon." *Beyond the Edge: National Geographic Adventure Blog*. 8 May. Retrieved 12/27/2014 from http://adventureblog.nationalgeographic.com/2014/05/08/hiking-below-the-north-rim-in-the-grand-canyon/.

Melville, Herman. 1851. *Moby Dick*. New York: Norton.

Motavalli, Delia. 2013. "Find a Good Frog." *This I Believe*. 22 March. Retrieved 1/10/2015 from http://thisibelieve.org/essay/101469/.

Myers, Walter Dean. 2004. *Monster*. New York: Armistad.

Nowak, Mark. 2009. *Coal Mountain Elementary*. Minneapolis: Coffee House Press.

Ondaatje, Michael. 1996. *The Collected Works of Billy the Kid*. New York: Vintage.

Pitts, Leonard. 2013. "Social Media Can Be Deadly." *Miami Herald*. 12 October. Retrieved 1/10/2015 from http://www.miamiherald.com/opinion/opn-columns-blogs/leonard-pitts-jr/article1956196.html.

Poehler, Amy. 2014. *Yes Please*. New York: Dey Street.

"Questions for . . . A. O. Scott." *New York Times*. Retrieved 1/3/2015 from http://www.nytimes.com/ref/readersopinions/questions-scott.html.

Quindlen, Anna. 1987. "Life in the 30's." *New York Times*. 9 September. Retrieved 1/10/2015 from http://www.nytimes.com/1987/09/09/garden/life-in-the-30-s.html.

Ray, Katie Wood. 1999. *Wondrous Words*. Urbana: National Council of Teachers of English.

———. 2006. *Study Driven*. Portsmouth, NH: Heinemann.

Rief, Linda. 2014. *Read Write Teach*. Portsmouth, NH: Heinemann.

Robinson, Keith, and Angel L. Harris. 2014. "Parental Involvement Is Overrated." *New York Times*. 12 April. Retrieved 1/20/2015 from http://opinionator.blogs.nytimes.com/2014/04/12/parental-involvement-is-overrated/.

Roethke, Theodore. 1942. "My Papa's Waltz." *Collected Poems of Theodore Roethke*. Retrieved 1/10/2015 from http://www.poetryfoundation.org/poem/172103.

———. 1974. "Vernal Sentiment." *Collected Poems of Theodore Roethke*. Retrieved 1/10/2015 from http://writersalmanac.publicradio.org/index.php?date=2014/06/16.

Romano, Tom. 2000. *Blending Genre, Altering Style: Writing Multigenre Papers*. Portsmouth, NH: Heinemann.

———. 2013. *Fearless Writing: Multigenre to Motivate and Inspire*. Portsmouth, NH: Heinemann.

Rosenthal, Amy Krouse. 2004. *Encyclopedia of an Ordinary Life*. New York: Crown.

Rylant, Cynthia. 1982. *When I Was Young in the Mountains*. New York: Puffin.

"The Science of Raising Happy Kids." *Happify*. Retrieved 1/10/2015 from http://www.happify.com/hd/the-science-of-raising-happy-kids/.

Scott. A. O. 2014. "Young Love, Complicated by Cancer." *New York Times*. 5 June. Retrieved 1/10/2015 from http://www.nytimes.com/2014/06/06/movies/the-fault-in-our -stars-sets-out-to-make-you-cry.html?_r=0.

Scott, Delano, and Daniel Vecchitto. 2013. "The Kids Are All Right—How Teens Read [Infographic]." *Random House Random Notes*. 6 November. Retrieved 1/10/2015 from http://randomnotes.randomhouse.com/how-teens-read/.

Sedaris, David. 2005. *Dress Your Family in Corduroy and Denim*. New York: Back Bay Books.

Seitz, Matt Zoller. 2014. "How *Seinfeld* Paved the Way for Tony Soprano." June 26. Retrieved 1/1/2015 from http://www.vulture.com/2014/06/how-seinfeld-paved-the -way-for-tony-soprano.html.

Shapton, Leanne. 2009. *Important Artifacts and Personal Property from the Collection of Lenore Doolan and Harold Morris, Including Books, Street Fashion, and Jewelry*. New York: Sarah Crichton Books.

Sherman-Jones, Carol. 2002. "A Lesson Not Learned." *I Thought My Father Was God: And Other True Tales from NPR's National Story Project*. Paul Auster, ed. New York: Picador.

Smith, Ryan. 2014. "*Titanfall* Supplants Its Ancestors with Speed and Scale." *A.V. Club*. 18 March. Retrieved 1/10/2015 from http://www.avclub.com/article/titanfall -supplants-its-ancestors-speed-and-scale-202272.

Stein, Josh. 2013. "The Triumph of Kindness." *This I Believe*. 15 March. Retrieved 1/10/2015 from http://thisibelieve.org/essay/83477/.

Temple, Emily. 2013. "20 Great Writers on the Art of Revision." January 8. Retrieved 1/1/2015 from http://flavorwire.com/361311/20-great-writers-on-the-art-of -revision/3.

The Onion. 2014. "Obama Spends Another Night Searching Behind White House Paintings for Safes." *The Onion*. 22 April 2014. Retrieved 1/10/2015 from http://www .theonion.com/articles/obama-spends-another-night-searching-behind-white,35850/.

Tucker, Ken. 2014. "Pharrell Williams: Just Exhilaratingly Happy." *Fresh Air*. *NPR,* March 6. http://www.npr.org/2014/03/06/286864627/pharrell-williams-new-album-is-as -happy-as-its-hit-single.

Wells, Pete. 2014. "Fred and Barney Would Feel Right at Home." *New York Times*. 28 January. Retrieved 1/10/2015 from http://www.nytimes.com/2014/01/29/dining /restaurant-review-m-wells-steakhouse-in-long-island-city-queens.html.

White, E. B. 1952. *Charlotte's Web*. New York: HarperCollins.

Wiedeman, Reeves. 2014. "Child's Play." *New Yorker*. 2 June. Retrieved 1/10/2015 from
http://www.newyorker.com/magazine/2014/06/02/childs-play-6.

Wilkins, Alasdair. 2014. "*Doctor Who*: 'Listen.'" *A.V. Club*. 13 September. Retrieved
1/10/2015 from http://www.avclub.com/tvclub/doctor-who-listen-209034.

Wissemann, William. 2008. "Accomplishing Big Things in Small Pieces." *This I Believe*. 14
September. Retrieved 1/10/2015 from http://thisibelieve.org/essay/39318/.

Zack, Andrew. 2011. "Bullying: Why Zero-Tolerance Policies Don't Work." *Huffington Post*.
8 February. Retrieved 1/10/2015 from http://www.huffingtonpost.com/andrew
-zack/bullying-zero-tolerance_b_815231.html.